普通高等教育仪器科学与技术系列"十二五"规划教材
编审委员会

名誉主任　中国工程院院士　金国藩

主　　任　王化祥

副 主 编　戎 蒙 　王雪林

委　　员　（以姓氏笔画为序）
王世忠　王向朝　尤宗杰　尤政　尤其昌　尤 文
何秀丽　吴学礼　张 潮　陈仁　夏学孔　林 丁
胡立华　战忠武　温雅芹　魏向明

普通高等教育测控技术与仪器"十二五"规划教材编审委员会

名誉主任 叶声华

主　　任 王化祥

副 主 任 孔　力　王建林

委　　员（按姓氏笔画排序）

　　　　　　王华忠　王晓荣　付家才　孙自强　杜　坚　李宏光
　　　　　　何苏勤　吴学礼　陈　娟　杨　帆　孟　华　尚丽平
　　　　　　郝立军　谌海云　韩建国　穆向阳

本书荣获中国石油和化学工业优秀出版物奖（教材奖）二等奖

普通高等教育测控技术与仪器"十二五"规划教材

测控技术与仪器专业英语

第二版

韩建国　主　编　　金翠云　汪晓男　副主编

化学工业出版社

·北京·

全书分为 4 章、20 个单元和 21 个阅读材料。第 1、2 章分别综合介绍测量与控制技术的背景、基本理论、基本技术概念及全貌；第 3 章较具体地介绍检测技术的基本内容；第 4 章重点介绍当前国内外一些新的测量技术与方法。

每篇课文之后设置有词汇表、注释、练习和阅读材料；每篇阅读材料之后也设有词汇表和注释。全书后设有词汇总表，并附有关于如何撰写英文的学术论文、关于如何参加一次国际 IEEE 学术会议、关于工程索引 "EI" 的介绍。

本书可供测控技术与仪器、自动化、电子信息工程以及仪器仪表类等相关专业学生作为阅读教材用，也可供相关领域的教师、科技人员作为参考材料用。

图书在版编目（CIP）数据

测控技术与仪器专业英语/韩建国主编．—2 版．
北京：化学工业出版社，2011.2（2022.1重印）
普通高等教育测控技术与仪器"十二五"规划教材
ISBN 978-7-122-10452-6

Ⅰ．测⋯　Ⅱ．韩⋯　Ⅲ．①测量系统：控制系统-英语-高等学校-教材②电子测量设备-英语-高等学校-教材　Ⅳ．H31

中国版本图书馆 CIP 数据核字（2011）第 012661 号

责任编辑：郝英华　　　　　　　　装帧设计：张　辉
责任校对：郑　捷

出版发行：化学工业出版社（北京市东城区青年湖南街 13 号　邮政编码 100011）
印　　装：天津盛通数码科技有限公司
787mm×1092mm　1/16　印张 13¾　字数 334 千字　2022 年 1 月北京第 2 版第 6 次印刷

购书咨询：010-64518888　　　售后服务：010-64518899
网　　址：http://www.cip.com.cn
凡购买本书，如有缺损质量问题，本社销售中心负责调换。

定　　价：36.00 元　　　　　　　　　　　　　　　　　　　　版权所有　违者必究

第二版前言

《测控技术与仪器专业英语》一书自 2002 年 6 月首版至今，受到了为数众多的读者的欢迎，已在一系列理工科高等院校的相关专业学科领域中被教师选定为本科生固定规范教材，历年来销售册数有增无减。同时，也得到了许多同学、教师、专业人员针对教材内容与模式给予的意见与建议，使笔者从中受益匪浅。

考虑到近十年来，随着微电子、数字电路、计算机及其网络通信、现代信息技术等多个领域的飞速发展，国内外测控领域已出现一系列崭新的成果。为了让我们的读者也能够在专业英语知识与技能上与时俱进地跟进并超越国内外的发展，特组织新生力量，对本书内容进行了补充和更新。本次修订主要内容如下。

Unit 15　Signal Sensoring and Data Record/ Display（信号传感器内容）；

Reading Material 15-1　Digital Temperature DS18B20（数字测温仪）；

Reading Material 16　Fuzzy Neural Control（模糊神经控制）；

Unit 19　Bionics Measurement（增加生物仿生量测量）；

Reading Material 19　Optical Polarization Based Navigation Technology（基于光偏振的定位技术）；

Unit 20　Embedded System Supporting Control Process（控制过程的嵌入式支持系统）；

Reading Material 20　The High-performance Microcontroller of Embedded System——ATmega 8（嵌入式系统高性能微控制器——ATmega 8）；

附录二　关于如何参加一次国际 IEEE 学术会议；

附录四　总词汇表（补充部分新内容）。

本次修订由韩建国担任主编，金翠云、汪晓男担任副主编，林冬蔚、杜毅、赵红亮参编。

我们恳请各位同行、专家和读者再次给予更多的建议、指正与帮助，并热切期望新版教材给读者带来更多的收益与方便。

编者
2011 年 1 月

第一版前言

自 1997 年起至今，全国大部分工科院校已按教育部制定的专业调整方案陆续开设了"测控技术与仪器"专业，并正式纳入教学常规。此学科覆盖了以往的电子、测量、计量、精密仪器等近十个专业，在全国构成了数以十万计的师生队伍。本教材正是适应了这样的教学、科研形势要求，遵照"全国部分高校化工类专业英语阅读教材编委会"1999 年、2000 年两届会议的精神及编写要求编写而成。全书具有以下特色。

1. 从课文、词汇、阅读材料三个方面合理地覆盖测控技术与仪器领域的基本理论和主要技术的内容和信息；
2. 引用国际上较高水平的理论、思想和观点；
3. 采用具有较深厚的教学与学术背景的资料来源；
4. 词汇水平保持在四级以上。

内容与结构 全书共分为 4 章、18 个单元。第 1 章综合地介绍了测量技术的背景、基本理论、基本概念及全貌；第 2 章介绍了控制技术的背景、基本理论、基本概念及全貌；第 3 章较具体地介绍测试技术的具体内容；第 4 章重点介绍了当前国内外的一些新的测量技术及方法。

每篇课文之后设置了词汇表、注释、练习和阅读材料；每篇阅读材料之后也设有词汇表和注释。全书后设有总词汇表，并附有文献查阅指导、产品与技术说明书阅读指导及专业论文书写指导。

适用范围 可供电子、信息、测量、计量、自控专业的大本、大专或硕士研究生作为阅读教材用，也可供相关领域的教师、科技人员作参考教材用。

本书由北京化工大学韩建国与四川大学廖俊必主编。北京化工大学信息学院张杰老师和四川大学成都分校机械制造学院测控系张涛老师参加了本教材的部分内容编写及全书的审核、整编工作。

清华大学肖德云教授担任了本书的主审工作，并提出了一系列指导性意见，在此表示深切的谢意。

本教材的出版得到了北京化工大学化新教材建设基金的资助。

由于作者水平有限，书中难免会有疏漏，希望得到广大读者的批评指正。

编 者
2002 年 3 月

CONTENTS

CHAPTER. 1　Introduction to Measurement ·· 1
　Unit 1　Definition of Measurement and Measurement Theory ············· 1
　　　　　Reading Material 1　Descriptions of Measurement ················ 6
　Unit 2　Measurement of Quantities and Measurement Data ················ 9
　　　　　Reading Material 2　Significant Digits and Rounding Numbers ······ 14
　Unit 3　Measurement Methods and Strategies ································· 16
　　　　　Reading Material 3　Some Concepts of Measurement Method and Strategy ········ 23
　Unit 4　Calibration ··· 28
　　　　　Reading Material 4　Calibration Records ····························· 30
　Unit 5　Operating Characteristic ··· 32
　　　　　Reading Material 5　Static Characteristics ··························· 35
CHAPTER. 2　Introduction to Control System ··································· 38
　Unit 6　Introduction ··· 38
　　　　　Reading Material 6　Describing Control System Using Transfer Function ··· 47
　Unit 7　Process Control System ·· 49
　　　　　Reading Material 7　Control System Drawings ····················· 54
　Unit 8　Computer Network Based Industrial Control Systems ············· 58
　　　　　Reading Material 8　On PLC's Registers and Selecting a PLC ···· 66
　Unit 9　Levels of Industrial Control ··· 70
　　　　　Reading Material 9　Network Communications and Architecture Model ······ 73
　Unit 10　Fieldbuses and Interoperability ·· 75
　　　　　Reading Material 10　Fieldbus ·· 77
CHAPTER. 3　Introduction to Measurement/test Technology and Equipment ············ 79
　Unit 11　Typical Measurement Technology ···································· 79
　　　　　Reading Material 11　Some Advantaged Measurement Technologies ········ 83
　Unit 12　Simple Instrument Model ·· 88
　　　　　Reading Material 12　Some Advantaged Instrument Model ······· 93
　Unit 13　Signal Process ·· 96
　　　　　Reading Material 13　Spectrum Analysis and Correlation ········· 100
　Unit 14　Basic Concepts of Communication and Networking ·············· 104
　　　　　Reading Material 14　Additional Concepts of Communication and Networking ············ 108
　Unit 15　Signal Sensing and Data Record/Display ··························· 112
　　　　　Reading Material 15-1　Digital Temperature DS18B20 ············ 120
　　　　　Reading Material 15-2　Other Data Record and Display ·········· 122

CHAPTER. 4　Modern Measurement and Control Technology ………………………… 127
　Unit 16　Intelligent Control Systems ……………………………………………… 127
　　　　　　Reading Material 16　Fuzzy Neural Control ……………………………… 133
　Unit 17　Machine Vision Systems ………………………………………………… 136
　　　　　　Reading Material 17　Theoretical Basis of Image Processing …………… 145
　Unit 18　Virtual Reality Applications ……………………………………………… 149
　　　　　　Reading Material 18　Human Factors Modeling ………………………… 157
　Unit 19　Bionics Measurement ……………………………………………………… 161
　　　　　　Reading Material 19　Optical Polarization Based Navigation Technology ……… 164
　Unit 20　Embedded System Supporting Control Process ………………………… 170
　　　　　　Reading Material 20　The High-performance Microcontroller of Embedded
　　　　　　　System—ATmega 8 …………………………………………………… 174
附录 ………………………………………………………………………………………… 181
　附录一　关于如何撰写英文的学术论文 ……………………………………………… 181
　附录二　关于如何参加一次国际 IEEE 学术会议 …………………………………… 188
　附录三　关于"工程索引"EI …………………………………………………………… 195
　附录四　总词汇表 ……………………………………………………………………… 198

CHAPTER. 1 Introduction to Measurement

Unit 1 Definition of Measurement and Measurement Theory

> Before reading the text below, try to answer the following questions:
> 1. What is necessary but not sufficient definition, and how to give a necessary and sufficient definition to measurement?
> 2. What is a satisfying definition and under what condition can a definition of measurement be considered as a satisfying one?
> 3. What a concept is the measurement established based on?
> 4. What a point on measurement results is set up in this theory?
> 5. What is the theoretically restricted definition of measurement?
> 6. What is an empirical relational system?

1. Definition of Measurement

A possible operational description of the term measurement which agrees with our intuition is the following: "measurement is the acquisition of information"; the aspect of gathering information is one of the most essential aspects of measurement; measurements are conducted to learn about the object of measurement; the measurand. This means that a measurement must be descriptive with regard to that state or that phenomenon in the world around us which we are measuring. There must be a relationship between this state or phenomenon and the measurement result. Although the aspect of acquiring information is elementary, it is merely a necessary and not a sufficient aspect of measurement: when one reads a textbook, one gathers information, but one does not perform a measurement.

A second aspect of measurement is that it must be selective. It may only provide information about what we wish to measure (the measurand) and not about any other of the many states or phenomena around us. This aspect too is a necessary but not sufficient aspect of measurement. Admiring a painting inside an otherwise empty room will provide information about only the painting, but does not constitute a measurement.

A third and necessary aspect of measurement is that it must be objective. The outcome of the measurement must be independent of an arbitrary observer. Each observer must extract the same information from the measurement and must come to the same conclusion. This, however, is almost impossible for an observer who uses only his/her senses. Observations made with our senses are highly subjective. Our sense of temperature, for example, depends strongly on any sensation of hot or cold preceding the measurement. This is demonstrated by trying to determine the temperature of a jug of water by hand. If the hand is first dipped in cold water, the water in the jug will feel relatively warm, whereas if the hand is first dipped in warm water, the water in the jug will feel relatively cold. Besides the subjectivity of our observation, we human observers are also handicapped by the fact that there are many states or phenomena in the real world around us which we cannot observe at all (e. g. magnetic fields), or only poorly (e. g. extremely low temperatures or high-speed movement). In order to guarantee the objectivity of a measurement we must therefore use artefacts (tools or instruments). The task of these instruments is to convert the state or phenomenon under observation into a different state or phenomenon that cannot be misinterpreted by an observer. In other words, the instrument converts the initial observation into a representation that all observers can observe and will agree on. For the measurement instrument's output, therefore, objectively observable output such as numbers on an alpha-numerical display should be used rather than subjective assessment of such things as colour, etc.. Designing such instruments, which are referred to as measurement systems, is the field of (measurement) instrumentation.

In the following, we will define measurement as the acquisition of information in the form of measurement results, concerning characteristics, states or phenomena (the measurand) of the world that surrounds us, observed with the aid of measurement systems (instruments). The measurement system in this context must guarantee the required descriptiveness, the selectivity and the objectivity of the measurement. We can distinguish two types of information: information on the state, structure or nature of a certain characteristic, so-called structural information, and information on the magnitude, amplitude or intensity of a certain characteristic, so-called metric information. The acquisition of structural information is called a qualitative measurement, the acquisition of metric information is called a quantitative measurement. If the nature of the characteristic to be measured is not (yet) known, it must be determined first by means of a qualitative measurement. This can then be followed by a quantitative measurement of the magnitude of the respective characteristic.

2. Measurement Theory

In the previous section we have seen that measurements form the essential link between the empirical world and our theoretical, abstract image of the world. This concept forms the basis of a theory of measurement. In this theory a measurement result is considered to be a representation of the actual empirical quantity. Measurement theory treats measurements as a mapping of elements of a source set belonging to the empirical domain space (see Fig. 1.1) onto the elements of an image (or outcome) set which is part of the abstract range (or image) space[1]. The quantity to be measured (the measurand) is an element of the source set. For instance, in the electrical domain we measure electrical current (source set) but only within a certain range of magnitude (elements). The result of the measurement process[2] is abstract; it forms an element of the image set in the abstract range space. For example, the magnitude of the electrical current to be measured in the above example is (by measurement) assigned a certain number (element) out of the set of real numbers (image set). In other words, the elements of the source set are empirical characteristics of states and phenomena of the world around us; the elements of the image set are symbols of the abstract image set of symbols. The symbols can be numbers (quantitative measurements) but can also be, for example, names (quantitative measurements).

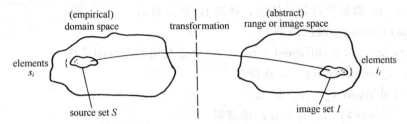

Fig. 1.1 Measurement constitutes the mapping between an empirical domain and a range space

Restricting the definition of measurement further, measurement theory states that measurement is the mapping of elements from an empirical source set onto elements of an abstract image set according to a particular transformation function. The transformation function consists of the assignment algorithms, rules or procedures that define the representation of empirical quantities by abstract symbols. In practice the assignment algorithm, rule or procedure is implemented by the employed measurement system. The measurement system therefore determines the representation. As stated earlier, this representation must be done in a descriptive, objective and selective way. Thus, the image set must consist of elements (measurement outcomes) which are abstract symbols with a unique meaning about which, by definition, all observers agree.

A measurement must be descriptive. In measurement theory this is described in terms of set theory: the relations that exist between the elements of the source set must be maintained under the transformation in the image set, for example, "larger than", "equal to" and "smaller than". The set of relations between the elements of the source set is referred to as the relational system (of the source set).

This empirical relational system determines the structure of the source set. Likewise, an abstract relational system determines the structure of the image set (for instance, the set of relations that apply to the set of integer numbers). A measurement (representation) is now called descriptive if the relational system or structure of the empirical source set is invariant under the transformation (measurement). The measurement only represents that which is measured if the two relational systems are identical; otherwise information is lost in the mapping. An example is measuring with a very low resolution; two different current magnitudes are mapped onto the same outcome, and are indistinguishable from each other.

Selected from "Electronic measurement and instrument, by Klassen, Klass B., Cambridge University Press, 1996".

Words and Expressions

1. operational description 操作描述
2. acquisition of information 信息采集
3. object of measurement 测量目标
4. measurand n. 被测物理量［性质，状态］，被测对象
5. measurement result 测量结果
6. a necessary and not a sufficient aspect 一个必要而非充分的条件
7. selectivity ［ˌsilek'tivəti］ n. 选择性
8. objective ［əb'dʒektiv］ adj. 客观的
9. observer ［əb'zɜːvə］ n. 观察者；观察器
10. extract ［'ekstrækt］ vt. 吸取，摘取
11. arbitrary ［'ɑːbitrəri］ adj. 专横的，专断的，反复无常的
12. conclusion ［kən'kluːʒ(ə)n］ n. 结论
13. highly subjective 高度主观的
14. handicapped ［'hændikæpt］ adj. 残疾的
15. magnetic fields 磁场
16. objectivity ［ˌɔbdʒek'tivəti］ n. 客观性
17. artefact ［'ɑːtifækt］ n. 人工品
18. misinterpret ［misin'təːprit］ vt. 曲解
19. measurement instrument's output 测量装置的输出
20. structural information 结构信息
21. metric information 公制信息
22. qualitative measurement 质量测量
23. quantitative measurement 数量测量
24. nature ［'neitʃə(r)］ n. 本性，本质
25. respective characteristic 各自的特性
26. empirical world 经验的世界
27. abstract image 抽象的映像
28. actual empirical quantity 实际经验的数量
29. mapping of elements 元素的映射
30. source set 源集
31. empirical domain space 经验域空间
32. image set 映像集
33. abstract range space 抽象域空间
34. electrical domain 电气域
35. measurement process 测量过程
36. symbol ［'simb(ə)l］ n. 符号，记号，象征
37. transformation function 转换功能
38. assignment algorithm 分配算法

39. abstract symbol 抽象符号
40. employed measurement system 被使用的测量系统
41. descriptive [di'skriptiv] adj. 描述的，叙述的
42. set theory 集合论
43. relational system 相关系统

Exercises

1. Complete the summary of the text, using no more than 3 words for each answer.

    The definition for measurement such as "measurement is the acquisition of information" and "it must be selective" is _____, because when one gathers information, he _____ a measurement. The definition of measurement such as "it must be selective" is _____ because when one obtains a selected information, he _____ a measurement. A satisfying definition must be _____. The third and necessary aspect of measurement is that it _____. The results of the measurement must be _____. Each observer must fetch the same information _____ and must be led to _____. This is almost impossible, because an observer may use only _____.

    From the previous section an important concept is developed that measurements sets up the essential link between _____ and _____ graphic comprehension of the world. Based on this concepts the _____ of measurement is developed. In this theory a measurement result is a _____ of the actual empirical quantity, and a measurement is treat as _____, which attributes to the _____. The measurand is an element of the _____. The result of the measurement process is abstract; it forms an element in _____. According to the theoretical definition, measurement is a _____ from _____ onto _____ of _____ according to a _____, which consists of _____. The measurement system is _____, which must be done in a _____, _____ and _____ way. The image set must consists of _____ which are _____ with a unique meaning.

2. Describe why the condition listed for the third definition of measurement mentioned in the text is impossible to be realized?
3. Illustrate the satisfying definition for measurement in your own words and using your own examples.
4. Describe what a role the qualitative measurement plays.
5. Illustrate the theoretically restricted definition of measurement.

Notes

① "Measurement theory treats…of the abstract range (or image) space.": 全句可译为：测量理论把测量理解为属于经验域空间的源集的元素到作为一个抽象范围（或称影像）空间的一部分的影像集元素的映射。句中"映射源"是"elements of a source set belonging to the empirical domain space", 映像是 "elements of an image (or outcome) set which is part of the abstract range (or image) space"

② process：这个词在下文中常常出现。当它作为名词出现时，常常指 "过程"，与 "系统" 相近，但强调了动态特性；当它作为动词出现时，常常指 "处理"，如，对信号进行处理等。

Reading Material 1

Descriptions of Measurement

1. Why measuring?

Why is there so much measuring going on? Apparently to provide information about the world that surrounds us, the observers. One reason may therefore be that we wish to add to and to improve our perception of that world. Abstractly speaking, our aim is to increase our knowledge of the surrounding world and the relationships that exist between characteristics, states and phenomena in this world. This is the case even when we measure such day to day quantities as tire pressure, body temperature (fever), etc. The gathered information enables us to reduce seemingly complex characteristics, states, phenomena and relationships to simpler laws and relations. Thus, we can form a better, more coherent and objective picture of the world, based on the information measurement provides. In other words, the information allows us to create models of (parts of) the world and formulate laws and theorems. We must then determine (again by measuring) whether these models, hypotheses, theorems and laws are a valid representation of the world. This is done by performing tests (measurements) to compare the theory with reality. We have actually described the application of measurement in the "pure" sciences. We assume that "pure" science has the sole purpose of

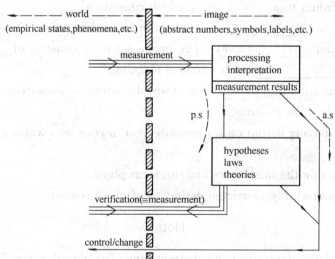

Fig. 1.2 Measurement as the link between the real world on the one hand and its concept in the "pure" sciences (p.s) and "applied" science (a.s) on the other

describing the world around us and is therefore responsible for our perception of the world. Fig. 1.2 illustrates this schematically.

In Fig. 1.2 the role of measurements in "applied" sciences is also indicated We consider "applied" science as science intended to change the world. Thereto, it will use the models, laws and theorems of "pure" science to modify the world around us. In this context, the purpose of measurement to regulate, controller alter the surrounding world, directly or indirectly based on the results of measurements and (existing) models, laws and theorems.

2. A Formal Description of Measurement

Let us now try to put this more formally: Assume that an empirical source set S consists of n elements s_i, so that $S = \{s_1, s_2, \cdots, s_n\}$. Let there exist k empirical relation R_j between the elements $s_i \in S$, so $R_j \subset E^{mj}$. Further, let the abstract image set I consist of m elements i_i, $I = \{i_1, i_2, \cdots, i_m\}$. Between these elements there are l relations N_j, so that $N_j \subset I^{mj}$. Clearly, if $k \neq l$, for instance, if l is large than k, the measurement outcome will suggest more information than is actually present in the measurand. Similarly, if the number of elements of the two sets is not equal($m \neq n$), for instance, $n > m$, the resolution of the mapping process may be inadequate. Therefore, for simplicity, let us assume $k = l$ and $m = n$. Now, let there be a function f that maps the elements of S onto I. We have to assume that this function is a single-valued, monotonic function in s_i. This will ensure a unique mapping onto I. The two relational systems $(S, R_1, R_2, \cdots, R_k)$ and $(I, N_1, N_2, \cdots, N_L)$ are isomorphic if:

$$\{s_1, s_2 \cdots s_{nj}\} \in R_j \Leftrightarrow \{f(s_1), f(s_2), \cdots, f(s_{nj})\} \in N_j$$

Again, the function f is implemented by the employed measurement system in the form of an algorithm, rule or procedure.

If we require isomorphism, we ensure that the relations between the elements of S are preserved; the structure remains the same. In other words, the information contained in the relations is not lost during the measurement. Although the requirement for isomorphism may preserve the structure of S, it does not define the representation entirely. It allows a certain amount of freedom in choosing the measurement procedure. This freedom can be demonstrated by transforming the measurement results using 'legal' transformations into new results which contain the same information. The requirement for isomorphism does not yield a single, unique representation, but rather a group of congruent representations. The results obtained with each of these representations can be transformed into one another, without loss of information. Such allowed transformations do not affect the structure of the empirical domain S. The information contained in the measurement results is invariant with respect to the allowed transformations. The allowed transformations therefore show exactly how unique the assignment of measurement values is.

Selected from "Electronic measurement and instrument, by Klassen, Klass B., Cambridge University Press, 1996".

Words and Expressions

1. gathered information   收集到的信息

2. enable [iˈneib(ə)l] vt. 使……有能力
3. theorem [ˈθiərəm] n. 定理；法则
4. valid representation 有确凿根据的陈述
5. hypothesis [haiˈpɔθisis] n. 假说，假设，学说； pl. hypotheses
6. schematically [skiˈmætikəli] 概要地
7. simplicity [simˈplisiti] n. 简单地
8. single-value 单值
9. monotonic function 单调函数
10. measurement constitute 测量组成
11. isomorphic [aisəuˈmɔːfik] adj. 同形的，[数] 同构的
12. preserve [priˈzɜːv] vt. 保护，保存
13. legal transformation 合法转换
14. yield [jiːld] v. 出产，生长，生产
15. congruent representation 适合的表述法
16. monotonic [ˌmɔnəˈtɔnik] adj. 单调的；没有变化的
17. invariant [inˈveəriənt] adj. 无变化的，不变的； n. [数] 不变式，不变量

Unit 2 Measurement of Quantities and Measurement Data

> Before reading the following text, try to answer the questions:
> 1. What physical quantities are often used in test and measure technology?
> 2. What energy system do physical quantities attribute to?
> 3. How do people make standards for these physical quantities?
> 4. What important usages are there for the quantities?
> 5. What do people mean with the term "data"?
> 6. What are qualitative data and quantitative data?
> 7. How do people categorize numerical data?
> 8. What stages will the data go through after it is collected?

1. Measurement of Physical Quantity

The physical quantities listed bellow are often used in test and measure technology. The first 2 are commonly called as electrical quantities and the other are commonly called as electrical parameters.

Usually the sensors receive the information of quantities under measurement (QUM) and convert it into variation of electrical parameters or electrical potential, which will normally be conditioned, and then converted into the electrical quantities, specially the current, and sent to the A/D converters.

Electrical potential difference

The primary standard for electrical potential difference used to be provided by an electrochemical standard cell (the Weston standard cell). The voltage of a Weston cell is approximately 1.01860 V at 20℃, with an inaccuracy of 3×10^{-6} under optimal conditions. Optimal conditions mean a variation of temperature less than 10^{-3} K, no load, no vibrations or jolting. The cell must remain in an upright position. A Weston standard cell has a very long thermal after-effect. After the cell has been heated to 30℃ it can take 6 months before it is totally stable within 0.3 μV of the original value at 20 degrees. Furthermore, a Weston cell will age, resulting in an increase in the internal resistance ($R_I \approx 500 \sim 1000\Omega$), and a small decrease of a few μV in the output voltage (during the first years).

Electrical current

Electrical current is standardized by measurement with an instrument called a "current balance". This device measures the electromagnetic force between two current carrying coils (one fixed, one moving) by balancing it with the force of gravity, acting on a known mass. The force between the coils is given by $F = I^2 \mathrm{d}M/\mathrm{d}x$, in which M is the known mutual induction of the coils and x is the known distance between them. The differential quotient $\mathrm{d}M/\mathrm{d}x$

is determined by the known geometry of the coils.

Electrical resistance

Standards of electrical resistance are resistors wound of special alloy wire giving a minimal temperature effect. An example of such an alloy is evanohm, consisting of 74% nickel, 20% chromium and 6% aluminium and iron. This alloy is frequently used for high resistance standards (10 kΩ). For low resistance values (1 Ω) manganine (86% Cu, 12% Mn, 2% Ni) or constantan (54% Cu, 45% Ni, 1% Mn) is often used. Higher-order resistance standards are kept at very accurately stabilised temperatures by thermostats.

Capacitance

It is possible to construct a capacitor from four coaxial cylinders, whose capacitance only depends on the length of the cylinders. Such a capacitor is particularly suitable as a standard of capacitance, since only the length has to be determined accurately. With the aid of optical interferometry this can be done extremely accurately. These so-called Thompson-Lampard cylinder capacitors can achieve an inaccuracy of less than 10^{-8}. A disadvantage, however, is the fact that the capacitance is small (approximately 1.9pF per metre). For lower-order standards other configurations of electrodes are used, which provide larger capacitance values (10~1000 pF), but also come with larger uncertainties.

Inductance

Accurate standards of inductance are difficult to realise. This is caused by the many parameters that determine the relatively complex geometry of a coil, all of which influence the accuracy of the inductor. Furthermore, power losses occur, due to wire resistance, proximity effects and eddy currents, which add to the inaccuracy. Currently available standards of inductance have an inaccuracy of about 10^{-5}.

Frequency

The standard of frequency is based on the quantum mechanical effect that electrons in an atom can only occupy one of a limited number of discrete energy levels. If an electron jumps to a higher or a lower energy level, the difference in energy ΔE of the photon that is absorbed or emitted, respectively, is related to the frequency of the photon by the expression $\Delta E = h f_0$. When atoms are irradiated with electromagnetic energy of frequency f_0, many electrons will pass to higher energy levels.

2. Measurement of non-physical quantities

Non-physical quantities found in non-technical fields are very difficult or even impossible to measure, mainly because they are part of very complex systems (people, organizations, societies, etc.). Cardinal measurements can therefore very rarely be made when dealing with the non-physical characteristics, states or phenomena in such systems.

When measuring complex systems or objects, the measurand often also depends on all kinds of other quantities. Usually, the nature and magnitude of these dependencies are unknown. Furthermore, these parasitic quantities, which influence the measurement result, are not constant during the measurement, making it impossible to correct any errors in the measurement. This means that the measurement is no longer selective; other factors are also being measured. Non-physical quantities are usually a part of a living organism or an organization of living beings. It is essential to the nature of an organism or an organization that they maintain (social, cultural, political) interactions with their environment. For this reason, it is usually not possible to perform an isolated measurement in the same way we can with inanimate things (putting in a thermostat, hooking up to a fixed supply voltage, etc.). It is, for example, not very practicable to isolate a section of the population from the rest of the world, for the sake of an economic measurement conducted to verify the relationship between the scarcity and the price of consumer goods. The object of the measurement continues to interact with its surroundings, to an extent and in a manner that remains unknown. These interactions obscure and corrupt the measurement results to some unknown degree, depending on the sensitivity to these interference.

Also, the repetition of an experiment is often not possible when dealing with such complex measurement objects. With physical measurements we often repeat a measurement to see how reproducible it is and to determine the magnitude of random errors. With non-physical measurements, however, the object often behaves differently the second time, because it has either learned from the first measurement, or it is no longer motivated to co-operate, has become tired, etc. Think, for example, of taking the same examination twice.

For ethical, political or financial reasons it is also usually not possible to freely modify variables to determine how they influence the measurement object, for example, increasing the scarcity of food in an economic community to determine the influence on the consumer's spending behavior.

As opposed to a physical measurement, the object of a non-physical measurement is often conscious of being measured. The mere fact that we measure influences the subject. The subject will behave differently in a laboratory than in daily life. An example for an often used (and abused) test animal: the rat. A measurement can even cause irrevocable processes in the object. Certain psychological experiments, for example, can cause catatonic states in certain patients, resulting in mental disorders or even chronic schizophrenia. The effects mentioned above will generally make it difficult to reproduce measurements in the fields of human and social studies accurately, assuming that these measurements can actually be made reasonably selectively and objectively.

Selected from "Electronic measurement and instrument, by Klassen, Klass B., Cambridge University Press, 1996".

3. The Nature of Data

Information you gather is called data. Data can be a factual statement of physical phenomena. For example, the statement "the copper was removed by the chemical reaction with ferric chloride" is descriptive data. When data is purely descriptive, it is said to be qualitative data. When a quantity is measured, we associate numerical values with it, and the information is more useful in a scientific way because more information is present. Information about the magnitude or intensity of a physical phenomenon is called quantitative data. Recall that the quantity that is being measured is called the measurand. Instrumentation extends the human senses by allowing a numerical value or values to be associated with the measurand.

Numerical data can be categorized in several ways. It can be an isolated value or can be dependent on time or location. Values recorded directly from an experiment or observation are called empirical data. Prior to processing, empirical data is often referred to as raw, or unprocessed data, whereas data that has been analyzed is called processed data. Data can also be generated by theoretical calculations. Frequently, theoretical data is compared to measured or processed data as a test of the theoretical model.

After data is collected, it may need to be processed either by applying mathematical computations to it or by arranging it in some meaningful manner. This procedure is called data processing or data reduction. Data may be entered into a computer for reduction, or, in some cases, the measurement instrument may perform the data reduction within the instrument. For example, a digital oscilloscope may present the rms value of a voltage as a displayed numeric value. As part of the process of data reduction, obvious errors or discrepancies should be looked for; sometimes statistical processing is applied to indicate the nature of experimental precision.

Selected from "Applied Electronic Instrumentation and Measurement, by David M. Buchla and Wayne C. McLachlan, Prentice-Hall, 1992" Englewood Cliffs, New Jersey.

Words and Expressions

1. physical quantity　物理量
2. electrical potential difference　电势差
3. cardinal measurement　最重要的测量
4. jolt [dʒəult]　v. 重击，摇撼
5. mutual induction　互感
6. quotient ['kwəuʃnt]　n. [数] 商数
7. alloy　合金；贱金属；成色
8. thermostat ['θə:məstæt]　n. 自动调温器
9. coil [kɔil]　n. 线圈；螺旋；vt. 盘绕
10. geometry [dʒi'ɔmitri]　n. 几何，几何学；几何图形，几何结构
11. coaxial [kəu'æksiəl]　adj. [数] 同轴的；[电] 同轴电缆的
12. cylinder ['silində]　n. 圆柱体；汽缸；圆柱形的容器
13. parasitic quantity　寄生量，附加量
14. dependency [di'pendənsi]　n. 从属，从属物
15. interaction [intər'ækʃn]　n. 交互作用，交感
16. isolated measurement　隔离测量，独立测量
17. inanimate [in'ænimət]　adj. 死气沉沉的，没生命的，单调的
18. practicable ['præktikəb(ə)l]　adj. 能实行的，行得通的，可以实行的
19. sake [seik]　n. 为了……之好处，出于对……的兴趣，缘故，理由
20. conduct [kən'dʌkt]　v. 引导，传导

21. consumer goods 消费商品
22. scarcity ['skeəsiti] n. 缺乏，不足
23. extent [ik'stent] n. 范围，程度
24. obscure [əb'skjuə] vt. 使暗，使不明显
25. corrupt [kə'rʌpt] vt. 使恶化
26. sensitivity [sensi'tiviti] n. 敏感，灵敏（度），灵敏性
27. repetition [repi'tiʃən] n. 重复性
28. reproducible [ˌriːprəˈdjuːsəbl] adj. 能繁殖的，可再生的，可复写的
29. random errors 随机误差
30. ethical ['eθik(ə)l] adj. 与伦理有关，民族的，民族特有的
31. modify variable 修改变量
32. irreversible process 不可改变的进程
33. psychological experiment 心理试验
34. catatonic state 紧张性精神病的状态
35. mental disorder 精神错乱
36. chronic schizophremia adj. 慢性的精神分裂症
37. oscilloscope [ə'siləkəup] n. 示波器，示波管（OSP）
38. rms abbr. root-mean-square 均方根
39. ferric ['ferik] adj. 铁的；含铁的
40. chloride ['klɔːraid] n. [化学]氯化物；漂白粉

Exercises

1. Complete the summary of the text, using no more than 5 words for each answer.

   In fact, all the physical quantities mentioned in the text are attributed to _____ energy system. Electrical quantities include _____ and _____. Electrical parameters include _____, _____, _____ and _____. The electrochemical cell called _____ provide _____ and _____.

   Optimal conditions for providing a standard to electrical potential difference mean a variation of temperature _____ or _____.

   The instrument called as "current balance" is used to _____.

   The standard of electrical resistance is provided by _____ with special _____. An important feature of this resistor is giving _____. Thermostats are used to keep the _____ at _____.

   The accuracy of a inductor is mainly influenced by _____.

   Information obtained by human is normally called _____. The data which is _____ is called as qualitative data. The data which is _____ is called as quantitative data. Information is related with numerical values through the method called _____. Empirical data is such values which are obtained by _____ or _____ directly. Data can be obtained by both methods, _____ and _____. After data is collected, it will be _____ by _____ or _____. The methods are called __

_____ or _____ . Data analysis is carried out in order to _____ and to _____ . The combination of the effects, _____ and _____ is used to _____ .

2. Illustrate the function of sensor related with quantities under measurement, electrical parameters or electrical potential and electrical quantities.
3. Illustrate an example of application of electrical parameters and electrical potential based on your measurement/test experiment in your own word.
4. Answer the following questions in your words:
   (1) Can all information obtained by us be called data? Why?
   (2) Is the data appears without variation and difference, also useful for us?
   (3) How to process data in term of test/measurement? What purpose is there for each process stage?

Reading Material 2

Significant Digits and Rounding Numbers

When a measurement contains approximate numbers, the digits known to be correct are called significant digits. The number of significant digits in a measurement depends on the precision of the measurement. Many measuring instruments provide more digits than are significant, leaving it to the user to determine what is significant. In some cases, this is done because the instrument has more than one range and displays the maximum number of significant digits on the highest range. If the instrument is set to a lower range, the instrument may show the same number of digits despite the fact that the rightmost digits are not significant. This can occur when the resolution of the instrument does not change as the range is changed. The user needs to be aware of the resolution of an instrument to be able to determine correctly the number of significant digits.

When reporting a measured value, the least significant uncertain digit may be retained, but other uncertain digits should be discarded. To find the number of significant digits in a number, ignore the decimal place and count the number of digits from left to right, starting with the first nonzero digit and ending with the last digit to the right. All digits counted are significant except zeros to the right end of the number. A zero on the right end of a number is significant if it is to the right of the decimal place; otherwise it is uncertain. For example, 43.00 contains four significant digits, but the whole number 4300 may contain two, three, or four significant digits. In the absence of other information, the significance of the right-hand zeros is uncertain. To avoid confusion, a number should be reported using scientific notation. For example, the number 4.30×10^3 contains three significant figures and the number 4.300×10^3 contains four significant figures.

The rules for determining if a reported digit is significant are as follows:
① Nonzero digits are always considered to be significant.
② Zeros to the left of the first nonzero digit are never significant.

③ Zeros between nonzero digits are always significant.

④ Zeros at the right end of a number and the right of the decimal are significant.

⑤ Zeros at the right end of a whole number are uncertain. Whole numbers should be reported in scientific notation to clarify the significant figures.

Since measurements always involve approximate numbers, they should be shown only with those digits that are significant plus no more than one uncertain digit. The number of digits shown is indicative of the precision of the measurement. For this reason, you should round a number by dropping one or more digits to the right. The rules for rounding are as follows:

① If the digit dropped is greater than 5, increase the last retained digit by 1.

② If the digit dropped is less than 5, do not change the last retained digit.

③ If the digit dropped is 5, increase the last retained digit if it makes it even, otherwise do not. This is called the round-even rule.

Selected from "Applied Electronic Instrumentation and Measurement, by David M. Buchla and Wayne C. McLachlan, Prentice-Hall, 1992".

Words and Expressions

1. significant digits　有效数字
2. rounding number　四舍五入数
3. decimal ['desiməl]　adj. 十进位的；小数的
4. nonzero [nɔn'ziərəu]　adj. 非零的
5. scientific way　科学方法
6. quantitative data　定量数据
7. measurable ['meʒərəbl]　a. 可测量的
8. categorize ['kætigəraiz]　vt. 分类
9. isolated value　分离量
10. empirical data　经验数据
11. raw or unprocessed data　原始或未处理数据
12. processed data　已处理过的数据
13. theoretical calculations　理论计算
14. theoretical model　理论模型
15. mathematical computations　数学计算
16. meaningful manner　有意义的方式
17. data processing　数据处理
18. data reduction　数据简化
19. measurement instrument　测量工具
20. discrepancy [di'skrepənsi]　n. 差异不一致，不符，差异
21. statistical processing　统计处理
22. experimental precision　精确实验
23. round-even　约偶，舍偶

Unit 3 Measurement Methods and Strategies

> Before reading the text below, try to answer the following questions:
> 1. What measurement methods are most important for measurement technology?
> 2. On what principles are the most important measurement methods developed based?
> 3. What is the problem of measurement strategies brought forward in addition to the measurement methods?
> 4. What can one do with the help of the three strategies mentioned in the text individually?
> 5. At what difficulties do these strategies have individually?
> 6. What principles are these strategies based on and what important methods are used regarding each strategy?

1. Measurement Methods

In order to conduct measurements in an optimal fashion, it is essential to be familiar with the most important methods, principles and strategies of measurement.

(1) Deflection method, difference method and null method

With the deflection method the read-out of the measurement device used entirely determines the result of the measurement. The difference method measures (indicates) only the difference between the unknown quantity and the known, reference quantity. Here, the result of the measurement is partially determined by the read-out of the measurement device used and partially by the reference quantity. Finally, with the "null method" the result is entirely determined by a known reference quantity. The read-out of the measurement instrument is used only to adjust the reference quantity to exactly the same value as the unknown quantity. The indication is then zero and the instrument is therefore used as a null detector or zero indicator.

(2) Compensation method and bridge method

On the basis of the number of power sources involved in a measurement, two other methods can be seen.

The compensation method is a method of measurement that removes the effect of the unknown quantity on the measurement system by compensating it with the effect of a known quantity. This is done in such a way that the unknown quantity is no longer influenced by the measurement system when full compensation is reached. If the unknown effect is compensated completely, no power is supplied to or withdrawn from the unknown quantity; the unknown quantity is not loaded by the measurement. The degree of compensation can be determined with a null indicator. The compensation method therefore requires an auxiliary power source that can supply precisely the power that otherwise would have been withdrawn from the measured quantity. Thus, for the compensation method, we need two power sources.

(3) Analogy method

This method makes use of a model of the object from which we wish to obtain measurement information. Measurements made on the model then provide information about the unknown object, as long as the model corresponds with the object in certain essential points. This analogy method is most often used when measurements of the actual object are not possible, extremely difficult, time consuming or costly.

(4) Repetition method

With this method several measurements of the same unknown quantity are conducted, each according to a different procedure. Most fundamental physical constants have been measured in several different ways, to prevent the possibility of making the same (systematic) errors, specific to a certain type of measurement. Different (correctly applied) methods of measurement will produce similar results, but the measurement errors in the results will be independent of each other. This will yield an indication of the reliability of the measurement.

(5) Enumeration method

The enumeration method is a method for determining the ratio of the magnitudes of two quantities (the known and the unknown) by counting. Only numbers of objects, patterns or events can be counted. Physical quantities of a given physical dimension must be *measured*. Measurement involves making errors, counting does not (mistakes excluded). The enumeration method is used, for instance, for measuring frequency. The frequency of a periodical signal is measured by simply counting the number of periods which fall within an accurately determined reference time interval.

Selected from "Electronic measurement and instrument, by Klassen, Klass B., Cambridge University Press, 1996".

2. Measurement Strategies

In addition to the methods of measurement discussed above, we will now examine several widely used measurement strategies. It is, in fact, not always possible to measure the desired physical quantity directly. If, for example, a quantity fluctuates more quickly than the measurement system can follow, correct information cannot be obtained; the frequency spectrum of the measured signal is wider than the bandwidth of the measurement system.

(1) Coherent sampling

This measurement strategy enables us to process a measurement signal with a spectrum width F, which is considerably larger than the bandwidth B of the measurement system, provided that the signal is periodic. By taking samples of the actual measurement signal at intervals that are just slightly larger than n periods of the signal (n integer), the shape of the signal can be preserved and a true representation can be obtained. If we denote the interval between the samples as $nT+\delta$, in which T is the period of the actual signal, the period of the reconstructed (from the samples) signal will be $(nT+\delta)T/\delta$. This means that the frequency has been reduced by a factor $\delta/(nT+\delta)$. Fig. 3.1 illustrates this principle. The number n of skipped periods and the ratio T/δ (the number of samples in one period of the reconstructed signal) are chosen in such a way that the reconstructed signal, which is the envelope of the peaks of the samples, has a frequency spectrum which is smaller than the bandwidth of the measurement system used to process the sampled signal. This type of sampling is used in stroboscopic measurements and in sampling oscilloscopes. A sampling oscilloscope with a bandwidth of 20 kHz, for instance, can display (periodic) electrical signals with a frequency of up to 15 GHz.

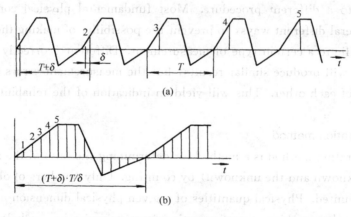

Fig. 3.1 Coherent sampling

(2) Random sampling

Coherent sampling, as discussed above, requires some kind of provision that ensures that the samples (1, 2, 3, ⋯, in Fig. 3.1) are taken at precisely the right instants. If we are only interested in amplitude information, however, and not in the shape of the signal, the samples can be taken at arbitrary moments: random sampling. In this manner it is very easy to determine, for example, the RMS-value of a signal with a wide frequency spectrum. The signal does not have to be periodic here. Another application is in obtaining the amplitude distribution function of a signal. More generally one may state that the statistical parameters of the signal amplitude are not affected.

(3) Multiplexing

This measurement strategy is a means of processing several signals, either simultaneously (frequency multiplexing) or sequentially (time multiplexing). This method can be used when the bandwidth of the measurement system is much wider than the frequency spectrum width of the measurement signals.

Selected from "Electronic measurement and instrument, by Klassen, Klass B., Cambridge University Press, 1996".

3. Error, Accuracy and Precision

Data measured with test equipment is not perfect; rather, the accuracy of the data depends on the accuracy of the test equipment and the conditions under which the measurement was made. In order to interpret data from an experiment, we need to have an understanding of the nature of errors. Experimental error should not be thought of as a mistake. All measurements that do not involve counting are approximations of the true value. Error is the difference between the true or best accepted value of some quantity and the measured value. A measurement is said to be accurate if the error is small-accuracy refers to a comparison of the measured and accepted, or "true," value. It is important for the user of an instrument to know what confidence can be placed in it. Instrument manufacturers generally quote accuracy specifications in their literature, but the user needs to be cautioned to understand the specific conditions for which an accuracy figure is stated. The number of digits used to describe a measured quantity is not always representative of the true accuracy of the measurement.

Two other terms associated with the quality of a measurement are precision and resolution. Precision is a measure of the repeatability of a series of data points taken in the measurement of some quantity. The precision of an instrument depends on both its resolution and its stability. Recall that resolution was defined in the previous section as the minimum discernible change in the measurand that can be detected. Stability refers to freedom from random variations in the result. A precise measurement requires both stability and high resolution. Precision is a measure of the dispersion of a set of data, not a measure of the accuracy of the data. It is possible to have a precision instrument that provides readings that are not scattered but that are not accurate because of a systematic error. However, it is not possible to have an accurate instrument unless it is also precise.

The resolution of a measurement is not a constant for a given instrument but may be changed by the measurand or the test conditions. For example, a nonlinear meter scale has a higher resolution at one end than at the other due to the spacing of the scale divisions. Likewise, noise induced in a system can affect the ability to resolve a very small change in voltage or resistance. Temperature changes can also affect measurements because of the effect on resistance, capacitance, dimensions of mechanical part, drift, and so forth.

Selected from "Applied Electronic Instrumentation and Measurement, by David M. Buchla and Wayne C. McLachlan, Prentice-Hall, 1992".

4. Systematic and Random Error

There are two classed of errors that affect measurements: systematic errors and random errors. Systematic errors consistently appear in a measurement in the same direction. These could be caused by inaccurate calibration, mismatched impedances, response-time error, nonlinearities, equipment malfunction, environmental change, and loading effects. Systematic errors are often unknown to the observer and may arise from a source that was not considered in the measurement. Sometimes a systematic error occurs because of the misuse of an instrument outside its design range, such as when a voltmeter is used to measure a frequency beyond its specifications. (This is also called an applicational error.) Another common type of systematic error is loading error. Whenever an instrument is connected to a circuit, it becomes part of the circuit being measured and changes the circuit to some extent. Measurements in high-impedance circuits can be significantly affected if this is not taken into account. Another possible systematic error is calibration error. For example, a frequency counter uses an internal oscillator to count an unknown frequency for a specific amount of time. If this oscillator runs too slowly, then the counter waits too long, giving a result that is consistently too high. This produces a systematic error for all readings made with that counter. Other systematic errors can occur because the calibration was performed under different environmental conditions than those present when the instrument is in service. These might include temperature, humidity, atmospheric pressure, vibration, magnetic or electrostatic fields, and so forth.

The best way to detect the presence of a systematic error is to repeat the measurement with a completely different technique using different instruments. If the two measurements agree, greater confidence can be placed in the correctness of the measurement.

Random errors (also called accidental errors) tend to vary in both directions from the true value by chance. These errors are unpredictable and occur because of a number of factors that determine the outcome of a measurement. Random errors are generally small and may be caused by electrical noise, interference, vibration, gain variation of amplifiers, leakage currents, drift, observational error, or other environmental factors. The best way to reduce random errors is to make repeated measurements and use statistical techniques to determine the uncertainty of the final result.

Selected from "Applied Electronic Instrumentation and Measurement, by David M. Buchla and Wayne C. McLachlan, Prentice-Hall, 1992".

Words and expressions

1. measurement strategy   测量策略
2. fluctuate ['flʌktjueit]   vi. 波动
3. frequency spectrum   频谱
4. coherent sampling   相干采样
5. periodic [piəri'ɔdik]   adj. 周期的，定期的
6. sample ['sɑ:mp(ə)l]   n. 采样值
7. actual measurement signal   实际测量信号
8. denote [di'nəut]   vt. 表示
9. skipped period   跳跃区间
10. reconstructed signal   重建的信号
11. envelope ['envələup]   n. 包络线

12. peak [pi:k]   n. 最高值，峰值
13. sampling oscilloscope   采样示波器
14. random sampling   随机采样
15. arbitrary moment   任意时刻
16. amplitude distribution function   振幅分布函数
17. statistical parameter   统计学参数
18. multiplex ['mʌltipleks]   v. 多路操作
19. simultaneously [ˌsiməl'teiniəsli]   adv. 同时地
20. sequentially [si'kwenʃəli]   adv. 顺序地
21. time multiplexing   时间多重操作
22. enumeration [iˌnjuːmə'reiʃən]   n. 计数，列举，细目
23. analogy [ə'nælədʒi]   n. 类推，类比，类推法
24. repetition [ˌrepi'tiʃən]   n. 重复，循环
25. denote [di'nəut]   vt. 指示，标志
26. stroboscopic [ˌstrəubəu'skɔpik]   adj. 频闪观测仪的
27. scatter ['skætə]   vt. 使分散，驱散，散布，挥霍； vi. 消散，溃散
28. nonlinearity   n. 非线性，非直线性
29. discernible [di'səːnəbl]   adj. 可看出的，可辨别的
30. class [klɑːs]   vt. 分类
31. systematic errors   系统误差
32. random errors   随机误差
33. consistently [kən'sistəntli]   ad. 一贯地，固守地
34. inaccurate calibration   不准确的刻度
35. mismatched impedance   不匹配的阻抗
36. response-time error   反应时间误差
37. malfunction [mæl'fʌŋkʃən]   n. 障碍；故障； vi. 发生故障
38. oscillator ['ɔsileitə]   n. 振动器，振动子，振荡器
39. humidity [hjuː'miditi]   n. 湿气；潮湿；湿度
40. calibration [ˌkæei'breiʃən]   n. 量口径；校准；测度；测定刻度

Exercises

1. Complete the summary of the text, using no more than 5 words for each answer.

   A common principle for measurement technology is to perform measurement in _____ _____.

   In order to be familiar with measurement technology, 3 most important factors must be well known, which are _____, _____ and _____. The key factor related to that a measurement method is attributed to Deflection Method, Difference Method or Null method lies in _____. The purpose of compensation measurement is to _____ by _____. The Analogy method uses _____. This method is often used when measurements of the actual object are _____. During the measurement with repetition method, different (correctly applied) methods of measurement will _____ , but the measurement errors in the result will _____. For enumeration method only _____ and _____ can be counted. This method is important not only for _____ but also for _____.

In order to measure some physical quantities which are normally _____ directly, some _____ are widely used. If a physical quantity varies _____ or the frequency spectrum _____ , then it is very difficult to measure. Because the correct information of it _____. Under the precondition that the physical quantities are periodical, the coherent sampling help us to measure them despite the fact that their frequency bandwidths are _____ than the frequency bandwidth of the _____ _____. According to coherent sampling strategy, the shape of the signal can be _____ and _____ can be obtained by taking sampling intervals that are n periods of the signal (n: integer). Random sampling method is used only for the measuring where only the information of _____ but not _____ is _____. When the bandwidth of the _____ of the measurement system is much _____ than the _____ of the measurement signals, the multiplexing method can be used. In such measurement strategy _____ signals, either _____ or _____ are processed.

The repeatability of a series of measurement depends on _____ and _____ of the instrument used. _____ and _____ determine the precision of instrument.

Two classes of errors that effect measurements are _____ and _____. Mean value of a large number of systematic errors can not be closed to the value _____ unless all values of the errors appear _____, because the values of all errors appear _____. The misuse of an instrument outside its range may cause a _____ error which is also called as _____ error. When an instrument is used under much different conditions than those present when it is _____, the _____ error appears. Such conditions include _____, _____, _____, _____, _____ or _____.

One _____ use mathematics equation to forecast the random errors. Random errors maybe caused by _____, _____, _____, _____, _____, _____ or _____.

2. Illustrate the means and application conditions of the 3 measurement strategies mentioned in the text in your own words with the help of the examples mentioned in the text.
3. List some practical examples to which the 3 measurement strategies can be applied.
4. Tell about the essential principles and effects of the measurements mentioned in the text.
5. Enumerate some possible application examples for these measurement methods according to their contents.
6. Define error accuracy, precision, stability, repeatability and resolution in your own words.

7. Discuss how to reach a good measurement accuracy in your own test/measurement experiment.

Reading Material 3

Some Concepts of Measurement Method and Strategy

1. Interchange Method and Substitution Method

In both the interchange method and the substitution method two measurements are performed in succession. With the interchange method the unknown quantity and the known quantity are both used simultaneously in each measurement. With the substitution method the known and unknown quantities are used separately and successively.

The substitution method first measures the unknown value of the measurand, which results in a certain indication deflection or reading of the measurement system. Then, the unknown quantity is replaced by a known and adjustable quantity, which is adjusted such that exactly the same measurement result is found. The indication of the measurement system is used here as an intermediate only. The characteristics of the measurement system should therefore not influence the measurement. Only the time stability and the resolution of the system are important. The resolution determines the "fineness" with which the unknown and known quantities can be made equal, the short-term stability determines the "drift" of the measurement system between the two measurements.

Calibration of a measurement system is, in fact, an application of the substitution method. First, the system is calibrated with a known quantity. An unknown quantity can then be measured accurately if its magnitude coincides with the calibrated points. A substitution method is also often used as a simple means for establishing equality, where the accuracy of the measurement system used to determine "equal" does not matter.

The interchange method is a method of measurement in which two, almost equal quantities in a measurement system are exchanged in a second measurement. This method can determine both the magnitude of the difference between the two quantities and the magnitude of a possible asymmetry in the measurement system. An example of this method is checking the equality of the two arms of a balance by swapping the weights on either side.

2. Time and Frequency Multiplexing

Fig. 3.2 gives an illustration of time multiplexing as it may be used, for instance, in an oil refinery. The analogue input signals come from various measuring points in the refinery where, say, temperature, pressure and flow are measured. These signals vary so slowly that a fast measurement and control system can process many of these signals sequentially and can put the resulting individual outputs on as many lines as there are inputs.

Frequency multiplexing shifts the frequency band of a narrow-band measurement signal, by modulation, to a different frequency band. This is done such that the spectra of several converted measurement signals will fit side by side in the frequency band, without overlap.

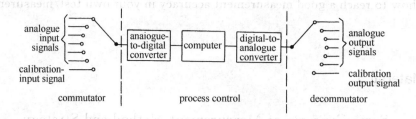

Fig. 3.2 Time multiplexing for process control

A demodulator at the output of the measurement system is necessary to restore each signal to its original frequency band. An example of this method is depicted in Fig. 3.3. This model is often used in telemetry (transmitting measurement signals) and telephony.

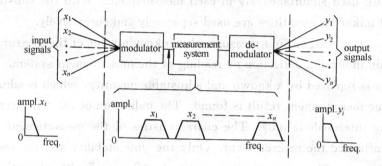

Fig. 3.3 Frequency multiplexing (F≪B)

Selected from "Electronic measurement and instrument, by Klassen, Klass B., Cambridge University Press, 1996".

3. The Normal Distribution

If a moderate-size group of measurements is tabulated, it can be difficult to see the significance of the data. A set of, for example, 60 data points for measurement of signal-to-noise ratio taken over several hours. The data can be rearranged in table from the smallest to the largest value. This may help clarify certain features of the data but has too many data points to show the overall pattern. If, instead, we tally the number of occurrences for each measurement that lie within some small interval, a frequency distribution of the results is obtained. The data can be listed as a frequency distribution in table. The frequency distribution sacrifices some details of the data but gives an overall representation of the results in a form that is easy to digest.

The normal distribution curve is important because many measurements are normally distributed or nearly so. As an example, a practical frequency distribution of some data is plotted as a histogram in Fig. 3.4. The histogram has the same information as tabulated frequency distribution; however, it is easier to interpret. If we make the measurement interval smaller and add many more observations, the frequency distribution curve will approach the famous bell-shaped curve called the **normal curve**, and the sample mean will approach the true value, as shown in Fig. 3.5. The normal curve extends indefinitely in both directions and is symmetrical about a vertical line drawn through the highest point. The vertical line represents the mean value of the measurement.

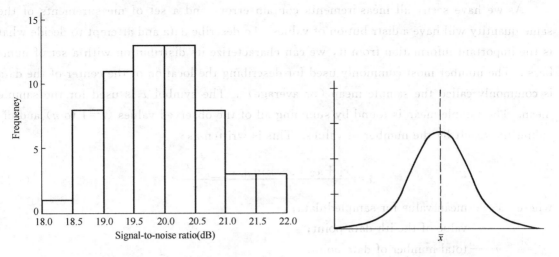

Fig. 3.4 Frequency distribution

Fig. 3.5 Bell-shaped normal distribution curve

There are some very useful relationships obtained from the normal distribution that allow us to make assumptions about the precision of the measurements. The most useful relationship is the **standard deviation**, which is a measure of the scatter of the data and permits us to assign a confidence range for the data. Standard deviation is abbreviated with the lowercase Greek letter sigma, $\hat{\sigma}$, shown with a circumflex to indicate an approximate value based on the measurements. If the data for the normal curve is tightly grouped about the mean, then the curve is narrow and the precision is high. As a result the standard deviation is small. On the other hand, if the data has large variations, then the normal curve is flatter, indicating that the results are less precise. As a consequence, the standard deviation is larger. Even though two different normal curves can have exactly the same mean, the standard deviations can be quite different, and the faith we place in the data is affected.

4. Statistic

Suppose you need to measure the upper cutoff frequency of an amplifier using an oscilloscope. You adjust the input frequency until the output amplitude drops to 70.7% of the midband amplitude and determine the frequency by counting the time for one cycle. You might decide to repeat the procedure several times to ensure that you have made the best possible measurement. Even though you have used the same procedure and equipment, the results are usually not identical because of random errors. The question arises, What is the best number to report and what is the precision of the result? The answer to this and other questions pertaining to observational data is given by a branch of mathematics called statistics.

Statistics is concerned with methods for handling data and drawing conclusions from it. There are two parts to the science of statistics. The first is called descriptive statistics and deals with collecting, processing, and analysis of data in a way that makes it comprehensible. The second is called statistical inference and has the goal of interpreting the data and drawing conclusions from it. The two parts are closely related. The drawing of inferences about data is meaningful only if we have previously collected, processed, and analyzed it.

As we have seen, all measurements contain error, and a set of measurements of the same quantity will have a distribution of values. To describe data and attempt to decide what is the important information from it, we can characterize its distribution with a set of numbers. The number most commonly used for describing the location of the center of the data is commonly called the sample mean (or average). The symbol $\bar{x}$ is used for the sample mean. The sample mean is found by summing all of the observed values ($i=1$ to n) and dividing the result by the number of values. This is written as

$$\bar{x} = \frac{x_1 + x_2 + x_3 + \cdots + x_n}{n} = \frac{\sum_{i=1}^{n} x_i}{n} \tag{1-1}$$

where $\bar{x}$——mean value for sampled data;
x_i——value of the ith data point;
n——total number of data point.

Selected from "Applied Electronic Instrumentation and Measurement, by David M. Buchla and Wayne C. McLachlan, Prentice-Hall, 1992".

Words and Expressions

1. interchange method 交换法
2. substitution method 代入法
3. indication deflection 指示偏差
4. adjustable quantity 可调量
5. intermediate [intəˈmiːdiət] n. 媒介; vt. 起中介作用
6. calibrated point 校正点
7. establish equality 建立等式
8. asymmetry [əˈsimitri] n. 不对称,不均匀
9. swap [swɔp] v. 交换
10. oil refinery 炼油厂
11. measuring point 测量点
12. flow [flou] n. 流量
13. frequency band 频率段
14. narrow-band 窄波段
15. overlap [əuvəˈlæp] v. (与……)交迭
16. modulation [mɔdjuˈleiʃən] n. 调制
17. demodulation [diːmɔdjuˈleiʃən] n. 解调
18. telemetry [tiˈlemətri] n. 遥感勘测,自动测量记录传导
19. tabulate [ˈtæbjuleit] vt. 把……制成表格;列表,制表(TAB)
20. tally [ˈtæli] n. 标签,记数器,记数; vt. 计算,记录,加标签; vi. 符合,记分
21. sacrifice [ˈsækrifais] n. 牺牲,献身; v. 牺牲,献出,供奉
22. histogram [ˈhistəgræm] n. 直方图,柱状图,矩形图

23. bell-shaped 钟形的
24. circumflex ['sə:kəmfleks] n. 昂低音符，长音符；音调符号；声调符号
25. transmitting measurement signal 测量信号发送
26. upper cutoff frequency 频段上截
27. midband amplitude 频带中心振幅
28. identical [ai'dentikəl] a. 同一的，相似的
29. observational data 观测数据
30. statistics [stə'tistiks] n. 统计学
31. descriptive statistics 描述性统计
32. comprehensible [ˌkəmpri'hensəbl] a. 可理解的
33. statistical inference 统计性推论
34. interpret [in'tə:prit] vt. 解释，翻译
35. distribution of value 数据分布
36. characterize ['kæriktəraiz] vt. 描绘……的特性
37. sample mean 样本均值

Unit 4   Calibration

> Before reading the text, try to answer the following questions:
> 1. What is calibration, and why do people perform it at specified intervals?
> 2. What are the standards, and what requirement must they satisfy?
> 3. What should the separate calibration groups do according to their tasks and office authorities?
> 4. What are calibration procedures and instrument performance check, and how are they implemented?

Calibration refers to the comparison of a measurement instrument to a standard or other instrument of known accuracy in order to bring the instrument into substantial agreement with an established standard. The established standard is normally of at least four times greater accuracy than the instrument being calibrated or the average of multiple standards if the four-times criterion is not feasible. To say that an instrument is calibrated means that it indicates measurements within specified limits of error for that instrument. To calibrate an instrument, the person doing the calibration should consider the limits of accuracy of the instrument to be calibrated, the methods that will be used to ensure that the required accuracy can be obtained, and the accuracy of the standard of instrument used as a reference. The accuracy of an instrument is dependent on three major contributing factors:

① The time since it was last calibrated;

② The difference between the calibration temperature and the operating temperature;

③ The uncertainty of the standard used for calibration.

In most organizations, calibration is the responsibility of a separate group. That group is responsible for maintaining working standards, keeping records of instruments for periodic calibration and certification, and being knowledgeable of the latest calibration procedures. The calibration facility is usually located in a separate standards laboratory, which is equipped to make the highest-accuracy measurements needed by the organization. The standards laboratory should have environmental controls to assure consistency because environmental factors can affect the accuracy of certain standards and the performance of instruments. Environmental factors that are controlled usually include temperature, humidity, vibration, dust, radio-frequency interference, grounding, and line voltage regulation.

The calibration procedure and instrument performance checks are generally specified by the instrument manufacturer in the manuals that are provided with the instrument. Sometimes calibration consists only of a performance check of the instrument to assure that it is operating within specified accuracy limits. Normally, if an instrument is operating well within its specified accuracy limits, adjustments to optimize its performance are unnecessary and should not be made. Frequent unnecessary adjustments may also interfere with the records for an instrument and accelerate progressive drift in values. An exception to this procedure can be made if the parameter is very near the tolerance limit and there is reason to believe it may be out of tolerance before the next calibration. The decision to adjust instruments that are close to the specified limits depends on the type of instrument and on the operating practice and philosophy of the laboratory doing the recalibration. The key factor is that the calibration laboratory is, in effect, guaranteeing that the instrument is calibrated and will remain calibrated until the next calibration due date (barring a breakdown). The technician making optimizing adjustments to an instrument needs to be aware that the adjustment of one parameter often has an interaction effect on another parameter. For example, if the power supply is "tweaked", it can have an effect on all other parameters and require a complete calibration check of the instrument.

Selected from "Applied Electronic Instrumentation and Measurement, by David M. Buchla and Wayne C. McLachlan, Prentice-Hall, 1992".

Words and Expressions

1. criterion [kraiˈtiəriən] n. 标准，准则，规律
2. known accuracy 已知精确度
3. substantial agreement 实质上的一致
4. established standard 现有标准
5. multiple standard 多重标准
6. feasible [ˈfiːzəbl] a. 可行的
7. specified limit 指定的限度
8. reference [ˈrefərəns] n. 参考
9. calibrate [ˈkæliˌbreit] vt. 校准
10. certification [ˌsəːtifiˈkeiʃən] n. 证明
11. calibration facility 校准装置
12. equip [iˈkwip] vt. 装备
13. environmental control 环境控制
14. performance check 性能检查
15. progressive drift 逐渐的漂移
16. tolerance limit 公差极限
17. key factor 关键因素
18. due date 期限，到期日
19. breakdown [ˈbreikdaun] n. 故障，损坏
20. tweak [twiːk] vt. 扭，捏，拧

Exercises

1. Fill in the blanks in the following sentences according to the text using your own words.

Calibration is defined as comparison of a _____ to a _____ or _____. Calibration is performed at a proper interval in order to keep the instrument _____. The standards must satisfy that it is _____. When an instrument can indicate measurements within _____, it is regarded as a _____ one. Three important factors, _____, _____ and _____, must be thought of by persons doing calibration. Three major contributing factors, _____, _____ and _____ determine the accuracy of an instrument.

The separate calibration groups have the task and right to make _____, and to control _____ in order to _____. Many factors such as _____, _____, and _____ influence the calibration interval, which may be _____ for stringent requirements or more typically _____. To keep instruments in a good working situation, generally the manufactures specified the _____ and _____ by using the _____.

Sometimes the instruments need neither to be completely calibrated nor to be adjusted to optimal performance when they satisfy the conditions that _____ and _____. The knowledge that _____ is important for the technicians to make _____.

2. List the calibration procedures or adjustment procedures of at least Three instruments of your own laboratories according to your instrument menus.
3. Explain how does the long term drift of instrument influences the calibration intervals referring to at least three instruments as examples.
4. Discuss with your classmates how to keep your instruments on a optimal performance and high accuracy without frequent calibration or adjustment.

Reading Material 4

Calibration Records

After an instrument's performance has been checked or it has been recalibrated, certain records should be completed. A label or other coding is attached to the instrument to indicate the instrument identification, date, person who performed the calibration, and the date when the instrument is to be rechecked. Different labels are used to indicate certain specific information about the calibration. A label may indicate conditions that affect the use of the instrument, such as a performance limitation, calibration deviation, that the instrument is traceable to NIST[①], or that no calibration is necessary.

In addition to the instrument label, a file record should be kept for each instrument belonging to an organization, listed by model and serial number. It should include the previously cited information plus any service work performed on the instrument. This record is valuable when troubleshooting an instrument, since it may point out likely problem locations. A similar record is often kept in a computer database to keep track of parts used on a particular instrument model, technician time, accounting charges, and the like. The computer record also simplifies the procedure for assuring that all instruments requiring calibration are recalled by the standards laboratory at the proper time interval. Careful monitoring of the calibration history of a model or class of instruments, including records on those that are out of tolerance and the repair history, can point to the need for corrective action, such as changing the recalibration interval, changing the recalibration procedure, derating the calibration, changing the specifications, or even removing an instrument from service.

Selected from " Applied Electronic Instrumentation and Measurement, by David M. Buchla and Wayne C. McLachlan, Prentice-Hall, 1992, Englewood Cliffs, New Jersey".

Words and Expressions

1. coding ['kəudiŋ] n. 编码
2. instrument identification 设备鉴定
3. performance limitation 性能限制因素，性能极限
4. calibration deviation 校验误差
5. traceable ['treisəbl] a. 起源于……的
6. file record 文件记录
7. serial number 序列号
8. cite [sait] vt. 引用
9. information [infə'meiʃən] n. 信息
10. valuable ['væljuəbl] a. 有用的，有价值的
11. troubleshoot ['trʌbl ʃu:tə] v. 排除故障
12. problem location 问题所在
13. computer database 计算机数据库
14. keep track of 跟踪，记录
15. accounting charge 结算费用
16. monitor ['mɔnitə] vt. 监控，监测，监听
17. calibration history 校验记录
18. corrective action 正确行为
19. derate [ˌdi:'reit] vt. 减免

Notes

① NIST = National Institute of Science and Technology 全国科学技术学会
　　　 = National Institute of Standard Technology （美国）国家标准技术研究所

Unit 5 Operating Characteristic

> Before reading the text, try to answer the following questions:
> 1. What are the meanings of range, span, and what are the differences between them?
> 2. How are resolution, dead-band and sensitivity related to an increase of measurement?
> 3. What are the reliability, over-range and drift?
> 4. What does environment of an experiment include?

Operating characteristics include details about the measurement by, operation of, and environmental effects on the measuring instrument.

1. Measurement

A measuring instrument can measure any value of a variable within its range of measurement. The range is defined by the lower range limit and the upper range limit. As the names imply, the range consists of all values between the lower range limit and the upper range limit. The span is the difference between the upper range limit and the lower range limit.

$$\text{Span} = \text{upper range limit} - \text{lower range limit}$$

Resolution, dead band, and sensitivity are different characteristics that relate in different ways to an increment of measurement. When the measured variable is continuously varied over the range, some measuring instruments change their output in discrete steps rather than in a continuous manner. The resolution of this type of measuring instrument is a single step of the output. Resolution is usually expressed as a percent of the output span of the instrument. Sometimes the size of the steps varies through the range of the instrument. In the case, the largest step is the maximum resolution. The average resolution, expressed as a percent of output span, is 100 divided by the total number of steps over the range of the instrument.

$$\text{Average resolution}(\%) = \frac{100}{N}$$

Where N represents the total number of steps.

The dead band of a measuring instrument is the smallest change in the measured variable that will result in a measurable change in the output. Obviously, a measuring instrument cannot measure changes in the measured variable that are smaller than its dead band. Threshold is another name for dead band.

The sensitivity of a measuring instrument is the ratio of the change in output divided by the change in the input that caused the change in output. Sensitivity and gain are both defined as a change in output divided by the corresponding change in input. However, sensitivity refers to static values, whereas gain usually refers to the amplitude of sinusoidal signals.

2. Operation

The reliability of a measuring instrument is the probability that it will do its job for a specified period of time under a specified set of conditions. The conditions include limits on the operating environment, the amount of overrange, and the amount of drift of the output.

Overrange is any excess in the value of the measured variable above the upper range limit or below the lower range limit. When an instrument is subject to an overrange, it does not immediately return to operation within specifications when the overload is removed. A period of time called the recovery time is required to overcome the saturation effect to the overload. The overrange limit is the maximum overrange that can be applied to a measuring instrument without causing damage or permanent change in the performance of the device. Thus one reliability condition is that the measured variable does not exceed the overrange limit.

Drift is an undesirable change over a specified period of time. Zero drift is a change in the output of the measuring instrument while the measured variable is held constant at its limit. Sensitivity drift is a change in the sensitivity of the instrument over the specified period. Zero drift raises or lowers the entire calibration curve of the instrument. Sensitivity drift changes the slope of the calibration curve. The reliability conditions specify an allowable amount of zero drift and sensitivity drift.

3. Environmental Effects

The environment of a measuring instrument includes ambient temperature, ambient pressure, fluid temperature, fluid pressure, electromagnetic fields, acceleration, vibration, and mounting position. The operating conditions define the environment to which a measuring instrument is subjected. The operative limits are the range of operating conditions that will not cause permanent impairment of an instrument.

Temperature effects may be stated in terms of the zero shift and the sensitivity shift. The thermal zero shift is the change in the zero output of a measuring instrument for a specified change in ambient temperature. The thermal sensitivity shift is the change in sensitivity of a measuring instrument for a specified change in ambient temperature.

Selected from "Introduction to control system technology, 4th Ed., by Robert N. Bateson, Macmillan Publishing Co., USA, 1993".

Words and Expressions

1. range [rendʒ]　n. 范围

2. lower range limit 范围下限
3. upper range limit 范围上限
4. span [spæn] vt. 跨度
5. resolution [ˌrezəˈluːʃən] n. 分辨率
6. dead band 死区
7. threshold [ˈθreʃəuld] n. 门限，阈值；临限
8. sensitivity [ˌsensiˈtiviti] n. 灵敏度
9. increment of measurement 测量值增量
10. discrete step 分离的步骤
11. continuous manner 连续方式
12. single step 单步
13. output span 输出范围
14. largest step 最大的刻度
15. measured variable 被测变量
16. static value 静态值
17. sinusoidal signal 正弦信号
18. reliability [rɪˌlaɪəˈbɪlɪti] n. 可靠度
19. specified period 特定时期
20. a specified set of condition 一系列的特定条件
21. operating environment 操作环境
22. amount of overrange 超出范围的数量
23. amount of drift 漂移量
24. overload [ˌəuvəˈləud] vt. 过载
25. recovery time 回复时间
26. saturation effect 饱和效应
27. permanent change 永恒的变化
28. reliability condition 可靠条件
29. undesirable change 不期望的变化
30. zero drift 零点漂移
31. sensitivity drift 敏感性漂移

Exercises

1. Fill in the blanks in your own words according to the text.

    The _____ and _____ are used to define the _____, and their _____ is used to define the _____.

    An increment of measurement is related by three considerable characteristics which are _____, _____ and _____.

    The maximum resolution is defined by the _____ of _____ in the case that _____ to the instruments which change their output in discrete steps corresponding to continuous input variables.

When a measured variable results in a measurable change in the output of a instrument, it must be _____.

The difference between sensitivity and gain consists in _____.

2. Express the following terms in English:
   (1) Overrange (2) Drift (3) Ambient temperature
   (4) Temperature effect (5) Resolution (6) Span
   (7) Dead band
3. List (in English) some examples for the terms mentioned in "2" above.
4. Explain the resolution of the television in comparision with the text.

Reading Material 5

Static Characteristics

Static characteristics describe the accuracy of a measuring instrument at room conditions with the measured variable either constant or changing very slowly. Accuracy is the degree of conformity of the output of a measuring instrument to the ideal value of the measured variable as determined by some type of standard. Accuracy is measured by testing the measuring instrument with a specified procedure under specified conditions. The test is repeat a number of times, and the accuracy is given as the maximum positive and negative error (deviation from the ideal value). The error is defined as the difference between the measured value and the ideal value:

$$\text{Error} = \text{measured value} - \text{ideal value}$$

Accuracy is expressed in terms of the error in one of the following ways:

① In terms of the measured variable (e. g. $+1℃/-2℃$);
② As a percent of span (e. g. $\pm 0.5\%$ of span);
③ As a percent of actual output (e. g. $\pm 1\%$ of out put).

The repeatability of a measuring instrument is a measure of the dispersion of the measurements (the standard deviation is another measure of dispersion). Accuracy and repeatability are not the same. Fig. 5.1 uses the pattern of bullet holes in a target to illustrate the difference between repeatability and accuracy. Notice that a rifle which is repeatable but not accurate produces a tight pattern——but that the pattern is not centered on the bull's-eye. The distance from the center of the bull's-eye to the center of the pattern is called the bias or systemic error. A shooter who is aware of the bias may adjust accordingly and produce an accurate and repeatable pattern on the next try. An experienced operator will make a similar adjustment to compensate for bias in a controller. Thus an automatic controller that is repeatable but not accurate may still be very useful.

Repeatability and reproducibility deal in slightly different ways with the degree of closeness among repeated measurements of the same value of the measured variable. Repeatability

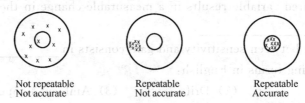

Fig. 5.1 Rifle target patterns illustrate the difference between repeatability and accuracy

is the maximum difference between several consecutive outputs for the same input when approached from the same direction in full range traversals.

Reproducibility is the maximum difference between a number of outputs for the same input, taken over an extended period of time, approaching from both directions. Reproducibility includes hysteresis, dead band, drift, and repeatability. The measurement of reproducibility must specify the time period used in the measurement. Reproducibility is obviously more difficult to determine because of the extended time period that is required.

The procedure of determining the accuracy of a measuring instrument is called calibration. The data from the calibration of a measuring instrument may be presented in tabular form in a calibration report or in graphical form in a calibration curve. The input is usually expressed as a percent of the input span. The output and the error are usually expressed as a percent of the ideal output span.

The measured accuracy and reproducibility of the measuring instrument are taken directly from the calibration report. Measured accuracy is the maximum negative and positive errors in any of the readings.

Selected from "Applied Electronic instrumentation and measurement, by David M. Buchla and Wayne C. Mchlachlan, Prentice Hall, USA, 1992".

Words and Expressions

1. static characteristics 静态特征
2. room condition 室内条件
3. degree of conformity 一致程度，相似度
4. ideal value 理想值
5. in terms of 就……而论，在……方面
6. actual output 实际输出
7. repeatable [ri'pi:təbl] a. 可重复的
8. dispersion [di'spə:ʃən] n. 分散
9. bullet hole 子弹孔
10. rifle ['raifl] n. 来复枪
11. tight pattern 紧凑的方式
12. bias ['baiəs] n. 偏差，偏见，偏爱
13. experienced operator 有经验的操作者

14. compensate ['kɔmpenseit] vt. 补偿
15. closeness ['kləusnis] n. 接近，近似
16. consecutive [kən'sekjutiv] a. 连续不断的
17. hysteresis [histə'ri:sis] n. 滞后现象
18. tabular form 表格形式
19. graphical form 图解形式

CHAPTER. 2　Introduction to Control System

Unit 6　Introduction

> Before reading the text, try to answer the following questions:
> 1. What is the control system?
> 2. How are the complex control systems behaving around us and within human bodies?
> 3. What functions do the practical control systems perform and how do their sensors and controllers act in your examples?
> 4. What is the controlled variable and the manipulated variable?
> 5. Depending on what basic facts and for what purposes are the methods-block diagram and transfer function developed?
> 6. What systems can usually be represented by mathematical methods, and what physical quantities can usually be input and output signals of the components involved in the systems?
> 7. Of what essential elements or parts do the block diagram and transfer function consist?
> 8. What are the frequency responds?
> 9. How are the open-loop and the close-loop control systems different from each other on the key point-relationship between input and output, and how is the difference embodied in a practical control system?
> 10. What are the advantages and drawbacks of the both control systems mentioned above?
> 11. Why is a close-loop control system called a feedback-control system?
>
> What would happen if a taxi driver could not see the speed display and could not feel the speed of the car, and of what type of control system would the taxi driving be at his moment?

1. An Overview for Control System

Control systems are everywhere around us and within us. * Many complex control systems are included among the functions of the human body. An elaborate control system centered in the hypothalamus of the brain maintains body temperature at 37 degrees Celsius (℃) despite changes in physical activity and external ambience. In one control system——the eye——the diameter of the pupil automatically adjusts to control the amount of light that reaches the retina. Another control system maintains the level of sodium ion concentration in the fluid that surrounds the individual cells.

Threading a needle and driving an automobile are two ways in which the human body functions as a complex controller. The eyes are sensor that detects the position of the needle and thread, or of the automobile and the center of the road. A complex controller, the brain, compares the two positions and determines which actions must be performed to accomplish the desired result. The body implements the control action by moving the thread or turning the steering wheel; an experienced driver will anticipate all types of disturbances to the system, such as a rough section of pavement or a slow-moving vehicle ahead. It would be very difficult to reproduce in an automatic controller the many judgments that an average person makes daily and unconsciously.

Control systems regulate temperature in homes, schools, and buildings of all types. They also affect the production of goods and services by ensuring the purity and uniformity of the food we eat and by maintaining the quality of products from paper mills, steel mills, chemical plants, refineries, and other types of manufacturing plants. Control systems help protect our environment by minimizing waste material that must be discarded, thus reducing manufacturing costs and minimizing the waste disposal problem. Sewage and waste treatment also requires the use of automatic control systems.

A control system is any group of components that maintains a desired result or value. From the previous examples it is clear that a great variety of components may be a part of a single control system, whether they are electrical, electronic, mechanical, hydraulic, pneumatic, human, or any combination of these. The desired result is a value of some variable in the system, for example, the direction of an automobile, the temperature of a room, the level of liquid in a tank, or the pressure in a pipe. The variable whose value is controlled is called the controlled variable.

To achieve control, there must be another variable in the system that can influence the controlled variable. Most systems have several such variables. The control system maintains the desired result by manipulating the value of one of these influential variables. The variable that is manipulated is called the manipulated variable. The steering wheel of an automobile is an example of a manipulated variable.

* An excellent idea of the scope of control systems is given in an Instrument Society of America film, "Principles of Frequency Response," 1958.

Control systems are becoming steadily more important in our society. We depend on them to such an extent that life would be unimaginable without them. Automatic control has increased the productivity of each worker by releasing skilled operators from routine tasks and by increasing the amount of work done by each worker. Control systems improve the quality and uniformity of manufactured goods and services; many of the products we enjoy would be impossible to produce without automatic controls. Servo systems place tremendous power at our disposal, enabling us to control large equipment such as jet airplanes and ocean ships.

Control systems increase efficiency by reducing waste of materials and energy, an increasing advantage as we seek ways to preserve our environment. Safety is yet another benefit of automatic control. Finally, control systems such as the household heating system and the automatic transmission provide us with increased comfort and convenience.

In summary, the benefits of automatic control fall into the following six broad categories.

① Increased productivity;
② Improved quality and uniformity;
③ Increased efficiency;
④ Power assistance;
⑤ Safety;
⑥ Comfort and convenience.

Control systems are classified in a number of different ways. They are classified as closed-loop or open-loop, depending on whether or not feedback is used. They are classified as analog or digital, depending on the nature of the signals——continuous or discrete. They are divided into regulator systems and follow-up systems, depending on whether the setpoint is constant or changing. They are grouped into process control systems or machine control systems, depending on the industry they are used in——processing or discrete-part manufacturing. Processing refers to industry they are used to produce products such as food, petroleum, chemicals, and electric power. Discrete-part manufacturing refers to industries that make parts and assemble products such as automobiles, airplanes, appliances, and computers. They are classified as continuous or batch (or discrete), depending on the flow of product from the process-continuous or intermittent and periodic. Finally, they are classified as centralized or distributed, depending on where the controller are located——in a central control room or near the sensors and actuators. Additional categories include servomechanisms, numerical control, robotics, batch control, sequential control, time-sequential control, time-sequenced control, event-sequenced control, and programmable controllers. These general categories are summarized below.

2. Classifications of Control Systems

(1) Feedback
　　① Not used——open-loop
　　② Used——closed-loop
(2) Type of signal
　　① Continuous——analog
　　② Discrete——digital
(3) Setpoint
　　① Seldom changed——regular system
　　② Frequently changed——follow-up system
(4) Industry

① Processing──process control
　　　　a. Continuous systems
　　　　b. Batch systems
　　　② Discrete-part manufacturing──machine control
　　　　a. Numerical control systems
　　　　b. Robotic control systems
　(5) Location of the controllers
　　　① Central control room──centralized control
　　　② Near sensors and actuators──distributed control
　(6) Other categories
　　　① Servomechanisms
　　　② Sequential control
　　　　a. Event-sequenced control
　　　　b. Time-sequenced control
　　　③ Programmable controllers

3. Block Diagrams and Transfer Functions

Although it is not unusual to find several kinds of components in a single control system, or two systems with completely different kinds of components, any control system can be described by a set of mathematical equations that define the characteristics of each component. A wide range of control problems-including processes, machine tools, servomechanisms, space vehicles, traffic, and even economics──can be analyzed by the same mathematical methods. The important feature of each component is the effect it has on the system. The block diagram is a method of representing a control system that retains only this important feature of each component. Signal lines indicate the input and output signals of the component. as shown in Fig. 6. 1.

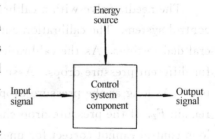

Fig. 6. 1　Block representation of a component

Each component receives an input signal from some part of the system and produces an output signal for another part of the system. The signals can be electric current, voltage, air pressure, liquid flow rate, liquid pressure, temperature, speed, acceleration, position, direction, or others. The signal paths can be electric wires, pneumatic tubes, hydraulic lines, mechanical linkages, or anything that transfers a signal from one component to another. The component may use some source of energy to increase the power of the output signal.

A block diagram consists of a block representing each component in a control system connected by lines that represent the signal paths. The driver's sense of sight provides the two input signals; the position of the automobile and the position of the center of the road. The driver compares the two positions and determines the position of the steering wheel that will maintain the proper position of the automobile. To implement the decision, the driver's hands and arms move the steering wheel to the new position. The automobile responds to the change in steering wheel position with a corresponding change in direction. After a short time has elapsed, the new direction moves the automobile to a new position. Thus, there is a time delay between a change in position of the steering wheel and the position of the automobile. This time delay is included in the mathematical equation of the block representing the automobile.

The loop in the block diagram indicates a fundamental concept of control. The actual position of the automobile is used to determine the correction necessary to maintain the desired position. This concept is called feedback, and control systems with feedback are called closed-loop control systems. Control systems that do not have feedback are called open-loop control systems because their block diagram does not have a loop.

The most important characteristic of a component is the relationship between the input signal and the output signal. This relationship is expressed by the transfer function of the component, which is defined as the ratio of the output signal divided by the input signal. (Mostly, it is the Laplace transform of the output signal divided by the Laplace transform of the input signal)

4. Open-loop Control

An open-loop control system does not compare the actual result with the desired result to determine the control action. Instead, a calibrated setting——previously determined by some sort of calibration procedure or calculation——is used to obtain the desired result.

The needle valve with a calibrated dial shown in Fig. 6.2 is an example of an open-loop control system. The calibration curve is usually obtained by measuring the flow rate for several dial settings. As the calibration curve indicates, different calibration lines are obtained for different pressure drops. Assume that a flow rate of F_2 is desired and a setting of S is used. As long as the pressure drop across the valve remains equal to P_2, the flow rate will remain F_2. If the pressure drop changes to P_1, the flow rate will change to F_1. The open-loop control cannot correct for unexpected changes in the pressure drop.

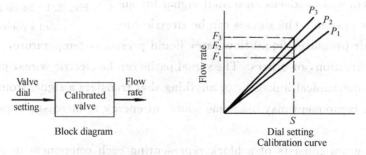

Fig. 6.2 A calibrated needle valve——an open-loop-control system

The firing of a rifle bullet is another example of an open-loop control system. The desired result is to direct the bullet to the bull's-eye. The actual result is the direction of the bullet after the gun has been fired. The open-loop control occurs when the rifle is aimed at the bull's-eye and the trigger is pulled. Once the bullet leaves the barrel, it is on its own: If a sudden gust of wind comes up, the direction will change and no correction will be possible.

The primary advantage of open-loop control is that it is less expensive than closed-loop control: It is not necessary to measure the actual result. In addition, the controller is much simpler because corrective action based on the error is not required. The disadvantage of open-loop control is that errors caused by unexpected disturbances are not corrected. Often a human operator must correct slowly changing disturbances by manual adjustment. In this case, the operator is actually closing the loop by providing the feedback signal.

5. Close loop Control: Feedback

Feedback is the action of measuring the difference between the actual result and the desired result, and using that difference to drive the actual result toward the desired result. The term feedback comes from the direction in which the measured value signal travels in the block diagram. The signal begins at the output of the controlled system and ends at the input to the controller. The output of the controller is the input to the controlled system. Thus the measured value signal is fed back from the output of the controlled system to the input. The term closed loop refers to the loop created by the feedback path.

6. Variable Names

The *controlled variable* (C) is the process output variable that is to be controlled. In a process control system, the controlled variable is usually an output variable that is a good measure of the quality of the product. The most common controlled variables are position, velocity, temperature, pressure, level, and flow rate.

The *setpoint* (SP) is the desired value of the controlled variable.

The *measured variable* (C_m) is the measured value of the controlled variable. It is the output of the measuring means and usually differs from the actual value of the controlled variable by a small amount.

The error (E) is the difference between the setpoint and the measured value of the controlled variable. It is computed according to the equation $E = SP - C_m$.

The controller output (V) is the control action intended to drive the measured value of the controlled variable toward the setpoint value. The control action depends on the error signal (E) and on the control modes used in the controller.

The manipulated variable (M) is the variable regulated by the final controlling element to achieve the desired value of the controlled variable. Obviously, the manipulated variable must be capable of effecting a change in the controlled variable. The manipulated variable is one of the input variables of the process. Changes in the load on the process necessitate changes in the manipulated variable to maintain a balanced condition. For this reason, the value of the manipulated variable is used as a measure of the load on the process.

The disturbance variables (D) are process input variables that affect the controlled variable but are not controlled by the control system. Disturbance variables are capable of changing the load on the process and are the main reason for using a closed-loop control system.

The primary advantage of closed-loop control is the potential for more accurate control of the process. There are two disadvantages of closed-loop control: (1) closed-loop control is more expensive than open-loop control, and (2) the feedback feature of a closed-loop control system makes it possible for the system to become unstable. An unstable system produces an oscillation of the controlled variable, often with a very large amplitude.

Selected from "Introduction to Control System technology, 4th Ed., by Robert N. Bateson, Macmillan Publishing Co., 1993".

Words and Expressions

1. control system 控制系统
2. function ['fʌŋkʃ(ə)n] n. 功能，作用
3. elaborate control system 精细控制系统
4. hypothalamus [haipə'θæləməs] n. 丘脑下部
5. physical activity 身体的运动
6. adjust [ə'dʒʌst] vt. 调整，调节，调理
7. celsius ['selsiəs] adj. 摄氏的
8. retina ['retinə] n. 视网膜
9. sodium ['səudiəm] n. 钠
10. needle [ni:dəl] n. 针
11. controller [kən'trəulə] n. 控制器
12. sensor ['sensə(r)] n. 传感器
13. disturbance [dis'tə:bəns] n. 骚动，打扰，干扰
14. automatic control system 自动控制系统
15. component [kəm'pəunənt] n. 成分，组成
16. desired value 期望值
17. variable ['vɛəriəbl] n. 变量；adj. 可变的，变量的
18. controlled variable 被控量
19. manipulated variable 操作量
20. elapse [i'læps] n. 过去，消逝
21. unimaginable [ˌʌni'mædʒinəb(e)l] adj. 想不到的，不可思议的
22. servo system n. 伺服系统
23. household ['haushəuld] adj. 普通的，平常的，家庭的
24. heating system 加热系统
25. automatic transmission 自动驾驶
26. closed-loop 闭环
27. open-loop 开环
28. feedback ['fi:dbæk] 反馈

29. analog ['ænələg]   adj. 模拟的
30. digital ['didʒitl]   adj. 数字的
31. continuous [kən'tinjuəs]   adj. 连续的
32. discrete [dis'kri:t]   adj. 离散的
33. regulator system   调节器系统
34. follow-up system   随动系统
35. setpoint [set'pɔint]   n. 给定值
36. process control system   过程控制系统
37. machine control system   机器控制系统
38. assemble product   装配产品
39. distribute [dis'tribju:t]   vt. 分发，分布
40. actuator ['æktjueitə]   n. 执行器
41. servomechanism ['sə:vəmetʃənizm]   n. 伺服机构（系统）
42. robotic [rəu'bɔtik]   n. 机器人
43. numerical control   数值控制
44. batch control   批量控制
45. sequential control   连续控制
46. time-sequential control   时间顺序控制
47. event-sequenced control   事件顺序控制
48. programmable controller   可编程控制器
49. regular system   调节系统
50. process control   过程控制
51. central control room   中央控制室
52. single control system   单回路控制系统
53. block diagram   方框图
54. signal line   信号线
55. flow rate   流通率
56. pneumatic tube   大气管道
57. hydraulic line   水力线
58. mechanical linkage   机械连接体
59. respond to   响应，作出反应
60. time delay   时延
61. correction [kə'rekʃən]   n. 改正 修正
62. output signal   输出信号
63. input signal   输入信号
64. Laplace transform   拉普拉斯变换
65. control action   控制动作
66. calibration procedure   标定过程，检验方法
67. calibration curve   标定曲线
68. pressure drop   压降

69. drive [draiv] vt. 驱动
70. process output variable 过程输出变量
71. measuring mean 测量值
72. controller output 控制器输出
73. setpoint value 设定值
74. change in the load 负载变化
75. balanced condition 平衡条件
76. closed-loop 闭环

Exercises

1. Fill in the blanks in your own words according to the text.

   Any control system can be described by _____ that _____. People develop the block diagrams in order to represent _____ that _____.

   In block diagrams the input and output signals of each component are indicated by _____. The signals can be _____, _____, _____, _____, _____, _____, _____, _____, or _____. The signal paths could be any thing that _____.

   The output signals may have stronger power than the input signals because their power may be _____ by the _____ using _____. The _____ play a role as _____ of he block diagram, and the output signal is _____. The block consists of: ① the brain of the driver, the function of which is _____; ② the arms and hands of the driver, the function of which is _____; ③ the mechanism of the car, the function of which is _____. The purpose of using a transfer function is to _____ of the component. Using Laplace Transform as tools, the transfer function is defined as _____.

   A control system normally consists of _____. The common task of control systems is to _____.

   A single control system may contain _____ components. The types of control systems may be _____, _____, _____, _____, _____, _____, _____ or any combination of them. The desired result is a _____ such as _____, _____, _____ or _____. Control variable is defined as _____. The manipulated variable is called _____ or _____ which is manipulated by _____ in order to _____.

   In the control system driving a car, the eyes also play the role as a _____, which _____, and the control action is _____.

   The comparison between the _____ and _____ will not be performed in an _____ system, instead, this performance is a key step of a _____ system.

   Another example for open-loop is _____, where the desired result is _____.

   An open-loop system often needs a person to _____ by _____. This human operating process is actually _____.

In a feedback-control system the difference between _____ and _____ must be _____.

2. Draw up a block diagram and write out a transfer function for a practical system.
3. Illustrate the practical processes of signal enter, arising of control action decision, control action and the respond of output signal of the block according to the control system mentioned in 2.
4. Illustrate some practical control systems running in your laboratories or in your houses, and indicate the sensors, controllers, manipulated variables and controlled variables of these control systems.
5. Imagine what would happen if there would be not natural and artificial control systems in the world.
6. Describe an open control system operated by human using an example.
7. Configure a close-loop control system for controlling the level of water lies in a water tank with one entrance and one exit using electromagnetism flow rate controller.

Reading Material 6

Describing Control System Using Transfer Function

The transfer function consists of two parts. One part is the size relationship between the input and the output. The other part is the timing relationship between the input and output. For example, the size relationship may be such that the output is twice (or half) as large as the input, and the timing relationship may be such that there is a delay of 2 seconds between a change in the input and the corresponding change in the output.

If the component is linear and the input signal is a sinusoidal signal, the size relationship is measured by gain and the timing is measured by phase difference. In a linear component with a sinusoidal input signal. The gain of the component is the ratio of the amplitude of the output signal divided by the amplitude of the input signal.

$$\text{Gain} = \frac{\text{amplitude of the output signal (output units)}}{\text{amplitude of the input signal (input units)}}$$

The phase difference of the component is the phase angle of the output signal minus the phase angle of the input signal.

$$\text{Phase difference} = \text{output phase angle} - \text{input phase angle}$$

Complex numbers (in polar form) are most conveniently used to represent values of the input, the output, and the transfer function.

Thus the transfer function, is represented by the complex number whose magnitude is the gain of the component, and whose angle is the phase of the output minus the phase of the input.

The gain of a component is often expressed as the ratio of the change in the amplitude of the output divided by the corresponding change in the amplitude of the input.

$$\text{Gain} = \frac{\text{change in output amplitude (output units)}}{\text{change in input amplitude (input units)}}$$

The gain of a component has the dimension of output units over input units. Thus an amplifier that produces a 10-volt (V) change in output for each 1-V change in input has a gain of 10V per volt. A direct-current (dc) motor that produces a change in speed of 1000 revolutions per minute (rpm) for each 1-V change in input has a gain of 1000 rpm per volt. A thermocouple that produces an output change of 0.06 millivolt (mV) for each 1℃ change in temperature has a gain of 0.06 mV/℃.

The gain and phase difference of a component for a given frequency are referred to as the frequency response of the component at that frequency. As an example, at a frequency of 1Hz, a certain control system component has a gain of 0.995 and a phase difference of 5.71°. At a frequency of 10 Hz, the gain is 0.707 and the phase difference is 45°. At a frequency of 100 Hz, the gain is 0.0995 and the phase difference is 84.29°.

Words and Expressions

1. size relationship   量值关系
2. timing relationship   时间关系
3. sinusoidal signal   正弦信号
4. gain ［gein］ n. 增益
5. phase difference   相位差
6. phase angle   相位角
7. complex number   虚数
8. magnitude ［'mægnitju:d］ n. 大小 量级
9. direct current   直流
10. revolution per minute   每分转数
11. millivolt ［'milivəult］ n. 毫伏
12. frequency response   频率响应
13. reference ［'refrəns］ n. 参考
14. forward path   前向路径
15. amplifier ［'æmplifaiə］ n. 放大器
16. transfer function   传输函数
17. passive device   被动装置
18. measured value   被测量
19. invert ［in'və:t］ vt. 转换
20. error detector   误差检测器
21. control mode   控制模型
22. be based on   基于

Unit 7 Process Control System

Before reading the text, try to answer the following questions:
1. What main stages does a typical processor include?
2. What important stages are involved in a typical control system?
3. What functions do the measuring transmitter, controller, manipulating element perform?
4. What basic controlling methods does a typical common controller have?
5. What is process, continuous process and batch process?
6. What features do most process controllers have?
7. What additional features are provided by microcontrollers?
8. What advantages are provided by microcontrollers themselves?

---

1. Process

The process block in Fig. 7.1 represents everything performed in and by the equipment in which a variable is controlled. The process includes everything that affects the controlled or process variable except the controller and the final control element.

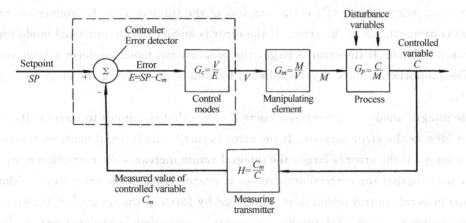

Fig. 7.1 Block diagram of a closed-loop process control system.

2. Measuring Transmitter

The measuring transmitter or sensor senses the value of the controlled variable and converts it into a usable signal. Although the measuring transmitter is considered as one block, it usually consists of a primary sensing element and a signal transducer (or signal converter). The term measuring transmitter is a general term to cover all types of signals. In specific cases, the word measuring is replaced by the name of the measured signal (e.g, temperature transmitter, flow transmitter, pressure transmitter, etc.).

The signal transducer receives the output of the primary element and produces an electric current signal. For example, a thermocouple converts temperature into a millivolt signal, and the thermocouple transducer converts the millivolt signal into an electric current in the range 4 to 20 mA. A resistance element converts temperature into a resistance value, and the resistance transducer converts the resistance value into an electric current signal. Other primary elements are handled in a similar manner.

3. Controller

The controller includes the error detector and a unit that implements the control modes. The error detector computes the difference between the measured value of the controlled variable and the desired value (or setpoint). The difference is called the error and is computed according to the following equation:

Error = setpoint − measured value of controlled variable

or $\quad E = SP - C_m$

The control modes convert the error into a control action or controller output that will tend to reduce the error. The three most common control modes are the proportional mode (P), the integral mode (I), and the derivative made (D). In this chapter you need only to know the names of the three modes and have an intuitive understanding of how they work. The following discussion will show that the names of the modes suggest the types of control action that is formed.

The proportional mode (P) is the simplest of the three modes. It produces a control action that is proportional to the error. If the error is small, the proportional mode produces a small control action. If the error is large, the proportional mode produces a large control action. The proportional mode is accomplished by simply multiplying the error by a gain constant, K.

The integral mode (I) produces a control action that continues to increase its corrective effect as long as the error persists. If the error is small, the integral mode increases the correction slowly. If the error is large, the integral action increases the correction more rapidly. In fact, the rate that the correction increases is proportional to the error signal. Mathematically, the integral control action is accomplished by forming the integral of the error signal.

The derivative mode (D) produces a control action that is proportional to the rate at which the error is changing. For example, if the error is increasing rapidly, it will not be long before there is a large error. The derivative mode attempts to prevent this future error by producing a corrective action proportional to how fast the error is changing. The derivative mode is an attempt to anticipate a large error and head it off with a corrective action based on how quickly the error is changing. Mathematically, the derivative control action is accomplished by forming the derivative of the error signal.

The proportional mode may be used alone or in combination with either or both of the other two modes. The integral mode can be used alone, but it almost never is. The derivative mode cannot be used alone. Thus the common control mode combinations are: P, PI, PD, and PID.

4. Manipulating Element

The manipulating element uses the controller output to regulate the manipulated variable and usually consists of two parts. The first part is called an actuator, and the second part is called the final controlling element. The actuator translates the controller output into an action on the final controlling element, and the final controlling element directly changes the value of the manipulated variable. Valves, dampers, fans, pumps, and heating elements are examples of manipulating elements. The valve that controls the fuel flow in a home heating system is another example of a manipulating element.

A pneumatic control valve is often used as the manipulating element in processes. The actuator consists of an air-loaded diaphragm acting against a spring. As the air pressure on the diaphragm goes, as an example, from 3 psi to 15 psi, the stem of the valve will move from open to closed (air to close) or from closed to open (air to open).

Selected from "Introduction to Control System technology, 4th Ed., by Robert N. Bateson, Macmillan Publishing Corp., 1993".

5. Process Control

Process control involves the regulation of variables in a process. In this context, a process is any combination of materials and equipment that produces a desirable result through changes in energy, physical properties, or chemical properties. A continuous process produces an uninterrupted flow of product for extended periods of time. A batch process, in contrast, has an interrupter and periodic flow of product. Examples of a process include a dairy, a petroleum refinery, a fertilizer plant, a food-processing plant, a candy factory, an electric power plant, and a home heating system. The most common controlled variables in a process are temperature, pressure, flow rate, and level. Others include density, viscosity, composition, color, conductivity, pH, and hardness. Most process control systems maintain constant processing conditions and hence are regulator systems.

Process control systems may be either open-loop or closed-loop, but closed-loop systems are more common. The process control industry has developed standard, flexible, process controllers for closed-loop systems. Over the years these controllers have evolved from pneumatic analog controllers to electronic analog controllers to microprocessor—based digital controllers (microcontrollers). The driving force in this evolution has been increased in capability and versatility of microcontrollers.

Most process controllers share a number of common features. They show the value of the setpoint, the process variable, and the controller output in either analog or digital format. They allow the operator to adjust the setpoint and switch between automatic and manual control. When manual control is selected, they allow the operator to adjust the controller output to vary the manipulated variable in an open-loop control mode. They allow the operator to adjust the control mode settings to "tune the controller" for optimum response. Many controllers also provide for remote setting of the setpoint by an external signal, such as the output of another controller. A local/remote settings.

Microcontrollers provide many additional features, some unique to one vendor and others common among a number of vendors. The following is a partial list of these features.

Choice of control modes: P, I, PI, PD, and PID
Detects and annunciates alarms
Accepts several analog inputs (about four)
Accepts several digital inputs (three or four)
Provides more than one analog output (can be used to manipulate process variables)
Provides several digital outputs (can be used for ON-OFF control of heating elements, . etc)
Direct input from a thermocouple or RTD temperature sensor
Linearizes thermocouple inputs
Performs ratio, feedforward, or cascade control
Bumpless transfer between local and remote modes
Front-panel configuration of the controller

Adaptive gain: automatic adjustment of the proportional mode gain based on some combination of the process variable, the error, the controller output, and a remote input signal.

Self-tuning by process model: determination of the control mode parameters from a model that is formed from observations of the response to step changes of the setpoint. The step change and modeling process is repeated until the model matches the actual process.

Self-tuning by pattern recognition: automatic adjustment of the control mode parameters after a disturbance by scanning the recovery pattern and applying tuning rules that are stored in the controller's memory.

Selected from "Introduction to Control System technology, 4th Ed., by Robert N. Bateson, Macmillan Publishing Co., 1993".

Words and Expressions

1. final control element　最终控制单元
2. sense [sens]　vt. 检测, 感知
3. sensing element　检测元件
4. signal transducer　信号变送器
5. temperature transmitter　温度变送器
6. flow transmitter　流量变送器
7. pressure transmitter　压力变送器
8. proportional mode　比例模型
9. integral mode　积分模型
10. derivative mode　微分模型

11. intuitive understanding　直觉理解
12. corrective effect　纠正作用
13. valve [vælv]　n. 阀
14. damper ['dæmpə]　n. 阻尼闸
15. fuel flow　燃料流量
16. pneumatic control valve　气动控制阀
17. diaphragm ['daiəfræm]　n. 振动膜
18. air to close　气关
19. air to open　气开
20. physical property　物理性质
21. chemical property　化学性质
22. in contrast　比较
23. fertilizer plant　化肥厂
24. food-processing plant　食品加工厂
25. level ['levl]　n. 液位，水平，水平面
26. conductivity [kʌndʌk'tiviti]　n. 传导性，传导率
27. composition [ˌkɔmpə'ziʃn]　n. 成分
28. hardness ['hɑːdnis]　n. 硬，硬度
29. flexible ['fleksibl]　adj. 柔性的
30. microcontroller [maikrəu'kəntrəulə]　n. 微控制器
31. versatility [ˌvəsə'tiləti]　n. 多功能性
32. share [ʃeə]　n. 共享，参与；　vt. 分享，共有
33. switch [switʃ]　n. 开关，转换；　vt. 转换，转变
34. manual control　手动控制
35. external signal　外部信号
36. pneumatic [njuː'mætik]　adj. 风力的，汽力的；　n. 气胎
37. local/remote setting　本地/远程设置
38. annunciate [ə'nʌnʃieit]　vt. 告示，通知
39. on-off control　开关控制
40. direct input　直接输入
41. cascade control　串级控制
42. bumpless transfer　无扰动切换
43. front panel　前面板
44. adaptive gain　适应性增益
45. self-tuning　自调谐 [校正]
46. pattern recognition　模式识别

Exercises

1. Fill in the blanks in the following sentences according to the text using your own words.

　　In a process there is a variable called _____ or _____ which is to be controlled and is affected by _____.

The value of the controlled variable is received by _____ or _____ and is converted into _____. The transmitter consists of _____ and _____.

The output of the primary element is received by _____ and is converted into an _____.

For example, the temperature is received by resistance element into _____, which is then converted by _____ into _____.

The controller consists of _____ and _____.

The error is defined by _____, and is computed by _____ according to the mathematical relationship described as _____.

The controller converts the error into a control action basically according to 3 modes: _____, _____, and _____. The controller output will _____ the error.

If a process control involves the _____ in it, then the process is defined as a _____ of _____ and _____. The equipment of the process produces a _____ though _____, _____ or _____.

Processes can be classified into 2 kinds which are _____ and _____. The first one produces _____ for _____, and the second one produces _____.

Process control may be sorted into 2 kinds which are _____ and _____. For the feedback control there are 2 kinds of controllers, _____ and _____ developed by controller industry.

Since years the controllers have gone through the course from _____ to _____ to _____.

The setpoint, the process variable, and the controller output can be shown in either _____ and _____ format. The setpoint can be _____ by _____. The modes of automatic and manual control can be _____ by process controller by using a _____.

During a manual control, the operation can _____ to _____ in an open-loop control mode.

2. Illustrate three control modes using an example from a practical control system.
3. List at lest 5 examples of manipulating elements and describe their functions.
4. List all types of mirocontrollers which you have met and describe their characteristic.
5. Illustrate some applications of microprocessors and mirocontrollers, and explain why they can not be replaced by each other.

Reading Material 7

Control System Drawings

The Instrument Society of America has prepared a standard, "Instrumentation Symbols and Identifications," ANSI/ISA—S5.1—1984, to "establish a uniform means of designating instruments and instrument systems used for measurement and control." This standard presents a designation system that includes symbols and an identification code that is "suitable for use whenever any reference to an instrument is required." Applications include flow diagrams, instrumentation drawings, specifications, construction drawings, technical papers, tagging of instruments, and other uses.

A circular symbol called a balloon is the general instrument symbol. The instrument is identified by the code placed inside its balloon. The identification code consists of a functional identification in the top half of the balloon and a loop identification in the bottom half. The first letter in the functional identification defines the measured or initiating variable of the control loop (e.g., flow, level, pressure, temperature). Up to three additional letters may be used to name functions of the individual instrument (e.g., indicator, recorder, controller, valve). The standard also defines symbols for instrument lines, control valve bodies, actuators, primary elements, various functions, and other devices.

Fig. 7.2 illustrates the use of the standard symbols and identification code in a process control drawing. The process blends and heats a mixture of water and syrup. This system has three control loops, with loop identification numbers of 101, 102, and 103. The first

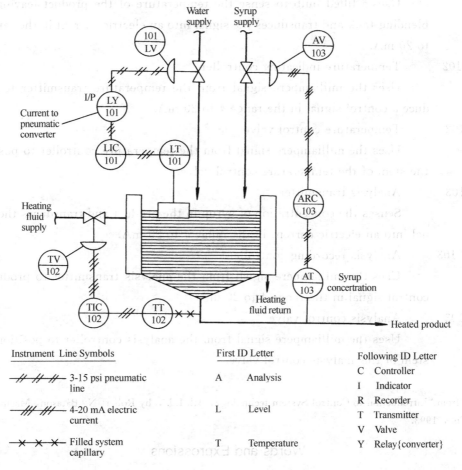

Fig. 7.2 Blending and heating system instrumentation drawing

two digits designate the area in the plant where this system is located. The third digit identifies a particular control loop. Loop 101 is a level control loop, as indicated by the first letter in the function code of each instrument in the loop. The meaning of each code is as follows:

LT-101　　Level transmitter

　　Uses a float to sense the level of the liquid in the tank and transduces the signal into an electric current in the range 4 to 20 mA.

LIC-101　　Level-indicating controller

　　Uses the milliampere signal from the level transmitter to produce a control signal in the range 4 to 20 mA.

LY-101　　Level current to pneumatic converter

　　Converts the milliampere output from the controller into a pneumatic signal in the range 3 to 15 pounds per square inch (psi).

LV-101　　Level control valve

　　Uses the pneumatic signal from the I/P converter to position the stem of the level control valve.

TT-102　　Temperature transmitter

　　Uses a filled bulb to sense the temperature of the product leaving the blending tank and transduces the signal into an electric current in the range 4 to 20 mA.

TIC-102　　Temperature-indicating controller

　　Uses the milliampere signal from the temperature transmitter to produce a control signal in the range 4 to 20 mA.

TV-102　　Temperature control valve

　　Uses the milliampere signal from the temperature controller to position the stem of the temperature control valve.

AT-103　　Analysis transmitter

　　Senses the concentration of syrup in the product and transduces the signal into an electric current in the range 4 to 20 mA.

ARC-103　　Analysis recording controller

　　Uses the milliampere signal from the analysis transmitter to produce a control signal in the range 4 to 20 mA.

AV-103　　Analysis control valve

　　Uses the milliampere signal from the analysis controller to position the stem of the analysis control valve.

Selected from "Introduction to Control System technology, 4th Ed., by Robert N. Bateson, Macmillan Publishing Co., 1993."

Words and Expressions

1. instrumentation [instrumen'teiʃn] n. 仪器使用

2. uniform means   统一方法
3. designation system   指定的系统
4. identification code   识别码
5. blend ［blend］ vt. 混合；n. 调和，合而为一；混杂
6. syrup ［'sirəp］ n. 糖浆，果汁
7. construction drawing   结构图
8. technical paper   资料
9. tagging of instrument   仪器标志
10. general instrument symbol   通用仪器符号
11. additional letter   附加字母
12. control valve   控制阀
13. level transmitter   液位变送器

Unit 8 Computer Network Based Industrial Control Systems

> Before reading the text below, try to answer the following questions:
> 1. What pattern of CIM is similarly followed by most companies?
> 2. What levels of computer integration are required for CIM to work, and what are their tasks?
> 3. What is the best way to develop a CIM system?
> 4. In what background are industrial controllers developed, and what role do they play?
> 5. What is PLC, and what functions does it perform?
> 6. What are the analogies and differences between PLC and PC?
> 7. What personal knowledges are required for mastering the PLC?
> 8. What major units are included in a typical PLC system and what roles do they platy individually?
> 9. What optional units are often added to PLC system ?

1. Types of Networking

Computer-integrated manufacturing (CIM) is a philosophy for integrating hardware and software in such a way as to achieve total automation. Although each company has its own idea of what CIM really means, most follow a pattern similar to that in Fig. 8.1. In this diagram, dedicated processing tasks are shown distributed around a factory. As computers are further removed form the actual manufacturing area, their function shifts from real-time control toward supervision.

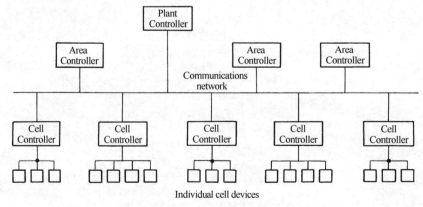

Fig. 8.1 Distribution of Processing Tasks in a Plant According to Function

It is generally agreed that at least three levels of computer integration are required for

CIM to work: the cell level, the area level, and the plant level. Each level has certain tasks within its range of responsibility Cell controllers, for example, are generally responsible for data acquisition and direct machine control. Area controllers are assigned the tasks of machine and tool management, maintenance tracking, material handling and tracking, and computer-assisted simulation and design facilities. The plant-level computers are responsible for such things as purchasing, accounting, materials management, resource planning, and report generation.

When you develop a CIM system, it is best to start at the lowest level. Refer to Fig. 8.1. Begin by completely developing the control for one cell. Then do the next cell, and so on. Then develop the area controllers. Only when the cell controllers function properly should you develop the plant controller. If CIM system fail, they do so for two major reasons. First, the design of the system is started at the top with the plant controller and works its way down. This does not work—it is backward. A second reason for the system's failure to come on line properly is using different machines made by various manufacturers. For example, We have 17 individual cell devices in four different cells. Your company procures 17 machines and 5 computers to be used as cell controllers. When connected, the machines and computers do not "talk" to each other, and nothing works together. When you call the computer manufacturer and the 17 cell device manufacturers, you find out no one is responsible for the communication between devices. Each manufacturer is only responsible for the programs of its own devices. In a CIM project, it is necessary to ascertain communication ability between devices before buying any device. One organization or person should write or procure the overall networking programs for the CIM cell early in the project time frame.

Technically speaking, any computer, including the PLC, is capable of performing both control and supervisory tasks. The trend, however, is toward customizing computers for specific applications. These customized controllers are called plant controllers. It can be seen from the hierarchical structure of CIM that specialized computers would be advantageous. In fact, many companies are already producing computers to satisfy the specific requirements of every CIM level. Invariably, mainframe computers are implemented at the plant level in large facilities. In some cases, those computers were already in place to handle such tasks as inventory and payroll. To promote them to the top of the CIM pyramid, one simply selects the proper software. These computers are usually in a location remote from the actual plant floor. All the information they require is available from the host of subordinate area controllers throughout the plant.

Area controllers are usually on the plant floor and are therefore subjected to a harsh environment. A special breed of computers, called industrial computers, has been developed specifically for this application. The main difference between a PC and an industrial computer lies in the physical construction. Very simply, industrial computers are built to withstand higher temperatures, greater vibration, electromagnetically noisy environments, and rough handling. Since their task is still supervisory in nature, their operating hardware does not differ significantly from that of a PC. Again, it is the software that turns a generic computer into an industrial computer. The PC should not be ruled out as a strong contender for the position of area controller. Personal computers are inexpensive, and with the myriad clones available, they are plentiful. An added advantage of using PCs for area control is that there is a large software base already established for such computers.

The most specialized computers are cell controllers, those used to control work cells. A cell is defined as a group of machine tools or equipment integrated to perform a unit of the manufacturing process. Therefore, the computer that coordinates action within the cell has special hardware requirements as well as special software requirements. Specifically such a computer must have multiple data paths (I/O ports) through which it may communicate with the various cell devices.

Traditionally, cell control has been accomplished with PLCs, which were designed for this very purpose. A CIM structure, however, requires that the cell coordinators communicate with other cell controllers, as well as with the area controller. The language of the PLC is somewhat restricting in this respect. In addition, most PLC languages do not lend themselves well to analysis and record keeping tasks.

2. The PLC System

Originally, the PLC was represented by the acronym PC. There was some confusion with using this acronym as it is commonly accepted to represent personal computer. Therefore, PLC is now commonly accepted to mean programmable logic controller.

A PLC is a user-friendly, microprocessor-based specialized computer that carries out control functions of many types and levels of complexity. Its purpose is to monitor crucial process parameters and adjust process operations accordingly. It can be programmed, controlled, and operated by a person unskilled in operating computers. Essentially, a PLC's operator draws the lines and devices of ladder diagrams with a keyboard onto a display screen. The resulting drawing is converted into computer machine language and run as a user program.

The computer takes the place of much of the external wiring required for control of a process. The PLC will operate any system that has output devices that go on and off (known as discrete, or digital, outputs). It can also operate any system with variable (analog) outputs. The PLC can be operated on the input side by on-off devices (discrete, or digital) or by variable (analog) input devices.

Today, the big unit growth in the PLC industry is at the low end—where small keeps getting smaller. When a few years ago the micro PLC entered the market, some thought that these devices had "bottomed out". Now, nano PLCs—generally defined as those with 16 or fewer I/O—are spreading. Some can fit into your shirt pocket, being no larger than a deck of cards and at the time of this writing, PLC*Direct* plans to introduce a PLC the size of a box of Tic-Tac candy that will include many features of current micro models.

The first PLC systems evolved from conventional computers in the late 1960s and early 1970s. These first PLCs were installed primarily in automotive plants. Traditionally, The auto plants had to be shut down for up to a month at model changeover time. The early PLCs were used along with other new automation techniques to shorten the changeover time. One of the major time-consuming changeover procedures had been the wiring of new or revised relay and control panels. The PLC keyboard reprogramming procedure replaced the rewiring of a panel full of wires, relays, timers and other components. The new PLCs helped reduce changeover time to a matter of few days.

There was a major problem with these early 1970s computer/PLC reprogramming procedures. The programs were complicated and required a highly trained programmer to make the changes. Through the late 1970s, improvements were made in PLC programs to make them somewhat more user friendly; in 1978, the introduction of the microprocessor chip increased computer power for all kinds of automation systems and lowered the computing cost. Robotics, automation devices, and computers of all types, including the PLC, consequently underwent many improvements. PLC programs, written in high-level language, became more understandable to more people, and PLCs became more affordable.

In the 1980s, with more computer power per dollar available, the PLC came into exponentially increasing use. Some large electronics and computer companies and some diverse corporate electronics divisions found that the PLC had become their greatest volume product. The market for PLCs grew from a volume of $ 80 million in 1978 to $ 1 billion per year by 1990 and is still growing. Even the machine tool industry, where computer numerical controls (CNCs) have been used in the past, is using PLCs. PLCs are also used extensively in building energy and security control systems. Other nontraditional uses of PLCs, such as in the home and in medical equipment, have exploded in the 1990s and will increase as we enter the new millennium.

A person knowledgeable in relay logic systems can master the major PLC functions in a few hours. These functions might include coils, contacts, timers and counters. The same is true for a person with a digital logic background. For persons unfamiliar with ladder diagrams or digital principles, however, the learning process takes more time.

A person knowledgeable in relay logic can master advanced PLC functions in a few days with proper instruction. Company schools and operating manuals are very helpful in mastering these advanced functions. Advanced functions in order of learning might include sequence/drum controller, register bit use, and move functions.

3. The Advantages of PLC

Following are 8 major advantages of using a programmable controller.

① Flexibility. In the past, each different electronically controlled production machine required its own controller; 15 machines might require 15 different controllers. Now it is possible to use just one model of a PLC to run any one of the 15 machines. Furthermore, you would probably need fewer than 15 controllers, because one PLC can easily run many machines. Each of the 15 machines under PLC control would have its own distinct program.

② Implementing Changes and Correcting Errors. With a wired relay-type panel, any program alterations require time for rewiring of panels and devices. When a PLC program circuit or sequence design change is made, the PLC program can be changed from a keyboard sequence in a metter of minutes. No rewiring is required for a PLC-controlled system. Also, if a programming error has to be corrected in a PLC control ladder diagram, a change can be typed in quickly.

③ Large Quantities of Contacts. The PLC has a large number of contacts for each coil available in its programming. Suppose that a panel-wired relay has four contacts and all are in use when a design change requiring three more contacts is made. Time would have to be taken to procure and install a new relay or relay contact block. Using a PLC, however, only three more contacts would be typed in. The three contacts would be automatically available in the PLC. Indeed, a hundred contacts can be used from one relay—if sufficient computer memory is available.

④ Lower Cost. Increased technology makes it possible to condense more functions into smaller and less expensive packages. Now you can purchase a PLC with numerous relays, timers and counters, a sequencer, and other functions for a few hundred dollars.

⑤ Pilot Running. A PLC programmed circuit can be prerun and evaluated in the office or lab. The program can be typed in, tested, observed, and modified if needed, saving valuable factory time. In contrast, conventional relay systems have been best tested on the factory floor, which can be very time consuming.

⑥ Visual Observation. A PLC circuit's operation can be seen during operation directly on a CRT screen. The operation or misoperation of a circuit can be observed as it happens. Logic paths light up on the screen as they are energized. Troubleshooting can be done more quickly during visual observation.

In advanced PLC systems, an operator message can be programmed for each possible malfunction. The malfunction description appears on the screen when the malfunction is detected by the PLC logic (for example, "MOTOR #7 IS OVERLOADED"). Advanced PLC systems also may have descriptions of the function of each circuit component. For example, input #1 on the diagram could have "CONVEY OR LIMIT SWITCH" on the diagram as a description.

⑦ Speed of Operation. Relays can take an unacceptable amount of time to actuate. The operational speed for the PLC program is very fast. The speed for the PLC logic operation is determined by scan time, which is a matter of milliseconds.

⑧ Ladder or Boolean Programming Method. The PLC programming can be accomplished in the ladder mode by an electrician or technician. Alternatively, a PLC programmer who works in digital or Boolean control systems can also easily perform PLC programming.

4. Overall PLC System

Fig. 8.2 shows, in block form, the four major units of a PLC system and how they are interconnected. The four major parts are

(1) *Central Processing Unit (CPU)*. The "brain" of the system, which has

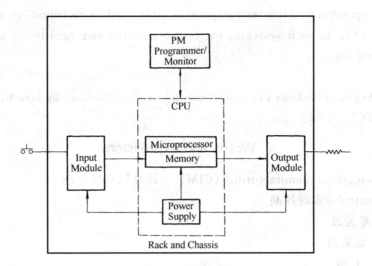

Fig. 8.2 PLC System Layout and Connection

three subparts.

a. Microprocessor. The computer center that carries out mathematics and logic operations.

b. Memory. The area of the CPU in which data and information is stored and retrieved. Holds the system software and user program.

c. Power supply. The electrical supply that converts AC line voltage to various operational DC values. In the process, the power supply filters and regulates the DC voltages to ensure proper computer operation.

(2) *Programmer/Monitor*. The programmer/monitor (PM) is a device used to communicate with the circuits of the PLC. Hand-held terminals, industrial terminals, and the personal computer exist as PM devices. In a hand-held unit, input takes place through a membrane keypad and the display is usually a liquid crystal (LCD) . With the industrial terminal or personal computer, more complex, type-writer-type keyboards and cathode ray tubes (CRTs) are employed.

(3) I/O Modules. The input module has terminals into which outside process electrical signals, generated by sensors or transducers, are entered. An electronic system for connecting I/O modules to remote locations can be added if needed. The actual operating process under PLC control can be thousands of feet from the CPU and its I/O modules.

(4) Racks and chassis. The racks on which the PLC parts are mounted and the enclosures on which the CPU, PM, and I/O modules are mounted.

Optional units often a part of the PLC system are:

• *Printer*. A device on which the program in the CPU may be printed. In addition, operating information may be printed upon command.

• *Program Recorder/Player*. Some older PLC systems use tape to provide secondary storage for CPU programs. Today, PLCs use floppy disks, with hard disks for secondary storage. The stored programs provide backup and a way to download programs written off-line from the PLC process system.

For large operations, a master computer is often used to coordinate many individual, interconnected PLCs. In such systems, the interconnecting electrical buses are sometimes referred to as data highways.

Selected from "Programmable Logic Controllers: principles and applications, by John W. Webb, Ronald A. Ress, No. 4, 1999".

Words and Expressions

1. computer-integrated manufacturing (CIM)　计算机集成制造
2. real-time control　实时控制
3. cell level　单元级
4. area level　装置级
5. plant level　厂级
6. direct machine control　直接机器控制
7. area controller　装置控制器
8. tool management　工具管理
9. maintenance tracking　跟踪维护
10. material handling　原料处理
11. computer-assisted simulation　计算机辅助仿真
12. on line　在线
13. specific application　特殊应用
14. frame [freim] vt. 构成，设计； n. 帧，画面，框架
15. customizing computer　用户化计算机
16. hierarchical structure　递阶结构，层次结构
17. pyramid ['pirəmid] n. 金字塔
18. mainframe computer　大型计算机
19. plant floor　装置层
20. harsh environment　恶劣的环境
21. industrial computer　工业计算机
22. physical construction　物理建筑
23. withstand [wið'stænd] vt. 抵挡，经受住
24. rough handling　粗处理
25. myriad clone　大量复制
26. acronym ['ækrənim] n. 只取首字母的缩写词
27. manufacturing process　制造过程
28. multiple data path　多路数据路径
29. restrict [ri'strikt] vt. 限制　约束
30. coil [kɔil] v. 盘绕　卷
31. relay ['ri:lei] n. 继电器
32. memory ['meməri] n. 内存　存储器

33. condense [kən'dens] v. 精简
34. modify ['mɔdifai] vt. 更改 修改
35. troubleshooting n. 发现并修理故障
36. malfunction [mæl'fʌŋkʃn] n. 故障
37. description [di'skripʃn] n. 描述
38. actuate ['æktjueit] vt. 开动，促使
39. scan time 扫描时间
40. Boolean programming method 布尔编程方法
41. membrane ['membrein] n. 膜，隔膜
42. liquid crystal (LCD) 液晶
43. cathode ray tubes (CRTs) n. 阴极射线管

Exercises

1. Fill in the blanks in your own words according to the text.

   Most companies of CIM follow a common PLC system pattern where dedicated processing tasks are _____, and the function of computers _____ because _____.

   A CIM system requires _____ to work properly, which are: _____, _____, and _____. The first one is generally responsible for _____; the second one is assigned for _____; the third one is responsible for _____.

   The best and basic process for developing a CIM system consists of 3 main steps: ①_____; ②_____; ③_____.

   The system's failure happens naturally for 2 major reasons. First, _____; second, _____.

   Although computers including PLC are capable _____, in fact, more and more computers are _____, but invariably a mainframe computer _____.

   The casting of computers which are implemented at device level are plied by _____, which are nothing new, in fact, had been used in _____.

   The original acronym of programmable logical controller was _____, but now it is commonly accepted to represent _____.

   The purpose of PLC is to _____ and _____.

   A PLC can be programmed and operated by a person who _____.

   The essential work of an operator of PLC is _____ with keyboard.

   The PLC can operate any system (s) which is (are) working with different types of signals including _____ or _____ and _____ or _____.

   For a few years, one of the significant developping directions of PLC is that _____.

   The first PLC system was evolved from _____ and applied _____ in _____ industry.

   By using PLC system, the traditional works such as rewiring a panel full of wires, relays, timers and other components could be replaced by _____.

The user friendly characteristics of PLC reflect in _____.

A person could master the major PLC functions quickly through _____, _____ or _____.

A PLC system includes 4 main units which are _____, _____, _____, and _____.

2. List some application examples of PLC systems and illustrate them according to your own experience or to your own imagine.
3. Summarize the development history and the further development direction of PLC system in your own words using at least 500 words.
4. List the different applications of PC and PLC, and point out the corresponding reasons.
5. Discuss the major units, their functions and the connections for them, according to the block form graphic Fig. 8.2.
6. Write out the full names of the following abbreviations according to the text.
CPU, DC, PM, LCD, CRT, I/O, PLC

Reading Material 8

On PLC's Registers and Selecting a PLC

1. General Characteristics of PLC's Registers

Within the PLC CPU, registers are found in two locations. The microprocessor has internal registers, most of which are not directly accessible by the user. These registers (3, 8, 16, or 32 bits wide, depending on the microprocessor) help the control and arithmetic and logic units within the processor to carry out their tasks. Accumulator registers, data registers, index registers, condition code registers, scratch pad registers, and instruction registers—all work to temporarily store data, which in turn is used to facilitate the carrying out of programmed functions.

In addition to these internal registers, the CPU's RAM also contains slots that are designated to hold variable information. These locations, or addresses, become external registers. Throughout this chapter and text we assume these registers are 16 bits wide. There can be a mere handful of such registers or hundreds, depending on the size of the CPU and complexity of the user program.

Each bit location in a register contains, of course, either a 1 or a 0. You can observe register contents on a VDT by calling up the register on a keyboard. In addition, on many models you can print the register contents on a typed printout. Various numbering systems are possible for reading register contents or printing them out. Depending on your PLC capabilities, you may choose to print register values based on one or more different numbering systems. For example, one model allows you to choose between 1—Decimal, 2—Binary, 3—Hex, or 4—ASCII. Other possibilities are Octal and special codes unique to the system being used. Still other PLCs are confined to displaying or printing in only one numbering system, usually the decimal system.

Registers are usually designated using prefixes followed by numbers, as is the case. HE256 represents holding register 256; OG2 represents output group register number 2. In other systems, a certain numerical series of addresses may be assigned to a specific task or function. One model of PLC has register addresses 901 through 930 assigned to timers and counters only. It is important to determine the functions for the addresses or your PLC registers form its operational manual.

2. Factors to Consider in Selecting a PLC

In the billion-dollar PLC industry, with over a hundred PLC manufacturers producing a thousand or more individual models, how do you choose the right machine for your needs? If you're a systems integrator, working as a consultant or for a large manufacturing company, it's your full-time job to know when, where, and what to acquire. But even if you are an electrician or electronics technician, hovering on the factory floor, you should have at least a rudimentary familiarity with the key factors that must be considered in selecting a PLC. Specifically, you should be cognizant of such issues as cost, serviceability/support, flexibility/expandability, and training/documentation. Not only might you be called upon to give advice on such matters, you might also become directly involved in implementing any purchasing decisions based on these factors.

When you consider cost, two factors are at work. First, you must determine the crossover point, where it becomes economically advantageous to go with a PLC as opposed to another (particularly a hard-wired) solution. Generally, given the high cost of quality, long-lasting industrial relays, if your application involves a half dozen or more of these electromagnetic components, it may be time to consider a PLC instead. With the latter below $200 in some cases, the PLC is becoming ever more cost-effective. This leads to the second consideration—overall cost. It is important to remember, especially when installing networked PLC systems, to weigh not only the initial cost of the PLCs, but installation, maintenance, and training costs as well.

In addition to cost (or, in fact, related to it) are the serviceability/support concerns that must be considered when purchasing a PLC. Of course, one wants the most reliable PLC for the money, but if failure occurs, is your PLC equipped with adequate self-diagnosis? And once the problem is found, can it be corrected with minimal effort and time? When it comes to vendor support, will the company that sold you the PLC be there with replacement parts for a quick turnaround? Keep such factors in mind when making any PLC selection decision.

Flexibility and expandability are also factors to consider in selecting a PLC. Your PLC system must be able to grow with your company's needs. Fortunately, most PLCs, even the "shoebox" variety, are designed with these two factors in mind. Memory, I/O, and system expansion, along with the communications infrastructure that goes with them, should not be taken for granted, however. Plan for the future by carefully analyzing your PLC system capabilities and limitations at the outset.

Finally, don't forget training and documentation when deciding what PLC vendor to deal with. At least five factors should be considered with regard to training: (1) Is training supplied at all? (2) Is traning provided on site, at your plant? (3) If training does not take place at your plant, what will it cost for employees to be away for training at a regional center or company home office? (4) Is training included when system upgrades are involved? (5) Is the training conducted by competent, industrially experienced instructors who know how to communicate with electricians and electronics technicians?

Documentation—user manuals, software support, and the like—is also extremely important and must accompany any hardware product. Unfortunately, too often documentation is an afterthought, something thrown together hurriedly as the product is being packaged for delivery. Actually, although that is a bit of an exaggeration, it is best to take the time to study any documentation at length before deciding on a particular PLC manufacturer. You will be glad you did.

Selected from "Programmable Logic Controllers: principles and applications, John W·Webb, Ronald A·Ress, No.4, 1999".

Words and Expressions

1. internal register　内部寄存器
2. location ［ləu'keiʃ(ə)n］　位置，特定区域
3. VDT＝Video Display Terminals　视频显示终端
4. arithmetic unit　算术单元
5. logic unit　逻辑单元
6. temporarily store　临时存储
7. ASCII　美国信息交换标准码
8. operation manual　操作指南
9. individual model　单独的模型
10. system integrator　系统集成器
11. consultant ［kən'sʌltənt］　n. 顾问
12. hover ［'hɔrə(r)］　v. 盘旋
13. rudimentary ［ru:di'mentəri］　adj. 根本的，未发展的，基本的
14. factory floor　厂地
15. be cognizant of　认识到
16. documentation ［dɔkjumen'teiʃn］　n. 文件
17. purchasing decision　采购决策
18. crossover point　交叉点
19. industrial relay　工业继电器
20. cost-effective　节省成本的
21. self-diagnosis　自诊断
22. minimal effort　最小的努力

23. system expansion   系统扩展
24. infrastructure [ˈinfrəstrʌktʃə]   n. 基础构造
25. upgrade [ʌpˈgreid] vt. 升级
26. instructor [inˈstrʌktə] n. 指导
27. user manual   用户手册
28. afterthought [ˈɑːftːθɔːt] n. 事后产生的想法
29. exaggeration [igzædʒəˈreiʃ(ə)n]   n. 夸张，夸大之词

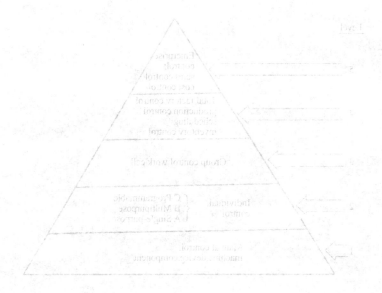

Unit 9　Levels of Industrial Control

> Before reading the text below, try to answer the following questions:
> 1. What general levels are included in a typical industrial factory, and what obvious characteristics are possessed by each level individually?
> 2. What contents are involved in each level of a typical industrial factory?
> 3. Under what conditions is each level reached individually?
> 4. Into what sublevels are level 2 divided, and why?
> 5. Is there any possibility to add more level (s) into the system?

Fig. 9.1 is a triangle showing the general levels of control of an industrial factory. At the bottom, only human control is involved. At the top, very involved computer analysis is used. Most smaller industrial operations go up through level 3. Larger factories are increasingly at level 4. Very large, multiplant operations are generally at level 5. A brief description of each level of control follows.

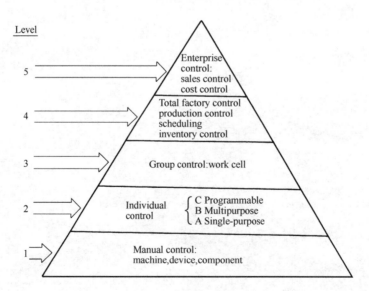

Fig. 9.1　Control System Level Triangle

Level 1 is the machine level. An example is a lathe with manual controls for moving the cutter through its path. Control is manual with cranks. The lathe may have power assists for more cutting power, but control is manual.

Level 2 is reached when electrical or other controls are added. Level 2 can be divided into three sublevels as shown in Fig. 9.1. Suppose an electronic, computer-based control operated the lathe. Such a control for automatic feed rate for cutting the metal would be level 2A. This level 2A rate would be automatically set for each part machined. Level 2B is reached when controls are programmed for machining more than one part. The control pattern for each part is called up from a master control as required. The master control has been preprogrammed for each part. The third sublevel is 2C, programmable control. At level 2C the machining pattern for each part is programmed in by an operator. When a part's machining program is first used, each step and motion is recorded as the process progresses. The steps and motions are stored in memory. The next time the same part is to be machined, the part's machining program is recalled form memory. This recall procedure saves redoing the setup each time the part is to be made. Machining patterns for many different parts can be stored and recalled as needed. Note that as you go from A to C of level 2, the cost of installation goes up accordingly. The cost of more control versus the possible benefits must be considered in determining economic feasibility.

Level 3 is where networking begins to be involved. Level 3 involves connecting the control of two or more individual machines or devices to work together. An example of this level is controlling a robot to load a lathe as well as controlling the lathe's operation. A master controller is needed to coordinate the two individual controllers of the robot and the lathe. In many manufacturing operations more than two devices are coordinated. An example might be on an automobile assembly line. Conveyors, positioners, robotic welders, and inspection devices are coordinated with a master computer. Such groups of machines and devices are called work cells.

Level 4 of automatic control involves a number of work cells hooked up to a master, coordinating automatic computer control. The entire factory is under the control of a large master computer. The master computer takes an order from sales input, checks for raw material availability in inventory, and prepares a production plan. It then causes the required parts to be made, by running them through the appropriate operations in the plant. The master computer does such other chores as reordering an appropriate amount of raw material as it anticipates the need. The master computer also carries out such tasks as scheduling part manufacturing in a given work cell for maximum machine utilization. One result of proper control at this level is reduced amounts of raw material and in-process inventory. Inventory takes up factory floor space as well as adding to costs.

Level 5 is one more step into sophisticated manufacturing. At this level, a computer looks at past demand for each product and predicts the number of items that will be needed at each time of the month or year. Sales forecasts are also factored in. The product to be manufactured is then scheduled and made accordingly. This level gets into an area called artificial intelligence, at a high cost. An analysis has to be made to determine whether people can make the same predictions at lower cost and with comparable accuracy. One result of proper use of level 5 would be reduced finished material inventory, if sales and production are matched properly. Another result would be timely availability of a product for prompt delivery. Other considerations, such as the time to buy raw material at lowest cost, would be included in the computer program at level 5.

Selected from "Programmable Logic Controllers: principles and applications, John W • Webb, Ronald A • Ress, No. 4, 1999".

Words and Expressions

1. general level 通用层
2. human control 人工控制
3. lathe [leið] n. 车床
4. computer analysis 计算机分析
5. industrial operation 工业操作
6. machine level 机器层
7. crank [kræŋk] n. 曲柄
8. power assist 辅助动力
9. sublevel ['sʌblevl] n. 子层，子级，次层，次能级
10. master control 主控制
11. process progress 进程
12. installation [ˌinstə'leiʃən] n. 安装
13. chore [tʃɔː(r)] n. 家务杂事
14. utilization [ˌjuːtəlai'zeiz(ə)n] n. 利用
15. inventory ['invəntəri] n. 详细目录，存货，财产清册，总量
16. sophisticated [sə'fistikeitid] adj. 久经世故的；高度发展的；富有经验的
17. cutter ['kʌtə] n. 刀具；切割机；快艇

Exercises

1. Fill in the blanks in the following sentences according to the text using your own words.

    A typical industrial factory includes 5 general levels. The first is _____, where the control is _____. When _____ the second level is reached, which can be divided into 3 sublevels, which are _____, _____ and _____. In level 3 the _____ is to be involved and the connecting of _____ is also involved, where _____, _____, and _____ are coordinated with _____. Level 4 involves _____. The _____ control the entire factory by performing the steps: 1) _____. 2) _____ and 3) _____. At level 5 a computer _____ and _____. This level is of the area called _____ and _____. For determining _____, a (n) _____ to _____.

2. Illustrate the 5 levels of control according to Fig. 9.1 using an example which you met in industrial system.

3. Sketch a block form diagram of a control system with 5 general control levels, which should be converted from Fig. 9.1 according to the illustration in the text, using symbols

of related computer (s), equipment and elements, and describe your diagram.

Reading Material 9

Network Communications and Architecture Model

1. Network Communications

The key to successful implementation of CIM is communication compatibility between all the computers involved in the process. This, in fact, poses quite a problem. Although communication standards do exist, each computer system may use a different standard. In addition, as the level of sophistication of communication increases, the need for more sophisticated standards arises. In anticipation of this problem, the International Standards Organization (ISO) has developed a model for what is called open systems interconnection (OSI). The OSI is a seven-layer model for communication network architecture (see Fig. 9.2). Each layer represents a different level of communication sophistication and provides the necessary support for the layers above it. Implementing such an architecture allows the user to connect virtually any data communication device to the network and be assured of compatibility.

| Application layer |
| Presentation layer |
| Session layer |
| Transport layer |
| Network layer |
| Data-link layer |
| Physical layer |

Fig. 9.2 Open System Interconnection (OSI) Model for Network Architecture

Buried within each OSI layer are communication protocols. A protocol is nothing more than an agreed-upon set of rules by which communication will take place. Protocols exist at all communication levels and are assigned to the appropriate OSI layer according to level of sophistication.

2. Model for Network Architecture

To illustrate the need for protocols at different levels, consider the simple action of making a telephone call. There must be some convention for how the wires are connected, the allowable bandwidth of the channel, and the signal levels used. Next, the sequence of signal exchange must be established. That is, the sequence of dial-tone transmission, dial-pulse or touch-tone detection, and ringing or busy signal transmission must be clearly defined. Finally, when connection has been made, the rules that govern human dialogue take over. There are three levels of protocols in this example: physical, transmission and user. Note that the physical protocol provides the necessary support for the transmission protocol, which in turn supports the user protocol. Additionally, if the physical protocol is changed, the transmission and user protocols should be unaffected. That is, changes within layers should be transparent to the other layers. This principle is the essence of OSI.

To date, only layers 1, 2, and 3 of the OSI model have been clearly defined and successfully implemented. Layer 1 contains physical-link protocols—those that define such things as signal level and connection conventions. Protocols RS-232C and RS-422 are examples that would fit into this layer. Layer 2, the data-link layer, contains protocols that address such problems as circuit establishment, transmission sequence, and error control. Protocols such as SDLC, HDLC, and BISYNC belong in this layer. The network layer (layer 3) defines procedures for data routing, packet switching, and error recovery. The X.25 protocol is the most pervasive in this layer.

Selected from "Programmable Logic Controllers: principles and applications, by John W. Webb, Ronald A. Ress, No.4, 1999".

Words and Expressions

1. compatibility [ˌkəmˈpætəbiliti] n. 兼容性
2. communication standard 通信标准
3. sophistication [səˌfistiˈkeiʃən] n. 混合
4. anticipation [ænˌtisiˈpeiʃən] n. 预期，预料
5. international standards organization (ISO) 国际标准化组织
6. open systems interconnection (OSI) 开放式系统互联
7. communication network architecture 通信网络层
8. communication sophistication 通信混合系统
9. rule [ruːl] n. 规则
10. allowable bandwidth 允许的带宽
11. channel [ˈtʃænəl] n. 通道，信道；频道
12. dial-tone 音频拨号
13. dial-pulse 脉冲拨号
14. touch-tone 音频按键
15. human dialogue 人对话，交互
16. user protocol 用户协议
17. physical-link 物理连接
18. network layer 网络层
19. data routing 数据路由
20. packet switching 分包交换
21. pervasive [pəˈveisiv] adj. 普遍深入的，渗透的

Unit 10 Fieldbuses and Interoperability

> Before reading the text below, try to answer the following questions:
> 1. What is the general meaning of Field bus?
> 2. How to describe the fieldbus from the perspective of computer communication system or of the designers?
> 3. What are the basic contents of all service layers of computer communication?
> 4. What situations related with the fieldbus exist today?

In the last six or eight years, the word "fieldbus" has been very widely used. Its common meaning is "a network for connecting field devices such as sensors, actuators, and field controllers such as PLCs, regulators, drive controllers and so on". But this is only an informal definition, and this paper will define the fieldbus services and their qualities of service more precisely. A fieldbus is a type of real time communication system, and, is then based on a layered structure deduced from the OSI seven-layer model (Zimmermann, 1980). However, many choices are possible in each of the layers, both for the services and for the protocols. Some of the services defined for each fieldbus are very similar (they allow the communication of data between the various devices), but the protocols chosen provide different qualities of service, essentially in term of timeliness.

Other services depend on the approach that had led to a given fieldbus specification or, in other words, depend on the primary objectives of the designers, which may be expressed as follows:
- a fieldbus is only a network for simplifying the wiring between devices, or
- a fieldbus is the spinal column of a distributed real-time system.

The fieldbus was initially presented at its beginning, as the network at the bottom level in a CIM architecture, the hierarchical organization of an automation system derived form the MAP task force. Today, the situation is rather different.

Firstly, the strictly pyramidal model of automation systems is now recognized as not being well suited to explaining or modelling all communication aspects. Indeed, it is necessary to distinguish the functional architecture from the real or operational architecture (Simonot-Lion et al., 1995). Therefore, a 3-axis model has been defined, in order to explain the different functional exchanges of information in an automation system. The complete application is structured in entities, providing different levels of service, and in flows between these entities (Simonot-Lion et al., 1995). Two types of traffic may be identified. The so-called "vertical traffic" is composed of requests from an upper entity to a lower one, and of confirmations associated with the requests in a similar way as in the "client-server" model. In the other sense (bottom-up), requests are called "indications" and confirmations, "responses". The so-called "horizontal traffic" is composed of exchanges of data between entities. Data may comprise state values or events. The exchanges are no longer defined according to the client-server model, but between a producer and one or more consumers (Thomesse and Noury, 1989).

The fieldbuses provide for one or both of these communication models. They have been extended to eight models by a combination of the previous basic models and the number of communicating entities (Vega-Saenz and Thomesse, 1995).

Secondly, new networks such as ASI, SDS and DeviceNet, sometimes called "subfieldbus", "sensorbus" or "devicebus" have been introduced into the architecture. They do not differ fundamentally from the others; they have only been designed in order to obtain very low-cost connections for a reduced number of simple items of equipment, and are then placed lower than the fieldbuses in the operational architecture.

Thirdly, fieldbuses may be used as cell networks or control-room networks. Indeed, if a given fieldbus provides good service and allows the management of the traffic required by entities with the right quality of service, it may be used at different levels of the architecture.

Selected from "Control Engineering Practice: Fieldbuses and interoperability, by Jean Pierre Thomesse, No. 7, 1999".

Words and Expressions

1. fieldbus   现场总线
2. interoperability   ['ɪntərˌɔpərə'bɪləti]   n. 互用性，协同工作的能力
3. drive controller   驱动控制器
4. layer structure   层次结构
5. timeliness   n. 合时，时
6. spinal column   脊柱
7. distributed real-time system   分布式实时系统
8. pyramidal model   金字塔模型
9. operational architecture   操作体系结构
10. entity   ['entiti]   n. 实体
11. confirmation   [kɔnfə'meɪʃ(ə)n]   n. 证实，确认
12. horizontal traffic   水平通信
13. client-server model   客户端服务器模型
14. combination   [kɔmbi'neɪʃ(ə)n]   n. 结合，合并

Exercises

1. Fill in the blanks in your own words according to the text.

   In common meaning, a fieldbus is _____ which includes _____ and so on.

   Exactly, a fieldbus is a _____ based on a _____, which is deduced from the _____.

   There are many possible choices in _____ for both _____ and _____.

   In the words of fieldbus designers, a fieldbus is only _____, or a fieldbus is the _____

Currently, people find that the pyramidal model of automation system is _____ suite to _____. Thus a _____ has been defined in order to _____ in an automation system.

Some new networks, sometime such as _____, _____ and _____ have been introduced into _____. They are used to _____.

Field bus may be placed at _____, thus the need for _____ must be solved.

2. Illustrate an industrial system including fieldbus and PLC according to your experience.
3. Describe the application of computer communication technology in field-bus.

Reading Material 10

Fieldbus

1. Research

Even though much work has been completed, and even though many products exits, not all the problems have yet been solved. Some important topics of current research are given below.

Services, protocols. It is not only of concern to create new services, but also to define more precisely and formally time-constrained services and their related quality of service. Now, from a protocol point of view, there is a place for new protocols and operating systems somewhere between completely static mechanisms and completely dynamic ones, that could integrate joint scheduling of tasks and messages in order to meet (as far as possible) the time constraints dynamically. Indeed, the solutions chosen for the design of all the fieldbuses favour either dynamic behaviour with some risk of not meeting the constrainst, or static behaviour to meet the constraints but without so much robustness. This is a problem of dynamic distributed systems control in which there is still much to be done.

Conformance testing and interoperability. Another research issue is to improve the conformance testing methods, including the characterization of the quality of Service. This may cover the QoS modelling, measurement and evaluation, and the definition of conformance classes that are based not only on the service availability, but also on their QoS (see also (ISO/IEC, 1996)), The interoperability is tested between communicating equipment, but this property depends on the applications being supported. Also it is only at the application integration stage that some problems can be detected. For this reason, it is of major interest to be able to prove this application interoperability before implementation. What is needed, then, are not only models but also a methodology to conduct the design, to choose a given distribution, and so on.

System design modeling and validation. It was mentioned earlier that the fieldbus is the spinal column of automation systems. It is known how to prove a fieldbus protocol and to test an implementation, but the proving or the testing of a complete system is always a problem. It would be interesting to be sure that a system designed with a fieldbus is correct before its implementation. That means that it would be important to define realistic models of fieldbuses, of operating systems and of applications and equipment, that are well suited for a formal validation. It is now of major importance to obtain very well suited computer-aided design tools, in order to cover all the stages from the specification to the implementation of a given application, including validations at each stage, and then to use realistic models of the fieldbus protocols, companion standards and distributed applications.

2. Standardization

From a standardization point of view, the first steps could be an extension of EN 50170 and a complete definition of EN 50254 with Interbus-S, and others. A final decision on the IEC 1158-3 and 1158-4 Data Link Layer and on the IEC 1158-5 and 1158-6 Application Layer, is necessary and the definition of IEC 1158-7 on network management should be finalized in the near future to ensure maximum interoperability.

The definition of companion standards, or interoperability guidelines, or function blocks, according to the different vocabularies used (even the 8th layer or user layer) is important to achieve interoperability. A new European project called NOAH (Network Oriented Application Harmonization) could improve the method and tools in this direction.

Recognition of a unique dream standard by the whole community cannot be left for tomorrow!

Selected from "Control Engineering Practice: Fieldbuses and interoperability, by Jean Pierre Thomesse, No. 7, 1999".

Words and Expressions

1. service ['səvis] vt. 保养，维修
2. operating system 操作系统
3. dynamic [dai'næmik] adj. 动态的，动力的
4. conformance testing 相似测试，一致性测试
5. robustness n. 鲁棒性
6. communicating equipment 通信设备
7. methodology [meθə'dɔlədʒi] n. 方法学
8. system design 系统设计
9. validation [ˌvæli'deiʃən] n. 确认
10. standardization [ˌstændədai'zeiʃən] n. 标准化
11. finalize ['fainəlaiz] v. 把……最后定下来
12. QoS=quality of service 服务质量

CHAPTER. 3　Introduction to Measurement/test Technology and Equipment

Unit 11　Typical Measurement Technology

> Before reading the text, try to answer the following questions:
> 1. How are radar and satellite used in height measurement for plane?
> 2. What kinds of technologies are used for thickness measurement?
> 3. Is the "position tracking" also one kind of distance measurement technology?
> 4. What is "Programmable switch", and where is it used?
> 5. What is vision measurement technology and how is it applied?

1. Altitude Measurement

Accurate monitoring of aircraft cruising height is required in order to reduce vertical separation to a minimum standard. Interest here focuses on the measurement of the distance between aircraft level and the sea surface level. This distance can be estimated onboard via barometric altimeters or it can be measured—either onboard or in ground stations—via electronic radio wave systems. The indication of the first equipment is referred to as pressure altitude, or simply altitude, whereas that of the second category is referred to as geometric height or simply height.

The altitude information at air traffic control (ATC) centers is based on pressure altitude measurement that the aircraft transponder system sends after it receives an appropriate interrogation—known as mode C interrogation—transmitted by a secondary surveillance radar. Actually, the altitude information is an atmospheric pressure measurement transformed to altitude indication through a formula expressing the pressure/altitude relationship. When a flight level is cleared for an aircraft, it actually means that the pilot must keep flying on an isobaric surface. However, the altimetry system may present systematic errors (biases) that are different for each airplane, and that significantly affect safety. Thus, the altimetry system performance as well as the aircraft height keeping performance must be monitored by an independent radar or satellite system.

2. Thickness Measurement

One can measure thickness on many scales. The galaxy is spiral disk about 100 Em (10^{20} m) thick. The solar system is pancake-like, about 1 Tm (10^{12} m) thick. The rings of Saturn are about 10 km thick. Closer to home, Earth's atmosphere is a spherical shell about

40 km thick; the weather occurs in the troposphere, about 12 km thick. The outermost shell of the solid Earth is the crust, about 35 km thick. The ocean has a mean depth of 3.9 km. In the Antarctic, the recently discovered objects believed to be microfossils indicative of ancient Martian life are less than 100 nm thick. In terms of the man-made environment, industry must contend with thickness varying from meters, for construction projects, to millimeters on assemble lines, to micrometers and nanometers for the solid-state, optical, and coatings industries. Perhaps the most familiar way of measuring thickness is by mechanical means, such as by ruler or caliper. Other means are sometimes called for, either because both sides of an object are not accessible, the dimension is either too big or too small for calipers, the object is too fragile, too hot, or too cold for direct contact, or the object is in motion on an assemble line — it may not even be a solid. Thickness may also be a function of position, as either the object may have originally been made with nonuniform thickness, deliberately or not, or the thickness may have become nonuniform with time due either to corrosion, cracking, or some other deterioration. The thickness may also be changing with time due to deliberate growth or etching, as example for thin films. Thus it follows that, in more general terms, measuring thickness might require measuring the topography or height profile of two surfaces and taking the difference. Alternatively, the measurement technique may produce a reading directly related to the difference.

3. Distance measurement

The tools and techniques of distance measurement are possibly one of humankind's longest-running inventive pursuits. This chapter concerns itself with methods to measure a relatively small segment of this range—from centimeters to kilometers. Even within this limited segment, it would hardly be possible to list, much less describe, all of the distance measurement approaches that have been devised. Nevertheless, the small sampling of technologies that are covered here should be of help to a broad range of readers.

Distance measurement, at its most basic, is concerned with determining the length of a unidimensional line joining two points in three-dimensional space. Oftentimes, a collection of distance measurements is called for, so that the shape, the orientation, or the changes in position of an object can be resolved. Therefore, one must consider not only the measurement of distances, but also their spatial and temporal distributions. The terminology "ranging" will be used in reference to systems that perform single sensor-to-target measurement, "range-imaging" for systems that collect a dense map or grid of spatially distributed range measurement, and "position tracking" for systems that record the time history of distance measurement to one or several targets.

4. Level Measurement

Level is defined as the filling height of a liquid or bulk material, for example, in a tank or reservoir. Generally, the position of the surface is measured relative to a reference plane, usually the tank bottom. If the product's surface is not flat (e.g., with foam, waves, turbulences, or with coarse-grained bulk material) level usually is defined as the average height of a bounded area.

Various classic and modern methods exist to measure product level in process and storage tanks in the chemical, petrochemical, pharmaceutical, water, and food industries, in mobile tanks on vehicles and ships, but also in natural reservoirs like seas, dams, lakes, and oceans. Typical tank heights are approximately between 0.5 m and 40 m.

Two different tasks can be distinguished: (1) continuous level measurements (level indication, LI), and (2) level switches (LS) (e.g., to detect an alarm limit to prevent overfilling). Fig. 11.1 shows the principal operational modes of level measurement. Every continuous system can also be used as a programmable switch. Many level devices are mounted on top of the tank and measure primarily the distance d between their mounting position and the product's surface. The level L is then calculated, defining the tank height h as constant, as shown in Fig. 11.1 and expressed as:

$$L = h - d \tag{11.1}$$

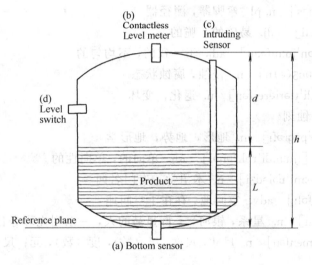

Fig. 11.1 Representation of a tank with a liquid or solid material (hatched area), the product to be measured. The level sensor can be mounted (a) contacting product at the bottom, (b) as a contactless instrument on top, (c) as an intrusive sensor, or (d) at the sides as a level switch

Words and Expressions

1. monitor ['mɔnitə(r)] n. 监听器,监视器,监控器　vt. 监控　v. 监控
2. cruising ['kru:ziŋ] vi. 巡游,巡航　n. 巡游,巡航
3. vertical ['və:tik(ə)] adj. 垂直的,直立的,顶点的,[解] 头顶的　n. 垂直线,垂直面,竖向
4. onboard [ɔn'bɔ:d] adj. 随车携带的
5. barometric [bærəu'metrik] adj. 大气压力
6. category ['kætigəri] n. 种类,别,[逻] 范畴

7. geometric [dʒiːəˈmetrik] adj. 几何的，几何学的
8. transponder [trænˈspɒndə(r)] n. [无] 异频雷达收发机
9. interrogation [ɪnterəˈgeɪʃ(ə)n] n. 审问，问号；询问
10. surveillance [səˈveɪləns] n. 监视，监督
11. isobaric [aɪsəʊˈbærɪk] adj. 表示等压的，同重元素的
12. altimetry [ælˈtɪmɪtri] n. 测高学，高度测量法（以海平面为基准）
13. systematic [sɪstəˈmætɪk] adj 系统的；规划的；有计划的
14. pancake [ˈpænkeɪk] n. 薄烤饼
15. saturn [ˈsætən] n. 土星
16. spherical [ˈsferɪk(ə)l] adj. 球的，球形的
17. troposphere [ˈtrɒpəsfɪə(r)] n. [气] 对流层
18. microfossils [maɪkrəʊˈfɒsəl] n. 微体化石，微化石
19. martian [ˈmɑːʃən] n. 火星人 adj. 火星的
20. nanometer n. 纳米（10^{-9} m）
21. calipers [ˈkælɪpəs] n. pl. 弯脚器，测径器
22. fragile [ˈfrædʒaɪl] adj. 易碎的，脆的
23. nonuniform [nɒnˈjuːnɪfɔːm] adj. 不一致的，不均匀的
24. corrosion [kəˈrəʊʒ(ə)n] n. 侵蚀，腐蚀状态
25. deterioration [dɪˌtɪərɪəˈreɪʃən] n. 退化，变坏
26. etch [etʃ] v. 蚀刻
27. topography [təˈpɒgrəfi] n. 地形，地势，地形学
28. unidimensional [ˌjuːnɪdɪˈrekʃənəl] adj. 单向的，单向性的
29. terminology [tɜːmɪˈnɒlədʒi] n. 术语学，专门名词
30. spatially [ˈspeɪʃəli] adv. 空间地，存在于空间地
31. galaxy [ˈgæləksi] n. 星系，银河，一群显赫的人，一系列光彩夺目的东西
32. dimension [dɪˈmenʃən] n. 尺寸，尺度，维（数），度（数），元；尺寸，量纲，维面积

Exercises

1. Translate the following words and phrases into Chinese:
    altitude measurement, cruising height, transform to, surveillance radar, secondary, isobaric surface, systematic error, nonuniform with time, related to, continuous system

2. Answer the following questions:
    ① What is accurate monitoring of aircraft cruising height required for?
    ② How does an aircraft contact with ground station for measuring its altitude?
    ③ What does it mean when a flight level is cleared?
    ④ What scales could be used for measuring thickness?
    ⑤ What units could be used to represent the thickness?
    ⑥ What tools and techniques are possibly applied to measure distance?
    ⑦ How is level defined and what modern methods are used for measuring it?

3. Describe the definitions of the following terms by using examples familiar to you.

   altitude measurement, thickness measurement, distance measurement and level measurement

Reading Material 11

Some Advantaged Measurement Technologies

1. Light Measurement

The foundation metric of light is luminous flux, which is the rate at which light energy is emitted from a source, and is expressed in lumens (lm). Luminous intensity is luminous flux per unit solid angle, and its unit of measurement is candela (cd). This is distinguished from illuminance, or illumination, which is simply luminous flux per unit area, expressed as lux (lx). Luminance, is a measure of the brightness, i. e., the amount of light, per unit area, either emitted by or reflected from a surface. Units of luminance measurement are candelas per square meter (cd/m^2) or nits. Finally, reflectance is a unitless ratio of the amount of light striking a surface to the amount of light leaving it:

$$R = \pi \times \frac{\text{lu min ance}}{\text{illu min ance}} \tag{11.2}$$

High reflectance can create glare, dramatically reducing visual performance.

2. Vision Measurement

The eye function very much like a conventional camera. Light enters the eye through a transparent cornea and is modulated by the pupil, a variable aperture opening controlled by muscles of the iris. The pupil grows larger in dark surroundings and smaller in bright surroundings to control the range of light intensity to the eye. Light rays are then refracted by an adjustable lens and brought into focus on the retina, where neural imaging begins. The retina contains both cones and rods, two distinctly different types of photoreceptors. Cones are concentrated near the fovea, or the central 2° of the visual field, and decrease rapidly with distance from this region. In contrast, rods are essentially absent in the fovea and increase in density with distance.

The eye is sensitive to three characteristics of electromagnetic radiation: (1) brightness (the intensity of ambient or incident light, measured in lux), (2) hue (the wavelength of light, measured in nm), and (3) saturation (relative concentration of specific hues in light, measured as a dimensionless ratio from 0 to 1). Cones are differentially sensitive wavelength, i. e., hue, and have greater resolving power than rods because of their one-to-one mapping onto visual nerves. Cones can be further divided into three type, each maximally sensitive to a different portion of the visible light spectrum: (1) red (670 nm peak), (2) green (470 nm peak), and (3) blue (400 nm peak). Rods are more sensitive to light than cones and have many-to-one connections with the nerves that exit the eye, a feature that permits neural summation of low light signals. Human ability to discriminate differences in levels of brightness, saturation, or hue is governed by a psychophysical function known as

Weber's law:

$$K = \frac{\Delta I}{I} \tag{11.3}$$

where, ΔI is the difference, or change, in intensity, I is the initial intensity, and K is the Weber fraction. Values of K have been experimentally determined for brightness (0.079), saturation (0.019 for red), and hue ($\approx$ 0.02 to 0.04, depending on the region of the visible spectrum).

Photopic vision occurs at light leases where both rods and cones are sensitive. The minimum light intensity required for photopic vision to is approximately 2 lx; colors are seen in this region. As brightness decreases, a transition from photopic to scotopic vision takes place and color perception drops out gradually, a phenomenon that can impact the interpretation of color-coded information in poor light. Perception of blues and reds is lost first, then cyan and yellow-orange, and finally green, i.e., the wavelengths where the eye is most sensitive. The eye becomes most sensitive to wavelengths of about 550 nm (green) near the limit of photopic vision. Scotopic vision occurs at low light levels (2×10^{-7} lx to 2 lx) and primarily involves the rods; only achromatic shades of gray are seen. The transition from photopic to scotopic vision occurs slowly, requiring approximately 30 min for complete adjustment from photopic to scotopic visual sensitivity.

Visual acuity is the ability to discriminate detail. The action of the lens, to change focus for objects at different distances, is called *accommodation*. *Minimum separable acuity*, the most common measure of discrimination, is determined by the smallest feature that the eye can detect, and is measured in terms of the reciprocal of the visual angle subtended at the eye by that feature. Visual angle, in minutes of arc, is calculated as

$$VA = \frac{3438H}{D} \tag{11.4}$$

where H is the height of the object and D (in the same units) is the distance from the observer. The ability to distinguish an object from its surroundings is known as visibility. The term is related to visual acuity, but implicitly combines factors of object size, contrast (i.e., including differences in hue and saturation), and brightness that all interact to determine true visual detection performance. On a more functional level, readability or legibility describe the ability to distinguish meaningful groups of objects (e.g., words extracted from groups of letters on a display).

Other parameters affecting visual performance include viewing angle and viewing distance. Viewing angle at the eye is measured from a line through the visual axis to the point being viewed, and determines where an object will register on the retina. The best image resolution occurs at the fovea, directly on the line of gaze, and visual acuity degrades with increasing angle away from this axis. Viewing angle at the display is the angle, in degrees, between a line normal to the display surface and the user's visual axis. The best viewing angle is, of course, on the visual axis and normal to the display surface, as luminance falls off for most display as the angle from normal increases. Luminance reduction with viewing angle can be calculated as

$$E = E_m \cos^4 \theta \qquad (11.5)$$

where E_m is the illuminance at the center of the display and θ is the viewing angle. Note that two viewing angles—at the eye and at the display—have been defined. Viewing distance is determined primarily by the minimum size requirements (i. e., visual angle) for objects that the user must see. A conventional reading distance is about 71 cm, although VDTs are frequently read at 46 cm. Most design criteria assume a viewing distance of between 50 and 70 cm.

Viewing fatigue is an imprecise term, but one in common use, referring to the annoyance, irritation, or discomfort associated with visual tasks performed under poor conditions or for extended periods of time. A common cause of visual fatigue is glare, which can be due to a combination of high brightness, high reflectance, and specular (mirrorlike) reflections causing source light to reflect directly into the eye. Minimizing or eliminating glare is essential for effective display performance, and usually involves a thoughtful placement of the display, proper positioning of room lights, control of ambient light (e. g., window shades), or the use of display hoods.

3. Ground-based Height Estimation

The radars used to derive the original measurements are either primary or secondary surveillance radars. A primary radar sends a signal and scans for the arrival of its reflection. The range to the object reflecting the signal is derived from the time elapsed between transmission and reception. With secondary radar, the radar sends an interrogation to aircraft—to all aircraft or to a selected one—and the appropriate aircraft sends a reply via its transponder. The range to the aircraft is computed from the time elapsed between the signal transmission and the signal arrival, taking into account the nominal delay time of the transponder. Most of the methods estimating the aircraft height make use of the SSR equipment because it is cost effective, the transponder reply signal is stronger than that reflected to a primary radar, and the system can operate more reliable in dense traffic areas.

Any systematic errors in the primary radar and in the ground equipment of the SSR can be corrected by calibration. However, the problem encountered with SSR is that it involves the transponder delay time in the range measurement process. Thus, any systematic error in the transponder delay time caused range bias errors that are different for each aircraft and thus suitable methods must be used to anticipate for it in the subsequent measurement data processing.

Navigation Accuracy Measurement System

Nagaoka has proposed an off-line height estimation system. It is composed of a primary marine radar located under an airlane and measures range R and depressing angle β. Fig. 11.2 shows the geometry of the system. The antenna rotates about a vertical axis and scans the area above it with rate equal to 1 rotation per 3s. The principle exploited to derive the height estimate is that the range varies as the aircraft passes through the data acquisition area. The rate of change of range is mainly a function of the flight height z and secondarily of depres-

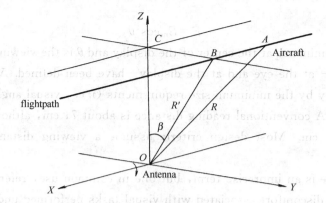

Fig. 11.2 Geometry of the Navigation Accuracy Measurement System (NAMS)
$BA=x$, $CB=y$, $OC=z$, $R'=z/\cos(\beta)$

sion angle. It is easily derived from Fig. 11.2, that the relation between the above quantities and the position x along the x axis at time t is:

$$R(t)=\sqrt{x^2(t)+R'(t)^2}=\sqrt{x^2(t)+\frac{z^2}{\cos^2\beta(t)}} \qquad (11.6)$$

Let x_0 denote the position of the aircraft at time t_0. Assuming the aircraft flies in straight and level flight, this means that the velocity V_x the depression angle, and the height h remain constant during the data collection period. The above quantities and the range measurement at time t_i are related through Equation 11.7

$$R_i=\sqrt{[x_0+V_x\ (t_i-t_0)]^2+\frac{z^2}{\cos^2\beta}}=f\ (t_i,\ \beta,\ q)\ =f_i\ (q) \qquad (11.7)$$

where q is the unknown quantities vector, $q=[x_0,\ V_x,\ z]^T$.

Measurements of R_i and β are collected at times t_0, t_1, ……, t_n, and their set is briefly expressed as a vector function of the unknown quantities with the following matrix equation:

$$R=f(q) \qquad (11.8)$$

where

$$R=\begin{bmatrix}R_0\\R_1\\\cdots\\R_n\end{bmatrix} \qquad f=\begin{bmatrix}f_0\\f_1\\\cdots\\f_n\end{bmatrix}$$

Equation 11.8 is nonlinear. Thus, a nonlinear least square method, such as the Gauss-Newton iterative method, must be used to estimate the unknown vector. Let $\hat{q}_k$ be the estimate at the k th iteration. Then, the next estimate is:

$$\hat{q}_{k+1}=\hat{q}_k+(F^TF)^{-1}F^T(R-f(\hat{q}_k)) \qquad (11.9)$$

where F is the partial derivatives (Jacobian) matrix:
that absorbs thermal radiation from a warmer object, an AFIR motion detector is active; that is, it radiates heat waves toward the surroundings. The sensor's surface temperature (T_s) is maintained somewhat above ambient. The element is combined with a focusing system, very much like the PIR detector, however, the function of that system is inverse to that of the

passive detectors. A focusing part in the AFIR detector projects a thermal image of the warm sensing element into its surroundings. The AFIR sensors have a significant advantage over the PIR: immunity against many interferences (such as RFI and microphonics).

The output voltage from the AFIR motion detector can be described by the following equation:

$$\Delta V \approx \frac{R}{V_0} \frac{\sigma \alpha \gamma}{\pi} b T_s^3 \frac{\Delta T}{L^2} \tag{11.10}$$

where R is the resistance of the sensor's heater and V_0 is the heating voltage. The minus sign indicates that for warmer moving objects, the output voltage decreases. There is an obvious similarity between Equations 11.9 and 11.10; however, sensitivity (detection range) of the AFIR sensor can be easily controlled by varying R or V_0. For better sensitivity, the temperature increment above ambient can be maintained on a fairly low level. Practically, the element is heated above ambient by only about 0.2℃.

Words and Expressions

1. luminous flux   n. [物] 光通量（其单位为流明 lumen）
2. illuminance [iˈljuːminəns] n. (=illumination) 照明 [度]，启发
3. candela [ˈkændilə] n. 烛光   adj. 小雪茄烟的
4. pupil [ˈpjuːpil] n. 瞳孔
5. cornea [ˈkɔːniə] n. [医] 角膜
6. iris [ˈaiəris] n. [解] 虹膜
7. refract [riˈfrækt] vt. 使折射，测定……的折射度
8. lens [lenz] n. 透镜，镜头
9. retina [ˈretinə] n. [解] 视网膜
10. cone [kəun] n. [数、物] 锥形物，圆锥体，（松树的）球果   vt. 使成锥形
11. rod [rɔd] n. 杆，棒
12. fovea [ˈfəuviə] n. 凹，小凹（尤指视网膜的中央凹）
13. hue [hjuː] n. 色调，样子，颜色，色彩
14. saturation [ˌsætʃəˈreiʃ(ə)n] n. 饱和（状态），浸润，浸透，饱和度
15. photopic [fəuˈtɔpik] n. 光适应，眼对光调节
16. scotopic [skəˈtɔpik] adj. [医] 暗适应的，暗视的
17. accommodation [əkɔməˈdeiʃən] n. （眼睛等的）适应性调节
18. subtend [səbˈtend] vt. 对着，对向
19. legibility [ˌledʒiˈbiliti] n. 易读性，易辨认，易理解
20. transponder [trænˈspɔndə] n. [无] 异频雷达收发机
21. off-line   adj. 不连接到线上的，脱机的，离线的
22. iterative [ˈitərətiv,-reit-] adj. 重复的，反复的，[数] 迭代的   n. 反复体
23. fatigue [fəˈtiːg] n. 疲乏，疲劳
24. ambient [ˈæmbiənt] adj. 周围的   n. 周围环境

Unit 12 Simple Instrument Model

> Before reading the text, try to answer the following questions:
> 1. What is null measurement and deflection measured?
> 2. What is the essential difference between analog sensors and digital sensors?
> 3. What important features do analog readout instrument and digital readout instrument have?
> 4. What a role does an analog sensor or a digital sensor play?

In addressing measurement problems, it is often useful to have a conceptual model of the measurement process. This unit presents. some of the fundamental concepts of measurement in the context of a simple generalized in strument model.

Fig. 12.1 presents a generalized model of a simple instrument. The physical process to

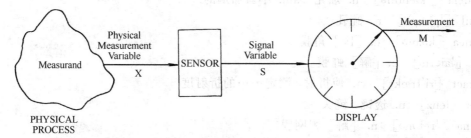

Fig. 12.1 Simple instrument model

be measured is in the left of the figure and the measurand is represented by an observable physical variable X. Note that the observable variable X need not necessarily be the measurand but simple related to the measurand in some known way. For example, the mass of an object is often measured by the process of weighing, where the measurand is the mass but the physical measurement variable is the downward force the mass exerts in the Earth's gravitational field. There are many possible physical measurement variables. A few are shown in Table 12.1.

Table 12.1 Normal Physical Variable

Common physical variables	Typical signal variables
• Force	• Voltage
• Length	• Displacement
• Temperature	• Current
• Acceleration	• Force
• Velocity	• Pressure
• Pressure	• Light
• Frequency	• Frequency
• Capacity	
• Resistance	
• Time	
• ...	

The key functional element of the instrument model shown in Fig. 12.1 is the sensor, which has the function of converting the physical variable input into a signal variable output. Signal variable have the property that they can be manipulated in a transmission system, such as an electrical or mechanical circuit. Because of this property, the signal variable can be transmitted to an output or recording device that can be remote from the sensor. In electrical circuits, voltage is a common signal variable. In mechanical systems, displacement or force are commonly used as signal variables. Other examples of signal variable are shown in Table 12.1. The signal output from the sensor can be displayed, recorded, or used as an input signal to some secondary device or system. In a basic instrument, the signal is transmitted to a display or recording device where the measurement can be read by a human observer. The observed output is the measurement M. There are many types of display devices, ranging from simple scales and dial gages to sophisticated computer display systems. The signal can also be used directly by some larger system of which the instrument is a part. For example, the output signal of the sensor may be used as the input signal of a closed loop control system.

If the signal output from the sensor is small, it is sometimes necessary to amplify the output shown in Fig. 12.2. The amplified output can then be transmitted to the display device or recorded, depending on the particular measurement application. In many cases it is necessary for the instrument to provide a digital signal output so that it can interface with a computer-based data acquisition or communications system. If the sensor does not inherently provide a digital output, then the analog output of the sensor is converted by an analog to digital converter (ADC) as shown in Fig. 12.2. The digital signal is typically sent to a computer processor that can display, store, or transmit the data as output to some other system, which will use the measurement.

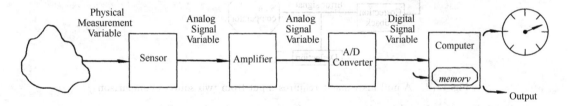

Fig. 12.2 Instrument model with amplifier, analog to digital converter, and computer output

1. Null Instrument

The null method is one possible mode of operation for a measuring instrument. A null instrument uses the null method for measurement. In this method, the instrument exerts an influence on the measured system so as to opposite in value, yielding a null measurement. Typically, this is accomplished by some type of feedback operation that allows the comparison of the measurand against a known standard value. Key features of a null instrument include: an iterative balancing operation using some type of comparator, either a manual or automatic feedback used to achieve balance, and a null deflection at parity [shown in Fig. 12.3].

A null instrument offers certain intrinsic advantages over other modes of operation (e.g., see deflection instruments). By balancing the unknown input against a know standard input, the null method minimizes interaction between the measuring system and the mea-

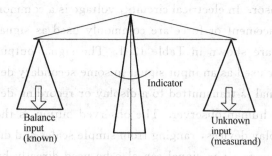

Fig. 12.3 The measurand and the known quantities balance one another in a null instrument

surand. As each input comes from a separate source, the significance of any measuring influence on measurand by the measurement process is reduced. In effect, the measured system sees a very high input impedance, thereby minimizing loading errors. This is particularly effective when the measurand is a very small value. Hence, the null operation can achieve a high accuracy for small input values and a low loading error. In practice, the null instrument will not achieve perfect parity due to the usable resolution of the balance and detection methods, but this is limited only by the state of the art of the circuit or scheme being employed [shown in Fig. 12.4].

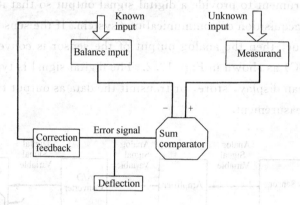

Fig. 12.4 A null instrument requires input from two sources comparison

A disadvantage of null instruments is that an iterative balancing operation requires more time to execute than simply measuring sensor input. Thus, this method might not offer the fastest measurement possible when high-speed of measurements are required. However, the user should weigh achievable accuracy against needed speed of measurement when considering operational modes. Further, the generally not the lowest cost measuring alternative.

2. Deflection Instrument

The deflection method is one possible mode of operation for a measuring instrument. A deflection instrument uses the deflection method for measurement. A deflection instrument is influenced by the measurand so as to bring about a proportional response within the instrument. This response is an output reading that is a deflection or a deviation from the initial condition of the instrument. In a typical form, the measurand acts directly on a prime element or primary circuit so as to convert its information into a detectable form. The name is derived from a common form of instrument where there is a physical deflection of a prime element that is linked to an output scale, such as a pointer or other type of readout, which deflects to indicate the measured value. The magnitude of the deflection of the prime element brings about a deflection in the output scale that is designed to be proportional in magnitude to the value of the measurand.

Deflection instruments are the most common of measuring instruments. The relationship between the measurand and the prime element or measuring circuit can be a direct one, with no balancing mechanism or comparator circuits used. The proportional response can be manipulated through signal conditioning methods between the prime element and the output scale so that the output reading is a direct indication of the measurand. Effective designs can achieve a high accuracy, yet sufficient accuracy for less demanding uses can be achieved at moderate costs.

An attractive feature of the deflection instrument is that it can be designed for either static or dynamic measurements or both. An advantage to deflection design for dynamic measurements is in the high dynamic response that can be achieved. A disadvantage of deflection instruments is that by deriving its energy from the measurand, the act of measurement will influence the measurand and change the value of the variable being measured. This change is called a loading error. Hence, the user must ensure that the resulting error is acceptable. This usually involves a careful look at the instrument input impedance for the intended measurement.

Words and Expressions

1. variable ['vєəriəb(ə)l] n. [数] 变数,可变物,变量 adj. 可变的,不定的,易变的; [数] 变量的
2. gravitational [grævi'teiʃənəl] adj. 重力的
3. interface ['intəfeis] n. [地质] 分界面,接触面;[物、化] 界面,接口
4. inherently [in'hiərəntli] adv. 天性地,固有地
5. transmit [trænz'mit, trɑː-] vt. 传输,转送,传达,传导,发射,遗传,传播 vi. 发射信号,发报
6. yield [jiːld] v. 出产,生长,生产 vi. (～to)屈服,屈从 n. 产量,收益
7. feedback ['fiːdbæk] n. [无] 回授,反馈,反应
8. iterative ['itərətiv,-reit-] adj. 重复的,反复的,[数] 迭代的 n. 反复体
9. parity ['pæriti] n. 奇偶
10. sophisticated [sə'fistikeitid] adj. 诡辩的,久经世故的
11. dial ['dai(ə)l] n. 刻度盘,钟面,转盘,(自动电话)拨号盘 v. 拨
12. gage [geidʒ] n. (＝gauge)标准度量,计量器 vt. (＝gauge)精确计量,估计
13. impedance [im'piːdens] n. [电] 阻抗,全电阻,[物] 阻抗
14. execute ['eksikjuːt] vt. 执行,实行,完成,处死,制成,[律] 经签名盖章等手续使(证书)生效
15. deviation [diːvi'eiʃ(ə)n] 背离
16. prime [praim] n. 最初,青春,精华 adj. 主要的,最初的,有青春活力的,最好的,第一流的,根本的,[数] 素数的 v. 预先准备好
17. detectable [di'tektəbl] adj. 可发觉的,可看穿的

18. proportional [prə'pɔːʃn(ə)l] adj. 比例的，成比例的，相称的，均衡的
19. magnitude ['mæɡnɪtjuːd;(US)-tuːd] n. 大小，数量，巨大，广大，量级
20. feature ['fiːtʃə(r)] n. 面貌的一部分（眼，口，鼻等）特征，容貌，特色，特写 vt. 是……的特色，特写，放映 vi. 起重要作用
21. dynamic [daɪ'næmɪk] adj. 动力的，动力学的，动态的
22. derive [dɪ'raɪv] vt. 得自 vi. 起源
23. involve [ɪn'vɒlv] vt. 包括，笼罩，潜心于，使陷于
24. response [rɪ'spɒns] n. 回答，响应，反应
25. moderate ['mɒdərət] adj. 中等的，适度的，适中的 v. 缓和
26. demanding [dɪ'mɑːndɪŋ;(US)dɪ'mændɪŋ] adj. 过分要求的，苛求的

Exercises

1. Translate the following sentences into chinese:
   physical process to be measured
   simple related to measurand
   gravitational field
   the Earth's gravitational field
   key function element
   instrument model
   the function of converting A into B
   the amplified output
   display device
   computer-based data acquisition
   null instrument
   deflection instrument
   balancing A against B
   measuring influence A by B
   input impedance
   low loading error
   being employed
   achieve perfect parity
   usable resolution
   detectable form
   output scale
   measured value

2. Answer the following questions with the help of analyzing Fig. 12.1 and 12.2:
   ① What key elements are included in a complete measurement process, and what functions do they perform?
   ② Why does a measurement system convert the physical variable, analog signal, amplified signal and digital signal from one into other orderly?

③ What might people do on the output signal after it comes out from the sensor output or computer output?
3. Describe the definitions, working principles and applications of the following instruments and technologies in English by using examples:
   null instruments
   deflection instruments
   balance in a measurement instrument
   deflection in a measurement instrument

Reading Material 12

Some Advantaged Instrument Model

1. Analog and Digital Sensors

Analog sensors provide a signal that is continuous in both its magnitude and its temporal (time) or spatial (space) content. The defining word for analog is "continuous". If a sensor provides a continuous output signal that is directly proportional to the input signal, then it is analog.

Most physical variables, such as current, temperature, displacement, acceleration, speed, pressure, light intensity and strain, tend to be continuous in nature and are readily measured by an analog sensor and represented by an analog signal. For example, the temperature within a room can take on any value within its range, will vary in a continuous manner in between any two points in the room, and may vary continuously with time at any position within the room. An analog sensor, such as a bulb thermometer or a thermocouple, will continuously respond to such temperature changes. Such a continuous signal is shown in Fig. 12.5, where the signal magnitude is analogous to the measured variable (temperature) and the signal is continuous in both magnitude and time.

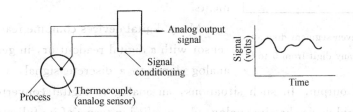

Fig. 12.5 A thermocouple provides an analog signal for processing

Digital sensors provide a signal that is a direct digital representation of the measurand. Digital sensors are basically binary ("on" or "off") device. Essentially, a digital signal exists at only discrete values of time (or space). And within that discrete period, the signal can representonly a discrete number of magnitude values. A common variation is the discrete sampled signal representation, which represents a sensor output in a form that is discrete both in time or space and in magnitude.

Digital sensors use some variation of a binary numbering system to represent and transmit the signal information in digital form. A binary numbering system is a number system using the base 2. The simplest binary signal is a single bit that has only one of two possible values, a 1 or a 0. Bits are like electrical "on-off" switches and are used to convey logical and numerical information. With appropriate input, the value of the bit transmitted is reset corresponding to the behavior of the measured variable. A digital sensor that transmits information one bit at a time uses serial transmission.

2. Analog and Digital Readout Instruments

An analog readout instrument provides an output indication that is continuous and directly analogous to the behavior of the measurand. Typically, this might be the deflection of a pointer or an ink trace on a graduated scale, or the intensity of a light beam or a sound wave. This indicated deflection may be driven by changes in voltage or current, or by mechanical, magnetic, or optical means, or combinations Of these. The resolution of an analog readout is defined by the smallest usable increment on its readout scale. The span of the readout is defined by the difference between the minimum values that it can indicate.

A digital readout instrument provides an output indication that is discrete. The value of the digital output is directly related to the value of the measurand. The digital readout is typically in the form of a numerical value that is either a fixed number or a number that is updated periodically. One means of displaying a digital number is the seven-segment digital display chip, shown in Fig. 12.6, whose output can be updated by altering the grounding inputs A through G. the resolution of a digital readout is given by its least count, the equivalent amount of the smallest change resolved by the least significant digit in the readout. The span and range are defined as for analog instruments.

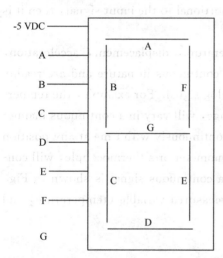

Fig. 12.6 A seven-segment display chip can display any digit from 0 to 9

Many digital devices combine features of an analog sensor with a digital readout or, in general, convert an analog signal to a discrete signal, which is indicated through a digital output. In such situations, an analog to digital converter (ADC) is required. This hybrid device has its analog side specified in terms of its full-scale analog range, E_{FSR}[①], which defines the analog voltage span over which the device will operate. The digital side is specified in terms of the bit size of its register. An M-bit device will output an M-bit binary number. The resolution of such a device is given by $E_{FSR}/2^M$[②].

Words and Expressions

1. hybrid ['haibrid]   n. 混合物   adj. 混合的，杂种的
2. binary ['bainəri]   adj. 二进位的，二元的

3. temporal ['tempər(ə)l] adj. 暂时的（现世的） n. 暂存的
4. spatial ['speɪʃ(ə)l] adj. 空间的
5. strain [streɪn] n. 过度的疲劳，紧张，张力，应变
6. bulb [bʌlb] n. 鳞茎，球形物
7. thermometer [θə'mɒmɪtə(r)] n. 温度计，体温计
8. serial ['sɪərɪəl] adj. 连续的
9. transmission [trænz'mɪʃ(ə)n, trɑː-] n. 播送，发射，传动，传送，传输，转播
10. span [spæn] n. 跨度，跨距，范围 v. 横越

Notes

① E_{FSR}: Full scale analog voltage span over which the device will operate. 设备工作的全程电压范围。

② $E_{FSR}/2^M$: The analog voltage resolution of an M-bit device. 一个 M 位设备的电压分辨率。

Unit 13 Signal Process

> Before reading the text, try to answer the following questions:
> 1. What is algorithmic method?
> 2. Can algorithmic method be applied in all domains?
> 3. Will algorithmic methods become obsolete along with the development of artificial intelligence?
> 4. How do you think of the idea "mapping of many to a few"?

While we appear to prefer the total objectivity of a mathematically formulated method of signal processing, it is now well proven that the AI methods often are better choices to use in terms of better speed of performance and often lower cost of processing. Often they are the only solution since the algorithmic approach cannot be deployed because of the lack of a suitable mathematical formulation or powerful enough processor to run the algorithm.

Signal processing in the modem instrument, therefore, will often make use of many different methods. This account is an introduction to the characteristics of the various forms and is written to assist selection.

Space limitations prevent presentation of each kind in detail.

1. Overview of Algorithmic Methods

Traditionally the most popular method used to develop mapping models is that of mathematical modeling. The mathematical model is usually what is sought, as it provides the highest level of understanding about the subject and the most precise representation of the behavior. The major disadvantage of mathematical models is that they can quickly become so complex that implementation of these models in measurement systems is often impractical.

In this class, the single, or set of multiple, input signal(s) to the data processor is converted to the output form using tightly formulated mathematical description. This relationship is called the algorithm. Strict relationships hold; the relationship is said to be formal, meaning that for any given input the output will always be the same. The algorithm supports only one interpretation.

This method of signal processing is the most highly developed method and is certainly one to aim for because it is devoid of ambiguity. All will agree on how it will respond. It carries a comforting level of understanding and, thus, acceptance.

Algorithmic methods can be very accurate, traceable, and can be calibrated with relative ease and agreement. They are the basis of many instrumentation systems. The origin of their use in instrumentation goes back to the early days of computing using, first, mechanical computational machines (late 1800s to around 1930) and then analog electric devices (early 1900s to 1960s), all of which were mostly replaced by the use of digital computers commencing around 1950. All of these algorithmic methods of processing can be simplistically regarded as embodiments of a mathematical equation inside a suitable technological machine.

As the demanded complexity and performance requirements grew over time, so the did the demands on the detail of the algorithm and the means to model it inside a computational machine. Mathematical description eventually reaches limits of definition as the models push the boundaries of mathematical methods and human development. Too often, this arises before adequate detail is able to be built into the model. The algorithm is then an inadequate model of the need.

As the algorithm increases in complexity, the processing power needed must be increased to maintain both fidelity and speed of processing.

Despite great advances being made in algorithm development and in computer power, the algorithmic methodology eventually encountered mathematical and technological barriers in many fields. The method is seen to not always be the best to use because of lack of an adequate algorithm or the high cost of computing.

In instrumentation, another factor also arises. Fast, detailed processing brings with it the need for increasing electrical bandwidth requirements in signal transmission. This increases implementation costs and also eventually reaches technological constraints.

2. Overview of Applied Intelligence Methods

Fortunately the solutions that may overcome these limiting constraints in many circumstances were developing in other fields under the general name of artificial intelligence (now called applied intelligence in engineering), as new forms of mathematics and in other fields, such as decision theory.

Principally, a key limitation of the algorithmic method is that its unforgiving level of formalism carries with it a depth of processing exactitude that is often not warranted.

Other methods have emerged that allow vaguely subjective, as opposed to tightly objective, processing to be applied to good effect.

These AI methods have gradually gained acceptance to the degree that many are now routinely used and are supported by dedicated applications software and electronic integrated circuitry.

At first, these many alternatives were seen to be isolated methods. Gradually, the literature has shown trends to merge them in pairs. Their use in a more widely mixed form is still limited. This account seeks to give a comprehensive appreciation of the commonly met AI processing methods by placing them into relative perspective.

It is interesting to contemplate that natural world computing in animals does not appear to make much use of algorithmic methods, but does make extensive use of the methods presented here in the AI class.

The paradigm invoked here is that experience has shown that informal methods based on knowledge-based systems (KBS) can produce mappings of many inputs to one by use of less than completely formal description.

The AI methods can yield surprisingly efficient solutions to previously unsolved needs. They often can outperform algorithmic methods or carry out a similar task with far less computing power. They are all associated with multiple input processing and can be applied to forming decisions from data supplied by sensors. Each situation has to be judged on the balance between use of computing effort and effective processing.

On the downside, they lack formality and thus may be very hard to calibrate and authenticate. They, not having adequate scientific foundation and a solid formal base of operation, are not easily accepted as "sound". They are often hard to comprehend by a second party, for their description is not always adequately documented or done to any agreed convention. As their principles vary widely, they must be well understood before application is developed.

For all of these negative factors, they often are able to provide "more performance for less cost" and thus will be increasingly adopted.

Their rising level of use should not suggest the algorithmic methods will become obsolete, but more that the instrument designer now has a much larger set of processing tools available.

3. Mapping in General

The high-level purpose of most signal processing is to yield knowledge of a situation so that decisions can be made.

For example, consider a health-monitoring system installed on an aircraft engine. A set of sensors of different measurand types and locations is installed at various critical points on the engine-temperatures, pressures, flow rates, metal content of the lubricating oil, and more. The data from these are collected and transmitted to a central processor using a common digital bus. The many inputs then need to be combined in some way to decide such conditions as emergency states, when to change the oil, and engine efficiency. This combination is a "mapping of many to a few".

These are not always simple mappings, for there is no adequate algorithm available to give a mathematical description for such things as degradation of oil condition. However, human intuition can be used quite effectively to obtain answers—the human mind is very capable of carrying out such mapping functions. This form of natural processing makes use of what are technically called "heuristics" -but more commonly known as "rules of thumb."

Consider the question, "How could we decide, using an automated measurement system, When loaves being made in a bakery are satisfactory to sell?" As the way to decide this almost all people asked would suggest that the weight, size, crustiness, appearance and softness inside would be the parameters that must all be satisfactory (that is, lie within a small range of values for each) to be declared suitable.

Words and Expressions

1. performance [pə'fɔːməns] n. 履行，执行，成绩，性能，表演，演奏
2. deploy [di'plɔi] v. 展开，配置
3. algorithm ['ælgərið(ə)m] n. [数] 运算法则
4. precise [pri'sais] adj. 精确的，准确的 n. 精确
5. impractical [im'prækti(ə)l] adj. 不切实际的
6. multiple ['mʌltrp(ə)l] adj. 多样的，多重的 n. 倍数，若干 v. 成倍增加
7. formal ['fɔːm(ə)l] adj. 外形的，正式的，合礼仪的，形式的，整齐匀称的 n. 正式的社交活动
8. interpretation [intə:pri'teiʃ(ə)n] n. 解释，阐明，口译，通译
9. ambiguity [æmbi'gjuːiti] n. 含糊，不明确
10. traceable ['treisəbl] adj. 可追踪的，起源于
11. calibrate ['kælibreit] v. 校准
12. simplistic [sim'plistik] adj. 过分单纯化的
13. adequate ['ædikwət] adj. 适当的，足够的
14. bandwidth ['bændwitθ] n. 带宽
15. formalism ['fɔːməliz(ə)m] n. 拘泥形式，（艺术或宗教上的）形式主义，虚礼
16. software ['sɔftweə(r)] n. 软件
17. circuitry ['səːkitri] n. 电路，线路
18. integrated ['intigreitid] adj. 综合的，完整的
19. contemplate ['kɔntempleit] v. 凝视，沉思，预期，企图
20. paradigm ['pærədaim] n. 范例
21. invoked [in'vəuk] v. 调用
22. mapping ['mæpiŋ] n. 映射，绘制……之地图，计划
23. lubricating oil 润滑油
24. outperform [ˌautpə'fɔːm] vt. 做得比……好，胜过
25. calibrate ['kælibreit] v. 校准
26. degradation [diːgreidə'ʃn] v. 鉴别
27. heuristic [hjuə'ristik] adj. 启发式的
28. crustiness ['krʌstinis] n. 外壳，硬壳，面包皮 vt. 盖以硬皮 vi. 结硬皮
29. parameter [pə'ræmitə(r)] n. 参数，参量 [口] 起限定作用的因素

Exercises

1. Describe the technological meanings of following terms refering to your understanding aboutthe text:
   mathematically formulated method
   signal processing
   well proven
   algorithmic approach

signal processing
   mapping model
   mathematical modeling
   mathematical description
   one to aim for
   be devoid of ambiguity
   suitable technological machine
   inadequate model
   increase in complexity
   processing power
   electrical bandwidth
   artificial intelligence
   decision theory
   vaguely subjective processing
   tightly objective processing
   available to give a mathematical description
2. Analyze the following sentences from the perspective of phraseological characteristic and structure:
   ① Traditionally the most popular method used to develop mapping models is that of mathematical modeling.
   ② In this class, the single, or set of multiple, input signal (s) to the data processor is converted to the output form using tightly formulated mathematical description.
   ③ The origin of their use in instrumentation goes back to the early days of computing using, first, mechanical computational machines (late 1800s to around 1930) and then analog electric devices (early 1900s to 1960s), all of which were mostly replaced by the use of digital computers.
   ④ They, not having adequate scientific foundation and a solid formal base of operation, are not easily accepted as "sound".
   ⑤ A set of sensors of different measurand types and locations is installed at various critical points on the engine-temperatures, pressures, flow rates, metal content of the lubricating oil, and more. The data from these are collected and transmitted to a central processor using a common digital bus.

Reading Material 13

Spectrum Analysis and Correlation

Most sensors and instruments can produce continuous measurements in time or sequential measurements at fixed or variable time intervals. The temporal patterns resulting from such measurements are usually referred to as signals. Signals can either be continuous or discrete in time. The main objective of spectral analysis is to provide an estimate of the distribution of signal power at different frequencies. Spectral analysis and correlation techniques are an aid to the interpretation of and to the systems that generate them. These methods are now widely used for the analysis and interpretation of measurements performed in medicine, geophysics, vibration analysis, communications, and several other areas.

Although the original concept of a signal involves measurements as a function of time, this term has been generalized to include measurements along other dimensions, e. g., distance. In addition, signals can have multiple dimensions-the instantaneous velocity of an airplane can be regarded as a four-dimensional signal since it depends on time and three spatial coordinates.

With the growing availability of signal-processing computer packages and dedicated instruments, most readers will perform spectral analysis and correlation at the "touch of a button," visualizing results on a screen or as a computer plot. These "black-box" systems are useful for saving time and money, but users should be aware of the limitations of the fundamental techniques and circumstances in which inappropriate use can lead to misleading results. This chapter presents the basic concepts of spectral analysis and correlation based on the fast Fourier transform (FFT) approach. FFT algorithms allow the most efficient computer implementation of methods to perform spectral analysis and correlation and have become the most popular option. Nevertheless, other approaches, such as parametric techniques, wavelet transforms, and time-frequency analysis are also available. These will be briefly discussed and the interested reader will be directed to the pertinent literature for application that might benefit from alternative approaches.

Practical applications of spectral and correlation analysis are performed on discrete-time signals. These are obtained either from a sequence of discrete measurements or from the transformation of a continuous signal to digital format using an analog-to-digital converter (ADC). When the latter is adopted to allow computer analysis of an originally continuous signal, two main characteristics of the ADC need to be considered. He first is the number of bits available to represent each sample, as this will determine the resolution and accuracy of the sampled signal. The second important consideration is the sampling interval Δt. From the Nyquist theorem, the maximum value of Δt must be such that the sampling frequency $f_s = 1/\Delta t$ is at least twice the highest frequency of interest in the original signal. If this rule is not followed, spectral and correlation estimations might be considerably distorted by a phenomenon called aliasing[1]. Low-pass filtering before ADC is always recommended to limit the bandwidth of the continuous signal to allow the correct choice of f_s or Δt. In practice, the sampling frequency is usually much higher than the minimum required by the Nyquist theorem to provide a better visual representation of the sampled data.

Let x_n represent a discrete-time signal with samples at $n = 0, 1, 2, \cdots, N-1$. The Fourier theorem states that it is possible to decompose x_n as a sum of cosine and sine waveforms of different frequencies using an appropriate combination of amplitude coefficients. Therefore,

$$x_n = a_0 + \sum_{k=1}^{N-1} a_k \cos\left(\frac{2\pi kn}{N}\right) + \sum_{k=1}^{N-1} b_k \sin\left(\frac{2\pi kn}{N}\right) \qquad (13.1)$$

where $k=1,2,\cdots,N-1$ determines the frequency of each cosine waveforms as $f_k = k/N\Delta t$. The corresponding coefficients are calculated from

$$a_0 = \frac{1}{N}\sum_{n=0}^{N-1} x_n \qquad (13.2a)$$

$$a_k = \frac{1}{N}\sum_{n=0}^{N-1} x_n \cos\left(\frac{2\pi kn}{N}\right) \qquad (13.2b)$$

$$b_k = \frac{1}{N}\sum_{n=0}^{N-1} x_n \sin\left(\frac{2\pi kn}{N}\right) \qquad (13.2c)$$

Note that Equation 13.2a represents the mean value of x_n and that the argument $2\pi kn/N$ is the same for direct (Equation 13.2) and inverse (Equation 13.1) discrete Fourier transforms (DFT).

From Euler's formula, it is possible to combine the cosine terms express the DFT in exponential form:

$$e^{j\theta} = \cos\theta + j\sin\theta \qquad (13.3)$$

leading to

$$x_n = \sum_{k=0}^{N-1} c_k e^{j\frac{2\pi kn}{N}} \qquad (13.4)$$

with

$$c_k = \frac{1}{N}\sum_{n=0}^{N-1} x_n e^{-j\frac{2\pi kn}{N}} \qquad (13.5)$$

Words and Expressions

1. spectrum ['spektrəm] n. 光，光谱，型谱，频谱
2. correlation [ˌkɔrə'leiʃən] n. 相互关系，相关（性）
3. frequency ['fri:kwənsi] n. 频率，周率，发生次数
4. interpretation [inˌtə:pri'teiʃən] n. 解释，阐明，口译，通译
5. vibration [vai'breiʃ(ə)n] n. 振动，颤动，摇动，摆动
6. velocity [vi'lɔsiti] n. 速度，速率，迅速，周转率
7. approach [ə'prəutʃ] n. 接〔逼〕近；近似法〔值〕；途径，方法
8. parametric [ˌpærə'metrik] adj. 〔数〕〔物〕〔晶〕参（变）数的，参（变）量的
9. alternative [ɔ:l'tə:nətiv] n. 二中择一，可供选择的办法，事物 adj. 选择性的，二中择一的
10. format ['fɔ:mæt] n. 开本，版式，形式，格式 vt. 安排……的格局（或规格），〔计〕格式化（磁盘）
11. Nyquist theorem 奈奎斯特定律
12. coefficient [kəui'fiʃnt] n. 〔数〕系数

Notes

① aliasing （混叠现象）：An effect that occurs when a signal is sampled at a rate less than twice the highest frequency present in the original signal. The subsequent signal recovered from the samples will not contain the high frequency component of the original signal and will display a false low frequency signal. 以低于信号中最高频率两倍的频率进行信号抽样时出现的一种效应，即当由抽样状态还原时，还原后的信号将不再含有原来信号中的高频成分，并将显示出虚假的低频信号。

Unit 14 Basic Concepts of Communication and Networking

> Before reading the text, try to answer the following questions:
> 1. What is a station on a network system?
> 2. What is media access control?
> 3. What is bandwidth of the network system?
> 4. How to identify each station in a network system ?
> 5. What is modulation?

In order to be able to select an appropriate network technology, it is necessary to understand some basic terminology so that the features and capabilities of various networks and technologies can be categorized and compared.

1. Station

A station represents a single communicating element on a network system. Each user of the network must access the communication capability of the network via a station. Each station will typically have some implementation of the open systems interconnection (OSI) network reference model as the means of utilizing the network system.

2. Media Access

Media access is the method by which individual stations determine when they are permitted to transmit, or "use" the media. Media access control (MAC) is a function that is usually performed in the data link layer of the OSI reference model. Some well-known methods of media access control include carrier sense multiple access with collision detection (CSMA/CD) and token passing. CSMA/CD systems (such as Ethernet) allow all stations on a network equal access. Each station must "listen" to the network to determine periods of inactivity before transmitting. Any station wishing to use the network may begin transmitting providing the network is inactive when it checks for activity. If multiple stations attempt to transmit simultaneously, a collision occurs. This is detected by all transmitting stations, which all must immediately stop transmitting and each wait a randomly determined period of time, before attempting to use the network again. Controller area network (CAN), for example, uses a variant of CSMA/CD for media access. Token-passing systems have a logical "token" which is exchanged among stations via network messaging. The station that holds the token has permission to transmit. All other stations are only permitted to receive messages. Stations wishing to transmit but not having the token must wait until the station holding the token passes it on. Another commonly used method of media access control is master-slave. In this method, one station on the network (designated the master) is generally in charge of, and originates, all communications. Slaves only respond to the master, and only respond when the master initiates communications with them via sending a message to the slave. Profibus-FMS (see below) is an example of a protocol which uses both token passing (in some cases) and master-slave (in some cases) to control media access.

3. Bandwidth

Bandwidth may have several different definitions. For digital communication systems, bandwidth describes the capacity of the system to transport digital data from one place to another. This term may be applied to the raw capability of the physical and data link layers to transport message data (raw bandwidth, closely related to the bit rate concept) or it may be applied to the effective rate at which user-meaningful information is transported (effective bandwidth). The bandwidth of a given system is generally inversely proportional to the worst-case node-to-node distance. The smaller the network span, the higher its bandwidth can be.

4. Addressing

Addressing is a concept that assigns generally unique identifiers to each station in a network system. This identifier (the address) can then be used by the network for a variety of purposes, including identifying the origin and/or destination of messages, or arbitrating access to a shared communications medium. Another addressing or identifier concept assigns unique identifiers not to stations, but to unique pieces of data or signals that will be carried by the network. Stations then use an identifier according to what type of data they will be transmitting. Many, but not all networking methods require establishment of an explicit address for each network station.

5. Arbitration

Arbitration is a function closely related to MAC. Arbitration is used by some networks to define the procedure followed When multiple stations wish to use the network simultaneously.

6. Signaling

Signaling refers to the actual physical (e.g., electrical, optical, or other) representation of data as it is carried on the media. For example, in some networks, data elements may be represented by certain voltage levels or waveforms in the media. In other networks, data elements may be represented by the presence of certain wavelengths of light in the media. The association of all the representable data elements (e.g., 0/1 or on/off) with the corresponding signal representations in the media is the signaling scheme or method. An important signaling method where electric wires are used as the medium is differential signaling. Differential signaling represents a particular data element (1 or 0) as two different states on a pair of wires. Determining the data element requires measuring the voltage difference between the two wires, not the absolute level of the voltage on either wire. Different data elements are then represented by the (signed) voltage difference between the two wires. For example, RS-485 represents a digital 1 data element as a 5-V signal level on the first wire and a 0-V signal level on the second wire, and a digital 0 as a 0-V signal level on the first wire and 5-V signal level on the second wire. One of the principal benefits of differential signaling is that it is possible to determine the data being transmitted without knowing the ground reference potential of the transmitter. This allows the transmitter and receiver to operate reliably, even when they have different ground potentials (within limits), which is a common occurrence in communication systems.

7. Encoding

Encoding refers to the process of translating user-meaningful information into data elements or groups of data elements to be transported by the network system. A code book refers to the set of all relationships between user-meaningful information and data carried by the network. Encoding may occur at several levels within the OSI reference model, as user-meaningful information is transformed successively until it becomes an actual network message, produced by the data link layer. Decoding is the reverse process, whereby a network message is successively translated back into user-meaningful information.

8. Modulation

Modulation in a classical sense refers to a signaling technique by which data or information is used to control some combination of the frequency, phase, and/or amplitude of a carrier signal. The carrier signal carries the information to a remote receiver where it will be demodulated to retrieve the information. Modulated network systems are outside the scope of this chapter.

9. Message

A message is the fundamental, indivisible unit of information which is exchanged between stations. User-meaningful information will be grouped into one or more messages by the OSI network reference model.

10. Multiplexing

Multiplexing refers to the ability to use the media in a network to carry multiple messages or information streams "simultaneously". Multiplexed systems allow several communication channels to use the same physical wire or media. Each message or information stream may have different sources and destinations.

Selected from "Programmable Logic Controllers: Principles and Applications, by John W. Webb, Ronald A. Ress, No. 4, 1999".

Words and Expressions

1. categorize ['kætigəraiz] n. 种类,别,[逻] 范畴
2. collision [kə'liʒ(ə)n] n. 碰撞,冲突
3. interconnection ['intəkə'nekʃən] n. 互相联络
4. multiple ['mʌltipəl] adj. 多样的,多重的 n. 倍数,若干 v. 成倍增加
5. implementation [,impli'mentəʃən] n. 执行
6. utilize [ju:'tilaiz] vt. 利用
7. individual [indi'vidjuəl] n. 个人,个体 adj. 个别的,单独的,个人的
8. randomly ['rædəmli] adv. 随便地,未加计划地
9. token ['təukən] n. 表示,象征,记号,代币 adj. 象征的,表意的
10. initiate [i'niʃiət] vt. 开始,发动,传授 v. 开始,发起
11. protocol ['prəutəkɒl;(US)-kɔ:l] n. 草案,协议
12. raw [rɔ:] n. 生的,未加工的
13. link layer [计] 链路层
14. inversely ['in'və:səli] adj. 倒转的,反转的 n. 反面 v. 倒转
15. identifier [ai'dentifaiə(r)] n. 标识符;标识号
16. arbitrate ['ɑ:bitreit] v. 做出公断
17. phase [feiz] n. 阶段,状态,相,相位 v. 定相
18. amplitude ['æmplitju:d;(US)'æmplitud] n. 广阔,丰富,振幅,物理学名词
19. carrier ['kæriə(r)] n. 载波,载流子
20. encoding ['kɔdiŋ] n. 译码器,编码器
21. decoding [,di:'kəudiŋ] n. 解码器
22. multiplexing n. 多路技术
23. destination [desti'neiʃ(ə)n] n. 目的地,[计] 目的文件,目的单元格

Exercises

1. Declare the concepts of following terms according to your understanding of the text: Station on network, Media Access, Bandwidth, Addressing, Arbitration, Signaling, Encoding, Modulation, Message, Digital communication systems, Network sensor, communication network, Network processor, Measurand variable, Electrical representation
2. Describe how the information or signals are received, converted or processed by network sensors and added communication components related to measurement system. according to your understanding about Fig. 14.1.
3. Write out the key points of the content described in the following text in English:

    Signaling refers to the actual physical representation of data as it is carried on the media. For example, in some networks, data elements may be represented by certain voltage levels or waveforms in the media or by the presence of certain wavelengths of light in the media. The association of all the representable data elements (e.g., 0/1 or on/off) with the corresponding signal representations in the media is the signaling scheme or

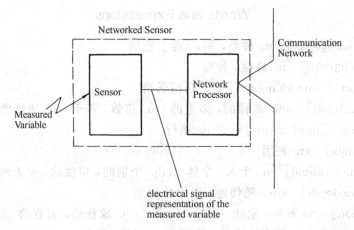

Fig. 14.1 A network sensor is an ordinary sensor with network communication components added

method. An important signaling method where electric wires are used as the medium is differential signaling. Differential signaling represents a particular data element (1 or 0) as two different states on a pair of wires. Determining the data element requires measuring the voltage difference between the two wires, not the absolute level of the voltage on either wire. Different data elements are then represented by the (signed) voltage difference between the two wires. For example, RS-485 represents a digital 1 data element as a 5V signal level on the first wire and a 0V signal level on the second wire, and a digital 0 as a 0V signal level on the first wire and 5V signal level on the second wire. One of the principal benefits of differential signaling is that it is possible to determine the data being transmitted without knowing the ground reference potential of the transmitter. This allows the transmitter and receiver to operate reliably, even when they have different ground potentials (within limits), which is a common occurrence in communication systems.

Reading Material 14

Additional Concepts of Communication and Networking

Multiplexing

Multiplexing may be accomplished using a variety of means. Time division multiplexing (TDM) involves breaking access to the media into a series of time quanta. During each time quantum, the media carries a separate message or information stream. The close arrangement of time quanta allow the network media to carry multiple messages "simultaneously". Code division multiplexing (CDM) involves the separation of the code book (see Encoding) into sections. Each section of the code book provides all of the messages that will be used for a particular information stream. Therefore, a particular information stream within the network media is distinguished by all of the messages that belong to the section of the code book for that stream. Frequency division multiplexing (FDM) divides an available bandwidth of a communication channel into several frequency ranges, and assigns one information stream to each frequency range.

Protocols

A protocol is a defined method of information exchange. Protocols typically are defined at several levels within the OSI network reference model, such as at the application layer and at the data link layer. Protocols are used to define how the services provided by a particular layer are to be exercised, and how the results of these services are to be interpreted.

Service

A service represents a specific function or operation that is supported by a particular layer in the OSI network reference model. For example, an application layer service might be provided for the reading of writing to a data element contained in another device (or station) on the network. This service might make use of a data link layer service which might be provided for supporting the exchange of a message with another device (or station) on the network.

Topology

Topology refers to the physical or geographic layout or arrangement of canonical topologies are commonly discussed in the context of networks, such as truckline/branchline, star (or hub), ring, and daisy chain.

Bit Rate

Bit rate refers to the speed at which binary pieces of information (bits) are transmitted on a particular network. The raw bit rate of a network generally refers to the actual speed transmission of bits on the network. The effective bit rate—or throughput—generally refers to the speed at which user information is transmitted. This number is less than or equal to the raw bit rate depending on what percentage of the bits transmitted is used for carrying user information. The bit carrying user information are overhead, used to carry protocol, timing, or other network information.

Duplex (Half and Full duplex)

Half duplex refers to a communication system in which station can either transit information or receive information, but not both simultaneously. A duplex network allows a station to transmit information and receive information simultaneously.

Internetworking

There are occasions when communications between two or more points are best handled by multiple networks. This may be the case when a single network has limitations that prevent it from tying the points together (e. g., distance limits) or when multiple networks are required for other reasons (e. g., to carry different types of data). When multiple networks are used to provide communications, there may be a need to pass messages or information directly from one network to another.

A repeater may be used when the networks to be joined are logically identical, and the purpose is simply to extend the length of the network or extend its capabilities in some way.

A repeater generally has no effect on messages, and simply carries all messages from one cable or port to another (i.e., a change of physical media). A repeater allows for connection of networks at the physical layer level.

A bridge is similar to a repeater, but allows for connection of networks at the data link layer level. Generally a bridge will pass all messages from one network to another, by passing messages at the data link layer level.

A router usually has the function of partitioning similar networks. Two networks may be based on the same technologies and protocol, but may not be logically identical. In these cases, some, but not all, of the messages on one network may need to be carried or transported to the other network. The router has the function of determining which messages to pass back and forth based on certain rules. Functions to enable efficient, automatic routing of messages may be included in layer 3 (the network layer) of the OSI network reference model, and a router allow for connection of networks at the network layer level.

A gateway may have a function similar to a router, or it may have the function of joining dissimilar networks, i.e., networks based on dissimilar technologies and/or protocols. When functioning like a router, a gateway usually performs its discrimination at a higher protocol level than a router. When a gateway joins dissimilar networks, generally a more complex set of rules must be designed into the gateway so that message translation, mapping, and routing can occur within the gateway as it determines which messages to pass from one network to the other.

ISO/OSI Network Reference Model

The explosion in the use and types of communication networks over the last several decades has led to more precise descriptions and treatment of communication networks in general. The International Organization for Standardization (ISO) has recognized one such method of precise description of networks, called the OSI reference model. As shown in Fig. 14.2, this model decomposes an arbitrary communication network into a "stack" of seven "layers." At each layer, certain types of network communication functions are described. The user of the communication system—usually another system that needs to communicate on the network—interacts with layer 7, the highest layer. The actual transmission medium (e.g., copper cable, fiber optic, free space, etc.) is connected to layer 1, the lowest layer. Most communication networks do not implement all of the layers in the reference model. In this case, formal definition, treatment, or inclusion of certain layers of the model in the actual network design are omitted. Layers 1, 2, and 7 are typically present in all networks, but the other

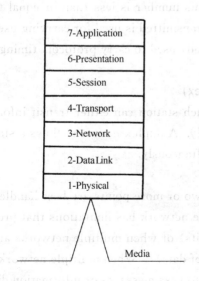

Fig. 14.2 The ISO-OSI Seven Layer Model provides a method for segmenting communication functions

layers may only be explicitly included or identifiable when their function is an important part of the network communications. In many sensor communication network, the functions performed by layers 3, 4, 5, and 6 are "collapsed" into vestigial additions to the functions of layer 7, the application layer.

Selected from "Programmable Logic Controllers: Principles and Applications, by John W. Webb, Ronald A. Ress, No. 4, 1999".

Words and Expressions

1. Multiplexing [mʌltipleksiŋ] n. 多路技术
2. simultaneously [siməl'teiniəsly;(US)saim-] adv. 同时地
3. quanta [kwɔnt, kwænt] n. pl. 量子（quantum 的复数）
4. protocol ['prəutəkɔl;(US)-kɔːl] n. 草案，协议
5. topology [tə'pɔlədʒi] n. 拓扑，布局　拓扑学
6. canonical [kə'nɔnik(ə)l] adj. 规范的
7. truckline ['trʌklain] n. 主干
8. branchline [brɑːntʃlain] n. 分支
9. daisy chain n. 雏菊花环,〈美〉链，环
10. hub [hʌb] n. 网络集线器，网络中心
11. duplex ['djuːpleks;(US)'duːpleks] [计]双方的 [修]双(向、重)，双工，二重
12. router ['ruːtə(r),'rəu-] [计]路由器（读取每一个数据包中的地址然后决定如何传送的专用、智能性的网络设备）
13. gateway ['geitwei] n. 门，通路，网关
14. stack [stæk] n. 堆，一堆，堆栈 v. 堆叠
15. interact [intər'ækt] vi. 互相作用，互相影响
16. collapsed [kə'læps] n. 崩溃，破裂；压缩；[微软]折叠
17. vestigial [ve'stidʒiəl] adj. 发育不全的，退化器官的

Unit 15 Signal Sensoring and Data Record/Display

> Before reading the text, try to answer the following questions:
> 1. In what kinds of sensors can the modern sensors appear?
> 2. What does the word "modern" mean?
> 3. In what cases are the modern sensors usually used?
> 4. What pushed the sensor technology to a new level of quantity?
> 5. What kinds of display technologies and devices do you know, and how do they operate?
> 6. What kinds of display could work better in sunlight and what kinds of display could work better in night?
> 7. What technical problems must be solved in performing the display functions?
> 8. Are portability, handheld operation, or group viewing required by industry?

15-1 Data Record and Display

The display system is the final link between the measuring process and the user. If the display is not easy to see and easy to understand, then that process is compromised. The user's sensory capabilities and cognitive characteristics, therefore, must both be addressed in display system selection. Furthermore, display technologies and performance capabilities are easier to evaluate in the context of their intended application.

1. Thermal Dot Array Recorders

In thermal dot array recorders, apart from the chart-pulling system, no moving parts are present; the writing transducer is essentially a rectilinear array of equidistant writing points which covers the total width of the paper. Although some apparatuses apply an electrostatic method, the thermal dot array and thermosensitive paper are generally used. In this array the writing styli consist of miniature electrically heated resistances; thermal properties of the resistances (in close contact with the chart paper) and the electric activating pulse form determine the maximal writing frequency. The latter ranges in real-time recorders from 1 to 6.4 kHz. Heating of the thermosensitive paper results in a black dot with good long-term stability. The heating pulse is controlled in relation to the chart velocity in order to obtain sufficient blackness at high velocities. Tracing blackness or line thickness is seldom used for curve identification; alphanumeric annotation is mostly applied. With the dot array a theoretically unlimited number of waveforms can be processed; the apparatus is thus programmed to draw its own calibration lines. Different types of grid patterns can be selected by the user. Moreover, alphanumeric information can be printed for indicating experimental

2. Magnetic Recording

At present, magnetic recording technology dominates the recording industry. It is used in the forms of hard disk, floppy disk, removable disk, and tape with either digital or analog mode. In its simplest form, it consists of a magnetic head and a magnetic medium, as shown in Fig. 15.1. The head is made of a piece of magnetic material in a ring shape (core), with a small gap facing the medium and a coil away from the medium. The head records (writes) and reproduces (reads) information, while the medium stores the information. The recording process is based on the phenomenon that an electric current i generates a magnetic flux Φ as described by Ampere's law[1]. The flux Φ leaks out of the head core at the gap, and magnetizes the magnetic medium which moves from left to right with a velocity V under the head gap. Depending on the direction of the electric current i, the medium is magnetized with magnetization M pointing either left or right. This pattern of magnetization is retained in the memory of the medium even after the head moves away.

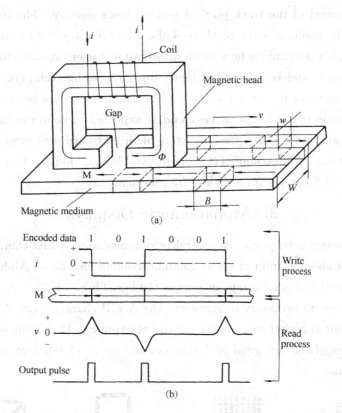

Fig. 15.1 Conceptual diagrams illustrating the magnetic recording principle (a), and recording/reproducing process (b)

Two types of head may be used for reproducing. One, termed the inductive head, senses magnetic flux change rate, and the other, named the magnetoresistive (MR) head, senses the magnetic flux. When an inductive head is used, the reproducing process is just the reverse of the recording process. The flux coming out of the magnetized medium surface is picked up by the head core. Because the medium magnetization under the head gap changes its magnitude and direction as the medium moves, an electric voltage is generated in the coil. This process is governed by Faraday's law[2]. Fig. 15.1 (b) schematically shows the digital recording/reproducing process. First, all user data are encoded into a binary format—a serial of 1s and 0s. Then a write current i is sent to the coil. This current changes its direction whenever a 1 is being written. Correspondingly, a change of magnetization, termed a transition, is recorded in the medium for each 1 in the encoded data. During the reproducing process, the electric voltage induced in the head coil reaches a peak whenever there is a transition in the medium. A pulse detector generates a pulse for each transition. These pulses are decoded to yield the user data.

The minimum distance between two transitions in the medium is the flux change length B, and the distance between two adjacent signal tracks is the track pitch W, which is wider than the signal track width W. The flux change length can be directly converted into bit length with the proper code information. The reciprocal of the bit length is called linear density, and the reciprocal of the track pitch is termed track density. The information storage area 1 density in the medium is the product of the linear density and the track density. This area 1 density roughly determines how much information a user can store in a unit surface area of storage medium, and is a figure of merit for a recording technique. Much effort has been expended to increase the area 1 density. For example, it has been increased 50 times during the last decade in hard disk drives, and is expected to continue increasing 60% per year in the foreseeable future. At present, state-of-the-art hard disk products feature area 1 densities of more than 7 Mbits/mm^2 ($B < 0.1\mu$m and $W < 1.5\mu$m). This gives a total storage capacity of up to 6 Gbytes for a disk of 95 mm diameter.

3. Alphanumeric Displays

The size of a letter is its pitch. A general recommendation is that characters should subtend a minimum of about 12 min of arc at common reading distances. Alphanumeric displays are usually constructed of pixel arrays or segmented bars (Fig. 15.2). A 5×7 pixel array is considered the minimum necessary to represent the ASCII character set. More pixels can increase legibility, but at higher cost for the control electronics. The seven-segment bar matrix is also common design and has good performance, but up to 16-segment arrays are available for better appearance.

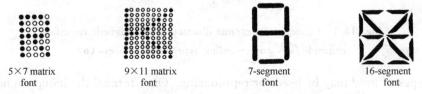

Fig. 15.2 Examples of alphanumeric displays

Stroke width is the ratio of the thickness of the stroke to the height of the letter. Recommendations for legibility are 1∶6 to 8 or 1∶8 to 10. As illumination is reduced, thick letters are easier to read than thin ones. With low illumination and low contrast, letters should be boldface type with low stroke width-height ratios (e. g. , 1∶5).

4. Quantitative and Status Displays

While numeric readout displays are easy to implement in software, analog pointer displays show an advantage when it is important to observe the direction or rate of change of the values presented. If the measurement application involves "more or less" or "up or down" interpretations, a straight-line or thermometer scale is preferred because it shows the measurement in relation to zero. Moving pointers are better able to convey minor changes in readings than fixed pointers or numeric readouts. Scale markings should reflect the length of the smallest unit to be read. It is desirable to have a marker for each unit, so that no interpolation is required.

Check reading indicators are used to determine whether a condition is "normal." The normal criterion point, therefore, should be clearly coded. If several indicators are grouped together, they should be arranged so that the deviant reading stands out (e. g. , by indicating a different column height or dial angle, etc.).

Color is an excellent method for organizing information on a display and for locating objects rapidly. Although display users can distinguish between many different colors, they usually cannot remember more than seven to ten of them, so the number should be limited if color is going to be used as a coding dimension.

Selected from "The Measurement, Instrumentation, and Sensors Handbook, CRC press LLC, 1999".

Words and Expressions

1. equidistant [ˈiːkwiˈdistən]　adj. 等距离的；同比例的
2. transducer [trænzˈdjuːsə(r), trɑː-]　n. 传感器，变频器，变换器
3. rectilinear [ˌrektiˈliniə]　n. 直线
4. thermosensitive [ˌθəːməuˈsensitive]　adj. [化] 热敏的
5. styli [ˈstailai] （留声机上的）唱针，日晷指针
6. miniature [ˈminitʃə(r);(US)ˈminiətʃuər]　n. 缩小的模型，缩图，缩影　adj. 微型的，缩小的
7. alphanumeric [ˌælfənjuːˈmerik]　adj. 文字数字的，包括文字与数字的
8. annotation [ˌænəuˈteiʃən]　n. 注释，注解
9. grid [grid]　n. 格子，栅格
10. storage [ˈstɔːridʒ]　n. 存储器，内存，存放处；[动] 存储
11. retrieval [riˈtriːvl]　n. 取回，恢复，修补，重获，挽救，拯救　检索，查找
12. transaction [trænˈzækʃ(ə)n, trɑː-]　n. 办理，处理，会报，学报，交易，事务，处理事务
13. credit [ˈkredit]　n. 信任，信用，声望，荣誉，[财务] 贷方，银行存款　vt. 相信，信任，把……归给

14. video tape n. 录像磁带
15. auxiliary [ɔːgˈziljəri] adj. 辅助的，补助的
16. servo [ˌsəːveu] n. 伺服，伺服系统
17. magnetic [mægˈnetik] adj. 磁的，有磁性的，有吸引力的
18. flux [flʌks] n. 磁通，（电，磁，光）通量；焊剂；流动
19. inductive [inˈdʌktiv] adj. 诱导的，感应的
20. magnetoresistive [mægˈniːtəriˈzistiv] a. [物] 磁滞电阻的
21. reciprocal [riˈsiprəkəl] adj. 互惠的 n. 倒数
22. pixel [ˈpiks(ə)l] n. （显示器或电视机图像的）像素
23. arc [ɑːk] n. 弧，弓形，拱；弧光；adj. 逆三角作用的
24. legibility [ˌledʒəˈbiliti] n. 易读性，易辨认，易理解
25. boldface [ˈbəuldfeis] n. [印刷] 黑体字，粗体铅字
26. matrix [ˈmeitriks] n. 矩阵
27. interpolation [inˌtəːpəuˈleiʃən] n. 篡改，填写，插补

Notes

① Ampere's law. 安培定律。
② Faraday's law. 法拉第定律。

Exercises

1. Describe the definitions, working principles, applications and use examples of the following devices or techniques in English according to your understanding of the content of the text:

   Thermal Dot Array Recorders, Magnetic Recording, Alphanumeric Displays, Quantitative and Status Displays

2. Express the key points of the content described in the following section:

   Two types of head may be used for reproducing. One, termed the inductive head, senses magnetic flux change rate, and the other, named the magnetoresistive (MR) head, senses the magnetic flux. when an inductive head is used, the reproducing process is just the reverse of the recording process. The flux coming out of the magnetized medium surface is picked up by the head core. Because the medium magnetization under the head gap changes its magnitude and direction as the medium moves, an electric voltage is generated in the coil. This process is governed by Faraday's law. Fig. 15.1b schematically shows the digital recording/reproducing process. First, all user data are encoded into a binary format—a serial of 1s and 0s. Then a write current i is sent to the coil. This current changes its direction whenever a 1 is being written. Correspondingly, a change of magnetization, termed a transition, is recorded in the medium for each 1 in the encoded data. During the reproducing process, the electric voltage induced in the head coil reaches a peak whenever there is a transition in the medium. A pulse detector generates a pulse for each transition. These pulses are decoded to yield the user data.

The minimum distance between two transitions in the medium is the flux change length B, and the distance between two adjacent signal tracks is the track pitch W, which is wider than the signal track width W. The flux change length can be directly converted into bit length with the proper code information. The reciprocal of the bit length is called linear density, and the reciprocal of the track pitch is termed track density. The information storage areal density in the medium is the product of the linear density and the track density. This areal density roughly determines how much information a user can store in a unit surface area of storage medium, and is a figure of merit for a recording technique. Much effort has been expended to increase the areal density. For example, it has been increased 50 times during the last decade in hard disk drives, and is expected to continue increasing 60% per year in the foreseeable future. At present, state-of-the-art hard disk products feature areal densities of more than 7 Mbits/mm^2 ($B<0.1\mu$m and $W<1.5\mu$m). This gives a total storage capacity of up to 6G bytes for a disk of 95 mm diameter.

3. Point out the commonness and characteristics of the four display technologies given in the text.

15-2 Modern Sensors

The so called "Modern sensors" can appear in different kinds of sensors, such as optical sensors, flow sensors, intelligent sensors, sensor networks, accelerometers and inclinometers, biosensors, physical parameter sensors, solid state gyroscopes, and so on.

Optical sensors are measuring devices in which a measured quantity is converted to an optical and, subsequently, an electrical signal by means of an optoelectronic transducer. Optical sensors belong to the class of contactless methods of measurement eliminating backward influence of a measuring device on an object of measurement.

As output signals from optical sensors are of an electronic nature and the methods of their further conditioning are generally known, the main attention will be devoted to the optical part of a sensor.

Measuring the flow of liquids, gases, steam of solids is important both for the processing industry and for occasional readings. In some processes inaccurate flowrate measurement can make the difference between profit and loss. In other cases inaccurate or erroneous flow measurements can have serious or even disastrous consequences.

Ordinary sensors, as described in other chapters of this book, were used for a long time and are still used in many applications. Thanks to the explosive progress in microelectronics in the final three decades of the 20th century, sensor technology moved to a completely new level of quality. The functionality of the ordinary sensors has been expanded in many ways and a new group of so-called *intelligent* sensors has appeared, providing a number of additional properties. They include higher accuracy, better immunity to environmental conditions, application flexibility and especially the possibility of easy integration into the industrial distributed systems.

Accelerometers have existed for several decades and they are always in constant evolution because they influence the performance of many devices in a strategic way. In the past 15 years in particular, thanks to micro technologies, there has been enormous progress in precision, linearity, stability and also size and electric consumption of the sensors.

The world in which we live is rapidly becoming dominated by digital information. Initially, the digital revolution primarily involved stand-alone computers that gradually became networked. More recently, the merging of computing with wireless communications systems has led to an enormous growth in accessibility to, and hence demand for, this information. At present, this demand is dominated by a mixture of text, audio and image-based data driven mainly by almost ubiquitous accessibility to the internet. However, the "web" communications that has been assembled over the past decade will fuel demand for more sources of information and data about important aspects of our lives-our health, our environment, our food, our work. Sensors provide portals between the "real" or analogue world in which we live, and the digital world of computers and modern communications systems. They make it possible for us to obtain real time information about things we can see, touch, smell and hear, and about other things that we cannot detect-things that can be harmful or beneficial to us.

A *biological sensor* (a biosensor) may be defined as "a device, consisting of a transducer and a film/membrane that contains a biological material e. g. an enzyme or an antibody, that generates a signal related to the concentration of a particular species in a given sample".

Measuring the level, position, distance and displacement of physical objects is essential for many applications: process feedback control, performance evaluation, transport, traffic control, robotics, security systems.

The sensors that can operate only when they are in direct contact with measured object belong to the class of contact sensors. By analogy, sensors which perform the measurement task without direct contact with a measured object form the class of non-contact sensors. Obviously the non-contact sensors offer many advantages as ideally they do not interfere with the measured object.

For measurement of time-varying quantities (e. g. vibrations) the dynamic properties of sensors are the key criteria for selection. The dynamic properties of sensors are determined by the frequency response of the sensor (the ratio of the amplitudes of output and input variables with sinusoidal waveform at the different frequencies).

Drawing a good glass of beer, pasteurizing milk or producing electricity are all processes that require accurate temperature measurement. Various methods of performing the measurement, each with its own characteristics and possibilities, are described in this module. In the first part, concepts that are commonly used in thermal measuring techniques are explained. We start with a definition of heat and temperature and then give different methods to measure a temperature. The necessity of thermal equilibrium is demonstrated with an example.

The second part deals with ways to measure temperature: glass thermometer, liquid filled thermometer, liquid filled expansion thermometer, pressure temperature detector, vapor-pressure temperature detector and bimetallic thermometer.

The first practical experiment with a gyroscope was carried out in 1865, thanks to the provision of movement by an electric motor. The first gyrocompass was patented in 1904. Since acceleration and angular rate are measurable physical quantities without an external reference, they can be used for navigation of autonomous systems. These sensors are constantly improving because of their strategic importance. In the last 15 years in particular, thanks to optical and to micro-technologies, there has been enormous progress made in precision, linearity and stability as well as in the size and electric consumption of these sensors.

Inertial navigation has evolved continuously with the first combined accelerometer and gyroscope being produced in 1923, the first platform with three axes in 1924 and the first operational equipment being launched in 1940s on V2 rockets.

Inertial navigation has evolved continuously with the first combined accelerometer and gyroscope being produced in 1923, the first platform with three axes in 1924 and the first operational equipment being launched in 1940s on V2 rockets.

The term "magnetic sensor" is broadly used for sensors using principles of magnetism. Magnetic sensors are usually contactless and robust and therefore they have reached a dominant position in the industrial and automotive sector.

Selected from "Modern Sensors Handbook, Pavel Riopa and Alois Tipek, ISTE Ltd, USA, 2007".

Words and Expressions

1. intelligent sensors 智能传感器
2. sensor networks 传感器网络
3. gyroscope [ˈdʒaɪərəskəup] n. 陀螺仪，回转仪
4. optoelectronic [ˌɔptəuilekˈtrɔnik] adj. 光电子的
5. disastrous [diˈzɑːstrəs] adj. 灾难性的，造成灾害的
6. microelectronics [ˌmaikrəuiˌlekˈtrɔniks] n. 微电子学
7. functionality [ˌfʌŋkʃəˈnæliti] n. 功能性，泛函性
8. immunity [iˈmjuːnəti] n. 免疫力
9. flexibility [ˌfleksəˈbiliti] n. 适应性，机动性
10. industrial distributed system 工业分布式系统
11. wireless communications system 无线通信系统
12. enormous [iˈnɔːməs] adj. 巨大的，极大的，庞大的
13. biosensor [ˌbaiəuˈsensə] n. 生物传感器
14. enzyme [ˈenzaim] n. [生化] 酶
15. robotics [rəuˈbɔtiks] n. 机器人技术
16. frequency response 频率响应
17. thermal equilibrium 热平衡
18. bimetallic [ˌbaimiˈtælik] adj. 双金属的；复本位制的
19. inertial navigation 惯性导航

20. accelerometer [æk,selə'rəmitə] n. 加速度计

Exercises

1. Fill in the blanks in your own words according to the text.

   Optical sensors (　) the class of (　) methods of measurement sensors. The main attention will be (　) the optical part of a sensor.

   The functionality of the ordinary sensors has been expanded in many ways and a new group of so-called intelligent sensors has appeared, providing a number of additional properties. They include (　), better immunity to (　) conditions, application (　) and so on.

   A biological sensor may be defined as a device consisting of a (　) and a film that contains a (　) material e. g. an enzyme or an (　), that generates a signal related to the concentration of a (　) species in a given sample.

   For measurement of time-varying quantities the dynamic properties of sensor are the key (　) for selection. The (　) properties of sensors are determined by the (　) of the sensor.

   The first practical experiment with a gyroscope was (　) in 1865. Since acceleration and (　) are measurable physical (　) without an external (　), they can be used for (　) of autonomous systems. Theses sensors are constantly improving because of their (　) importance.

   The term "magnetic sensor" is broadly used for sensors using principles of (　). Magnetic sensors are usually (　) and robust and therefore they have reached a (　) position in the (　) and automotive situation.

2. Put the following into Chinese.

   optical sensors　contactless methods　explosive progress　additional properties
   electric consumption　modern communication systems　real time information
   particular species　process feedback control　time-varying quantities

Reading Material 15-1

Digital Temperature DS18B20

1. DESCRIPTION

The DS18B20 digital thermometer provides 9-bit to 12-bit Celsius temperature measurements and has an alarm function with nonvolatile user-programmable upper and lower trigger points. The DS18B20 communicates over a 1-Wire bus that by definition requires only one data line (and ground) for communication with a central microprocessor. It has an operating temperature range of $-55°C$ to $+125°C$ and is accurate to $\pm 0.5°C$ over the range of $-10°C$ to $+85°C$. In addition, the DS18B20 can derive power directly from the data line ("parasite power"), eliminating the need for an external power supply.

Each DS18B20 has a unique 64-bit serial code, which allows multiple DS18B20s to function on the same 1-Wire bus. Thus, it is simple to use one microprocessor to control many DS18B20s distributed over a large area. Applications that can benefit from this feature include HVAC environmental controls, temperature monitoring systems inside buildings, equipment, or machinery, and process monitoring and control systems.

2. OVERVIEW

Fig. 15.3 shows a block diagram of the DS18B20, and pin descriptions are given in the *Pin Description* table. The 64-bit ROM stores the device's unique serial code. The scratchpad memory contains the 2-byte temperature register that stores the digital output from the temperature sensor. In addition, the scratchpad provides access to the 1-byte upper and lower alarm trigger registers (T_H and T_L) and the 1-byte configuration register. The configuration register allows the user to set the resolution of the temperature-to-digital conversion to 9, 10, 11, or 12 bits. The T_H, T_L, and configuration registers are nonvolatile (EEPROM), so they will retain data when the device is powered down.

The DS18B20 uses Maxim's exclusive 1-Wire bus protocol that implements bus communication using one control signal. The control line requires a weak pullup resistor since all devices are linked to the bus via a 3-state or open-drain port (the DQ pin in the case of the DS18B20). In this bus system, the microprocessor (the master device) identifies and addresses devices on the bus using each device's unique 64-bit code. Because each device has a unique code, the number of devices that can be addressed on one bus is virtually unlimited. The 1-Wire bus protocol, including detailed explanations of the commands and "time slots," is covered in the *1-Wire Bus System* section.

Another feature of the DS18B20 is the ability to operate without an external power supply. Power is instead supplied through the 1-Wire pullup resistor via the DQ pin when the bus is high. The high bus signal also charges an internal capacitor (C_{PP}), which then supplies power to the device when the bus is low. This method of deriving power from the 1-Wire bus is referred to as "parasite power." As an alternative, the DS18B20 may also be powered by an external supply on V_{DD} (see Fig. 15.3, Fig. 15.4).

Selected from "Products description DALLAS MAXIM, DS18B20 Programmable Resolution 1-Wire Digital

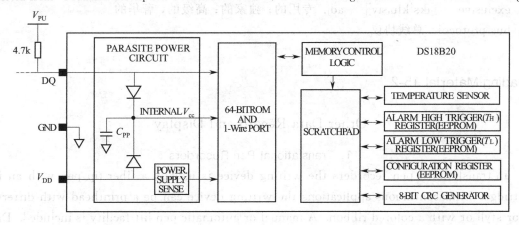

Fig. 15.3 DS18B20 Block Diagram

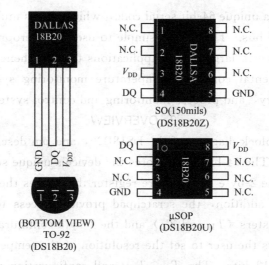

Fig. 15.4 Pin Configuration

Words and Expressions

1. alarm function 提示功能，警告功能
2. user-programmable 用户可编程的
3. central microprocessor 中心主处理器
4. operating temperature 操作温度，工作温度
5. external power supply 外部电源供应，外部供电
6. distribute [disˈtribjuːt] vt. 分布，分配，分给
7. machinery [məˈʃiːnəri] n.（总称）机器
8. block diagram 方块图，简图，结构图
9. scratchpad memory [计] 暂时存储器
10. trigger registers 触发寄存器
11. configuration register 配置寄存器
12. nonvolatile [nɒnˈvɒlətail] adj.（尤指物质）非挥发性的；不挥发，非易失的
13. exclusive [iksˈkluːsiv] adj. 专用的；独家的；高级的，奢华的
14. bus protocol 总线协议

Reading Material 15-2

Other Data Record and Display

1. Translational Pen Recorders

In translational pen recorders the writing device is usually a fiber-tip pen with an ink cartridge. In discontinuous applications the writing device can be a printhead with different color styli or with a colored ribbon. A manual or automatic pen lift facility is included. During recording, the writing device is translated along the y-axis as it is linked to a mechanical guidance and a closed-loop wire system. A motor and wheels system pulls the wire and thus the writing device. In some designs a motor and screw system is applied. Translational recorders are primarily designed as a servo type. The position of the pen is accurately measured, and the difference voltage between the input signal and the position magnitude (following appropriate amplification and conditioning) drives the servomotor. Servo motors can be DC or stepper types; servo electronics can be analog or digital. Position sensing can be potentiometric ("potentiometric" recorders): the pen carriage is equipped with a sliding contact on the resistor (wire wound or thick film) which covers the complete width of the paper. More recently developed methods use optical or ultrasonic principles for position sensing; with these methods contacts are absent resulting in less maintenance and longer lifetime. For example, in the ultrasonic method the pen position is sensed by a detector coil from the propagation time of an ultrasound pulse, which is imparted by a piezoelectric transducer to a magnetostrictive strip covering the chart width. Accordingly, brushless dc-motors are used in some apparatuses. In the servo system accuracy is determined for the larger part by the quality of the sensing system. A poor contact with the resistor can give rise to noise; there may be a mechanical backlash between pen tip and the sliding contact on the potentiometer. The velocity of the pen carriage is limited, about 0.5 to 2 m/s dependent on motor and mechanics design. This results in a bandwidth of the recorder depending on the amplitude of the tracing: the -3 dB frequency fits in the range from 1 to 5 Hz for a full-scale width of 200 to 250 mm. Alternatively, the pen response time to a full-scale step input is given (5% to 95% of full-scale tracing): 0.1 to 0.5s. Overshoot of the pen step response is extremely small in accurate designs.

2. Magnetooptic Recording

The primary drawback of a CD-ROM to an end user is its inability to record. This deficiency is remedied by MO recording technology, as depicted in Fig. 15.5. A linearly polarized laser beam is focused on a layer of magnetic material, and a coil provides a dc magnetic field on the other side of the medium. This dc magnetic field is too weak to affect the medium magnetization at normal temperature. The recording process utilizes the thermomagnetic property of the medium, and the reproducing process is achieved by using the Kerr effect. During recording, the medium is initially magnetized vertically in one direction, and the DC magnetic field is in the opposite direction. The laser heats up the medium to its Curie temperature, at which the coercivity becomes zero. During the cooling process, the dc magnetic field aligns the medium magnetization of the heated region to the magnetic field direction. In the process of reproducing, the same laser is used with a smaller intensity. The medium is heated up to its compensation temperature, at which the coercivity becomes extremely high. Depending on the direction of the magnetization, the polarization of the reflected light is rotated either clockwise or counterclockwise (Kerr rotation). This rotation of polarization is detected and decoded to get the data. The main disadvantage of MO recording is that a separate erasing process is needed to magnetize the medium in one direction before recording. Recently some technologies have been developed to eliminate this separate erasing process at the cost of complexity.

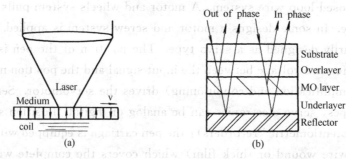

Fig. 15.5 Schematic illustrations of (a) MO recording/reproducing and (b) quadrilayer medium cross section

The medium used in MO recording must have a reasonable low Curie temperature ($<300\,^{\circ}\text{C}$). The materials having this property are rare earth transition metal alloys, such as $Tb_{23}Fe_{77}$ and $Tb_{21}Co_{79}$. Unfortunately, the properties of these materials deteriorate in an oxygen and moisture environment. To protect them from air and humidity, they are sandwiched between an overlayer and a underlayer, such as SiO, AlN, SiN, and TiO_2. Another issue with the rare earth transition metal alloys is their small Kerr rotation, about $0.3°$. To increase this Kerr rotation, multiple layers are used. In the so-called quadrilayer structure (Fig. 15.5 (b)), the overlayer is about a half-wavelength thick and the underlayer is about a quarter-wavelength thick. The MO layer is very thin (≈ 3 nm). Light reflected from the reflector is out-of-phase with the light reflected from the surface of the MO layer, and is in-phase with the light reflected from the inside of the MO layer. As a result, the effective Kerr rotation is increased several times.

3. Light-Emitting Diode Displays

Light-emitting diode (LED) displays involve single-crystal phosphor materials, which distinguishes them from the polycrystal EL materials discussed in the previous section. The basic physics behind their operation is, however, quite similar. LED displays are highly versatile and well suited to a variety of measurement applications. Advantages of LED displays include high reliability and graceful degrades; individual LED elements can fail without affecting overall display performance. LEDs are rugged, for operation in harsh environments, and they are more tolerant of temperature extremes than other technologies. LEDs demonstrate better viewing angles than LCDs, and excellent brightness for visibility in sunlight. Unfortunately, LED displays also have high power consumption when packaged in large, flat panel displays, and the cost is high for the complex assembly. Optical cross talk between array elements can occur if transparent substrates are used. LEDs are the most-restricted display in terms of color range (e.g., no blue device is commercially available).

4. Cathode Ray Tube Displays

The cathode ray tube (CRT) is by far the most common display technology in use today, and its widespread use in televisions and computer monitors should guarantee its continued presence throughout the foreseeable future. Advantages of CRT-based displays include (1) versatility (the same CRT can be used for alphanumerics, pictures, or graphics), (2) high-resolution capability and high luminous efficiency, extremely fast dynamic response (which can be important for rapidly changing signals), (3) extensive commercial availability (e.g., 2.5 to 64 cm, diagonally), (4) high reliability, (5) long life, and (6) relatively low cost. CRT displays can function well in high ambient illumination if filtering is used. Potential disadvantages of CRT displays are bulk (the depth of conventional CRT tubes can match or exceed their diagonal dimension, although flat CRTs are available), and vulnerability to ambient reflections and high illumination. Light falling on the smooth display surface can produce a veiling illuminance that washes out screen contrast and reduces the number of colors that can be perceived.

5. Liquid Crystal Displays

Liquid crystal displays (LCDs) belong to the class of nonemissive technologies, i.e., displays that do not generate light of their own but control the transmission or reflection of an external light source. LCDs alter the optical path of light when an electric field is placed across the liquid crystal (LC) material.

The principal advantages of LCDs include (1) very low power consumption (important for battery-operated and portable systems such as calculators), (2) a flat display package, (3) low cost of the basic materials, and (4) excellent contrast in high ambient illumination. Some LCDs, however, have slow dynamic response (i.e., for switching display elements on and off); 100 to 500 ms rise times, for example; are visually noticeable and such systems may be unacceptable for measurement applications. Low luminance is another drawback, and can make the display difficult to read in low-light conditions without an external light source. In addition, viewing angle is limited by inherent LC characteristics, and is usually less than 45° without special designs. Many LCD features, such as switching thresholds and response times, are temperature dependent.

Selected from "The Measurement, Instrumentation, and Sensons Handbook, CRC press LLC, 1999".

Words and Expressions

1. cartridge ['kɑːtridʒ] 盒式磁盘[带] (机); 夹头; (粉) 盒 [CART]
2. ribbon ['ribən] n. 带状电缆, 扁平柔性电缆; (打印机的) 色带; [微软] 带状条; 格式栏
3. motor ['məutə(r)] n. 发动机, 电动机
4. potentiometric [pəuˌtenʃi'ɔmitrik] n. 电位计, 分压计 adj 电势测定的
5. ultrasonic [ˌʌltrə'sɔnik] adj. 超音速的, 超声的 n. 超声波
6. magnetostrictive [mægniːtəu'tæktik] adj. 磁力控制的 磁致伸缩的
7. impart [im'pɑːt] vt. 给予 (尤指抽象事物), 传授, 告知, 透露
8. magneto optic [mægniːtəu] ['ɔptik] adj. [物] 磁光的, 磁场对光线的影响的
9. polarize ['pəuləraiz] v. (使) 偏振, (使) 极化, (使) 两极分化
10. coercivity [ˌkəuəː'siviti] n. [电] 矫顽 (磁) 力, 矫顽 (磁) 性
11. vertically ['vəːtikəli] adv. 垂直地

12. clockwise ['klɔkwaiz] adj. 顺时针方向的 adv. 顺时针方向地
13. erase [i'reiz] vt. 抹去，擦掉，消磁，〈俚〉杀死
14. moisture ['mɔistʃə] n. 潮湿，湿气
15. phosphor ['fɔsfə(r)] n. 磷，启明星
16. versatile ['vəːsətail] adj. 可使直立的，通用的，万能的，多才多艺的，多面手的
17. cathode ['kæθəud] n. 阴极
18. foreseeable [fɔː'siːəbl] adj. 可预知的，能预测的，能看透的
19. veiling ['veiliŋ] n. 罩以面纱，面纱，面纱布料，帐幔
20. crystal ['kristəl] adj. 结晶状的；n. 水晶，水晶饰品，结晶，晶体
21. threshold ['θreʃəuld] n. 阈，阈值，门限，门槛
22. kerr rotation 克尔旋度，克尔旋转

CHAPTER. 4 Modern Measurement and Control Technology

Unit 16 Intelligent Control Systems

> Before reading the text, try to answer the following questions:
> 1. What differences are there between adaptive systems and intelligent systems?
> 2. What functions do the intelligent systems incorporate?
> 3. What parts does an expert system consist of?
> 4. How is fuzzy control applied in consumer products?
> 5. What is neural network, and what does a standard neural network model consist of?

1. Overview

In the 1950's, we began to look again at differential equation models and Kalman, Bellman, and others introduced the state-space concept which lead to "optimal control" which had been introduced earlier by Weiner and Phillips. Sampled data systems were introduced to handle control systems which used digital computers. These developments are often cited as the beginning of "modern control."

In the 1960's, we began to address the problem of designing control systems for situations which varied with time (as the system ages, or as it's operating environment changes). Adaptive systems were designed which (1) measure their operation relative to an "index of performance" and (2) then modify controller parameters to approach optimal values (for whatever operating conditions may be present). Successful adaptive systems have been built for many applications, and there are no doubt many future control problems that will be solved with this powerful methodology.

Adaptive control systems readjust themselves to different operating conditions; however an adaptive controller does not "learn" from it's experiences. Even though the adaptive controller many adjust itself for optimal performance in a given circumstance, it must re-adjust itself again if it should return to the same circumstance. On the other hand, if "learning" were incorporated into an "intelligent" control system, then it could utilize it's past experience and more quickly achieve optimal performance, especially for "familiar" circumstances. This challenge (among others) has served to stimulate our current interest in "intelligent" control systems.

Intelligent systems attempt to incorporate functions which are normally contained in living beings; adaptation, learning, planning under large uncertainty, coping with unexpected changes handling large amounts of (possibly conflicting) information, self reliance, and so on. In addition to accommodating variable plants and unexpected changes in operating conditions, intelligent control is also directed toward improving our ability to accurately model non-linear systems. (We have a rich inventory of control technology that can be successfully applied if we have better mathematical models for the systems. Thus it is natural to look toward intelligent techniques as a means for generating better models.)

Today we have several artificial intelligent methods that are being examined for potential application to intelligent control systems.

- Expert Systems
- Fuzzy Logic
- Neural Networks

In addition to the above methods, several hybrid combinations of these (and other more conventional techniques) are also being examined. We will likely find that such combinations in fact yield the best results for selected applications. Over time, "intelligent techniques" will no doubt have great success.

2. Expert systems

Feigenbaum, a pioneer in expert systems, states:

An "expert system" is an intelligent computer program that uses knowledge and inference procedures to solve problems that are difficult enough to require significant human expertise for their solution. The knowledge of an expert system consists of facts and heuristics. The "facts" constitute a body of information that is widely shared, publicly available, and generally agreed upon by experts in a field. The "heuristics" are mostly private, little-discussed rules of good judgment (rules of plausible reasoning, rules of good guessing) that characterize expert-level decision making in the field. The performance level of an expert system is primarily a function of the size and quality of the knowledge base that it possesses.

It has become fashionable today to characterize any AI system that uses substantial domain knowledge as an expert system. Thus, nearly all AI applications to real world problems can be considered in this category, though the designation "knowledge-based systems" (KBS) is more appropriate.

An expert system consists of:

① A knowledge base (or knowledge source) of domain facts and heuristics associated with the problem.

② An inference procedure (of control structure) for utilizing the knowledge base in the solution of the problem.

③ A working memory, global database, for keeping track of the problem status. The input data for the particular problem, and the relevant history of what has thus far been done.

Expert systems use a set of "rules" to perform logical inferences about the state of a process operation or some other activity of interest. An early and highly visible demonstration project, the FALCON project, was a collaborative effort between Du Pont, Foxboro, and the University of Delaware during the period, 1983~1987. The objective was to develop and apply knowledge-based methods for fault diagnosis in a full-scale chemical plant, an adipic acid converter. Although this pioneering project was judged to be only a partial success, it paved the way for many future Du Pont KBS applications.

Stephanopoulos and Han note that industrial applications of KBS systems have largely been concerned with either diagnostic and monitoring activities or supervisory control. Supervisory control applications have included the following problems: complex control schemes; recovery from extreme conditions; and emergency shutdowns. They also describe a number of industrial KBS applications.

Future applications of expert systems will be facilitated by real-time KBS which enable the user to integrate plant data and process models in an expert system shell which has a sophisticated graphical interface. This combination provides a powerful vehicle for on-line process monitoring, especially diagnostics and fault detection. At the present time, the most widely used system in the G2 product from the GENSYM Corporation (Cambridge, MA). It has been reported that over 1000 G2 systems have been installed worldwide. In a recent application at a Monsanto-Krummich plant in Illinois, a G2 system provided the framework for a sensor and control loop validation system for over 600 measurement points. The diagnostic system was able to successfully identify a variety of actual faults and is being modified for use in other plants.

The early enthusiasm for KBS has been tempered by the realization that a considerable effort is required to codify the available expertise. Furthermore, if each potential application has a significant number of unique features, it is less feasible to spread the development costs over a large number of projects. Despite this inherent problem, the industrial employment of KBS for applications such as process diagnosis and supervisory control is significant and growing at an impressive rate.

3. Fuzzy control systems

Fuzzy logic provides a conceptual framework for practical problems where some process variables are represented as "linguistic variables" which have only a few possible values (e.g. very large, large, normal, small etc.). The linguistic variables can then be processed a set of rules. Thus applications of fuzzy logic and fuzzy control can be viewed as special cases of KBS which have fuzzy boundaries for the rules.

Unlike more general KBS and neural nets, fuzzy control strategies have appeared in the control literature for over 20 years. Early process control applications consisted of demonstrations that fuzzy control could be used to control simple laboratory apparatus. In recent years, the success of fuzzy control in Japan, especially in consumer products such as washing machines and camcorders, has generated a new wave of interest. Industrial applications of fuzzy control to process control problems have begun to appear more frequently in Japan and

Europe than in the U. S. But even in Japan, a survey has indicated that MPC has been more widely used in the process industries than any of the three AI techniques considered in this section (Yamamoto and Hashimoto 1991).

There has been considerable controversy concerning fuzzy controllers and their relative merits viz. conventional control and model-based control. One of the reasons for this controversy is that there is no theoretical framework for analysing the closed-loop properties of fuzzy control systems. As Stephanopoulos and Han aptly note, "Using fuzzy controllers takes a lot of testing and /or faith."

4. Neural networks

Pobert Hecht-Nielsen defined a neural network as: "…a computing system made up of a number of simple, highly interconnected processing elements, which process information by its dynamic state response to external inputs".

To put that definition into perspective, consider a serial computer, which is a single central processor that can address data and instructions stored in memory locations. The processor fetches an instruction and any data required by that instruction and saves the results at a specific memory location. In other words, everything happens in a deterministic sequence of operations. In contrast, a neural network is neither sequential not even necessarily deterministic. It is composed of many simple processing elements that usually do little more than take a weighted sum of all their inputs. Instead of executing a series of instructions, a neural network responds, in parallel, to the inputs given to it. The final result consists of an overall state of the network after it has reached a steady-state condition, which correlates patterns between the sets of input data and corresponding output or target values. The final network can be used to predict outcomes from new input data.

Neural networks provide a powerful approach for developing empirical nonlinear models for a wide variety of physical phenomena. In the area of process control, they have been used for a variety of traditional activities, such as developing nonlinear dynamic models and control system design. Neural networks also provide a promising approach for pattern recognition problems such as sensor data analysis and fault detection where traditional modeling techniques are not easily applied.

Standard neural network models consist of three layer networks with sigmoidal functions used as the "activation function" for each neuron in the hidden layer. However, networks which consist of linear combinations of radial basis functions offer significant theoretical and computational advantages over the standard neural networks. Furthermore, a priori physical information such as known steady-state relations and some types of constrains can easily be incorporated into the otherwise empirical models.

The commercial availability of neural networks software for use by non-specialists should continue the current widespread interest in neural network applications for process control. However, at the present time it is difficult to assess the extent to which process control applications of neural networks are being used in industry.

5. Summary

Regrettably, a high degree of "hype" was associated with the initial introduction of these three AI technologies and consequently, early expectations were not always fulfilled. But it is important to keep in mind that these are new approaches for process control and that software still tends to be "first generation". As the technology and available software continues to improve, widespread industrial applications are quite likely. Also, the individual AI techniques can be combined to good advantage, for example, by embedding neural networks and fuzzy logic in knowledge-based systems. In particular, neural networks have been proposed for the preliminary screening of data that are analyzed further by expert systems in diagnostic and monitoring applications.

Selected from "Electronics: The Intelligence in Intelligent Control, Edited by Michael K. Masten, IFAC PRESS 1997 and A perspective on advanced strategies for process control, Modeling Identification and Control, by D. E. Seborg, 1994".

Words and Expressions

1. stimulate ['stimjuleit] vt. 激励，鼓励
2. incorporate [in'kɔːpəreit] vt. 合并，包含
3. accommodate [ə'kɔmədeit] vt. 供应，供给，使适应
4. inventory ['invəntəri] n. 详细目录，存货，财产清册，总量
5. diagnosis [ˌdaiəg'nəusis] n. 调查；诊断
6. full-scale adj. 与原物大小一样的，全面的，未经删节的 n. 全尺寸，满标度
7. fuzzy ['fʌzi] adj. 失真的，模糊的
8. neural ['njuər(ə)l] adj. 神经的，神经系统的
9. hybrid [haibrid] adj. 混合的，杂种的
10. yield [jiːld] vt. 出产，生长，生产
11. expertise [ekspɜː'tiːz] n. 专家的意见，专门技术
12. heuristics [hjuə'ristiks] n. [计] 试探法
13. plausible ['plɔːzib(ə)l] adj. 似是而非的
14. substantial [səb'stænʃ(ə)l] adj. 坚固的，实质的，真实的，充实的
15. designation [dezig'neiʃ(ə)n] n. 指示，指定，选派，名称
16. collaborative [kə'læbəreitiv] adj. 合作的，协作的，协力完成的
17. adipic acid n. 己二酸
18. validation [væli'deiʃən] n. 确认
19. sigmoidal ['sigmɔidəu] n. S形曲线，S形的，反曲的
20. enthusiasm [in'θjuːziæz(ə)m] n. 狂热，热心，积极性
21. temper ['tempə(r)] v. (冶金) 回火，锻炼，调和，调节
22. linguistic [liŋ'gwistik] adj. 语言上的，语言学上的
23. camcorder ['kʌmkɔːdə(r)] n. 可携式摄像机

24. controversy ['kɔntrəvə:si] n. 论争，辩论，论战
25. perspective [pə'spektiv] n. 远景，前途，观点，看法，观察
26. constrain [kən'strein] n. 约束，强制，局促
27. hype [haip] n. 皮下注射，欺骗，骗局
28. embed [em'bed] vt. 使插入，使嵌入，深留，嵌入

Exercises

1. Fill in the blanks in your own words according to the text.

   　　　　Intelligent Systems attempt to _____ functions which are normally contained in living beings; _____, _____, _____ under large uncertainty, coping with _____ changes handling large amounts of (possibly _____) information, _____, and so on. Today we have several artificial intelligent methods that are expert systems, fuzzy Logic, neural networks.

   　　　　An expert system, also referred to as _____ (KBS), is an intelligent computer program that uses _____ and _____ to solve problems that are difficult enough to require significant human _____ for their solution. It consists of ①A knowledge _____ of domain facts and _____ associated with the problem. ②An _____ _____ procedure for utilizing the knowledge base in the solution of the problem. ③A working memory, _____, for keeping track of the problem status.

   　　　　Fuzzy logic provides a _____ for practical problems where some process variables are represented as "_____ variables" which have only a few possible values (e.g. very large, large, normal, small etc.). The linguistic variables can then be _____ _____ a set of rules. Thus applications of fuzzy logic and fuzzy control can be _____ _____ as special cases of KBS which have fuzzy _____ for the rules.

   　　　　A neural network is a computing system made up of a number of simple, highly _____ _____ processing elements, which process information by its dynamic state _____ to external inputs. Standard neural network models consist of three layer networks with __ _____ functions used as the "_____ function" for each neuron in the hidden layer. The final network can be used to _____ outcomes from new input data.

2. Put the following into Chinese.
   non-linear system　　optimal control　　knowledge-based systems
   knowledge base　　logical inferences　　supervisory control　　fault detection
   recovery from extreme conditions　　linguistic variables　　target value

3. Put the following into English.
   自适应系统　　推理程序　　紧急关闭　　专家系统　　微分方程模型故障诊断
   动态响应　　在线过程监控　　固有问题　　模糊逻辑　　闭环系统
   神经网络　　径向基函数　　经验模型　　模式识别

4. List some functions of intelligent system.
5. List some practical application examples for expert system.
6. Tell the essential operating principles of neural networks.

7. Enumerate some possible application examples for fuzzy control.

Reading Material 16

Fuzzy Neural Control

Classical logic and mathematics assume that we can assign one of the two values, *true* or *false*, to each logical proposition or statement. If a suitable formal model for a certain problem or task can be specified, conventional mathematics provides powerful tools which help us to solve the problem. When we describe such a formal model, we use a terminology which has much more stringent rules than natural language. This specification often requires more work and effort, but by using it we can avoid misinterpretations. Furthermore, based on such models we can prove or reject hypotheses or derive unknown correlations.

However, in our everyday life formal models do not concern the interhuman communication. Human beings are able to assimilate easliy linguistical information without thinking in any type of formalization of the specific situation. For example, a person will have no problems to accelerate slowly while starting a car, if he is asked to do so. If we want to automate this action, it will not be clear at all, how to translate this advice into a well-defined control action. It is necessary to determine a concrete statement based on an unambiguous value, i. e. step on the gas at the velocity of half an inch per second. On the other hand, this kind of information will not be adequate or very helpful for a person.

Therefore, automated control is usually not based on a linguistic description of heuristic knowledge or knowledge from one's own experience, but it is based on a formal model of the technical or physical system. This method is definitely a suitable approach, especially if there is a good model to be determined.

However, a completely different technique is to use knowledge formulated in natural language directly for the design of the control strategy. In this case, a main problem will be the translation of the verbal description into concrete values, i. e. assigning "step on the gas slowly" into "step on the gas at the velocity of a centimeter per second" as in the above mentioned example.

When describing an object or an action. usually use uncertain or vague concepts. In natural language we hardly ever find exactly defined concepts.

The notion *fuzzy logic* has three different meanings. In most cases the term fuzzy logic refers to fuzzy logic in the broader sense, including all applications and theories where fuzzy sets or concepts are involved. This includes also fuzzy controllers which are the subject of this book.

On the contrary, the second (and narrower) meaning of the term fuzzy logic focuses on the field of approximative reasoning where fuzzy sets are used and propagated within an inference mechanism as it is for instance common in expert systems.

Finally, fuzzy logic in the narrow sense, which is the topic of this section, considers fuzzy systems from the point of view of multi-valued logics and is devoted to issues connected to logical calculi and the associated deduction mechanisms.

We cannot provide a complete introduction to fuzzy logic as a multi-valued logic. In this section we will introduce some notions of fuzzy logic which are necessary or useful to understand fuzzy controllers. In the sections about logic-based fuzzy controllers, we discuss some further aspects of fuzzy logic in the narrow sense. We mainly need the concepts of (fuzzy) logic to introduce the set theoretical operations for fuzzy sets. The basis for operations like union, intersection and complement are the logical connectives disjunction, conjunction and negation, respectively. Therefore we briefly repeat some fundamental concepts from classical logic in order to generalise them to the field of fuzzy logic.

Promising approaches for optimization of existing fuzzy controllers and to learn a fuzzy system from scratch are approaches that combine fuzzy systems and learning methods of artificial neural nets. These methods are usually described with the terms *neural fuzzy* or *neurol fuzzy* systems. Nowadays, there are many specialized models. Beside the models for system control, especially systems for classification and more general models for function approximation have been developed.

In this section we only introduce systematics and discuss some approaches. Furthermore, we give a short introduction to the fundamental principles of neural nets to the extent, which is necessary to understand the following discussion about control engineering models. A detailed introduction to the fundamentals of artificial neural nets can be found in, e.g. (see Fig. 16.1~Fig. 16.3).

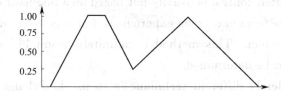

Fig. 16.1 The fuzzy set μ

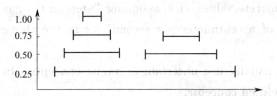

Fig. 16.2 The α-level sets of the fuzzy set μ for $\alpha=0.25, 0.5, 0.75, 1$

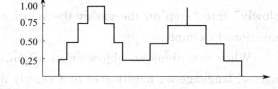

Fig. 16.3 The approximation of the fuzzy set μ resulting from the α-level sets

Selected from "Fuzzy Neural Control, Springer, 2006, London".

Words and Expression

1. misinterpretation ['misintə:pri'teiʃən] n. 误译，曲解
2. assimilate [ə'simileit] vt. & vi. 吸收，消化

3. linguistical [liŋˈgwistikəl] adj. 语言上的，语言学上的
4. unambiguous [ˌʌnæmˈbigjuəs] adj. 不含糊的；清楚的；明确的
5. heuristic [hjuəˈristik] adj. 启发式的
6. control strategy 控制策略
7. fuzzy logic 模糊逻辑
8. optimization [ˌɔptimaiˈzeiʃən] n. 最佳化，最优化
9. artifical neural nets (ANN) 人工神经网络
10. systematics [sistəˈmætiks] n. 分类学，分类法；系统学

Unit 17　Machine Vision Systems

> During reading the text, try to answer the following questions:
> 1. According to their functions, what the categories may machine vision systems be divided into?
> 2. What is the VGS?
> 3. What are the uses of the VIS?
> 4. Give some application examples of VRS, VIS, and their combination?
> 5. What are the popular working principles for 3D machine vision systems?
> 6. What are the advantages and the disadvantages of triangulation method?
> 7. What is the focal gradient method?
> 8. What are the advantages and the disadvantages of focal gradient method?

1. Introduction

Machine vision systems may be divided into three categories according to their functions, (1) visual recognition systems (VRS), (2) visual inspection systems (VIS), and (3) visual guidance systems (VGS). In practice systems may be a combination of two or three categories, for example VRS + VIS; VRS + VGS; VIS + VGS or VRS + VIS + VGS.

The emphasis of the VRS is to identify objects in a given area. Typical applications are vehicle recognition systems, object recognition by robots with vision function for the disabled and in the fields of medicine, arts, environmental monitoring and aviation.

VIS is commonly used in inspection applications for detecting deformations, deviations from specifications, or missing elements. Such systems have an emphasis on checking the size and shape of objects. The significance is that they have the ability to carry out 100 percent on-line inspection and measurement. Many successful application examples can be found in industry. For example, the 100 percent visual inspection system of valve-stem seals [Pham et al., 1995], 3D mechanical parts visual inspection [Wolfson et al., 1997] and automatic PCB inspection [Moganti et al., 1996].

VGS is concerned with the position of an object and directs a controller to move the object. The vision system in VGS is a measuring loop, which supplies positions and/or orientations of objects. All highly automated industries have a potential for applying VGS, for example, raw parts feeding and car screen insertion systems in Rover [Rooks, 1997].

Vision systems also can be divided into 1D, 2D and 3D systems, where 1D is for the measurement of width or height, a 2D can measure both width and height and 3D can measure geometry in 3 dimensions.

This CMM[①] vision system research is concerned with workpiece recognition, position and orientation determination in 3D space and then controlling the probe to align the workpiece. Therefore the system belongs to the combination type of VRS + VGS and is a 3D vision system. The structure of a vision system is depended on the requirements. For a 1D or 2D problem, usually a one-camera vision system will be employed, otherwise stereo vision system should be considered. Since the research presents a 3D problem both for the probe and workpiece the literature survey concentrated on stereo vision systems.

2. Moiré fringe technique

This popular method employs one camera and a projector. Fig. 17.1 shows a typical Moiré projection system. A bundle of light rays, in a pre-defined grating pattern, is projected onto the object to define a number of outward vectors to points on the object. The camera records an image of the projected grating, as it appears on the object, thereby defining a number of inward vectors from points on the object. Rather than directly determining the orientations of the outward and inward vectors, the image of the object, which shows the grating pattern deformed by the surface relief, is superimposed on a reference grating. Moiré fringes resulting from the interaction of the image with the reference grating represent the height contours of the object. Fig. 17.2 shows a Moiré interference pattern when the technique is applied to the surface of a propeller. A fairly accurate and qualitative assessment can be made as to the shape just from the examination of the interference pattern. An extremely accurate 3D surface contour can be extrapolated from the fringe pattern information to give a quantitative wire mesh representation of the object. Using electronic analysis techniques, high accuracy measurements (better than 1/250th of the contour interval) can be made.

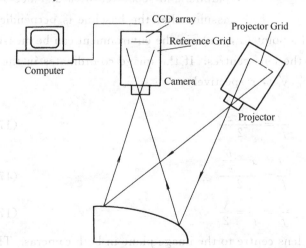

Fig. 17.1 Typical arrangement for moiré projection contouring

Fig. 17.2 Projection of moiré contour Pattern of a small propeller

The Moiré fringe technique can measure 3D space positions using one camera. The key point is that in the system, the projection grid and reference grid is employed in the light projector and camera respectively. The depth information can be obtained by calculating the Moiré interference pattern. This system is very useful for the location of deformations and faults. A major advantage of the system is that just by looking at the Moiré interference pattern, surface faults and abnormalities can be detected at a glance without having to compute the exact 3D surface contour. However the technique only works well on smooth single colour surfaces and in controlled lighting, as it is sensitive to ambient light. The special requirements for the camera and projector make the system expensive. In this research, the CMM vision system requires to recognise workpieces and determine their positions rather than measurement of deformations and faults. Due to this other techniques were investigated.

3. Triangulation method

There are four popular working principles for 3D machine vision systems: triangulation; Moiré fringe technique; shape from motion and focal gradient method. The triangulation method uses two or more cameras, others employ a single camera.

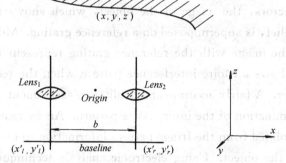

Fig. 17.3 3D vision geometry using 2 cameras [Horn, 1993]

The triangulation method imitates a human visual system. The (x, y) information can be obtained directly from image plane's co-ordinates in any one of the cameras. The position information in the z direction is extracted from the two cameras. Fig. 17.3 illustrates the basic geometry. Suppose two cameras' optical axes are parallel and separated by a distance b and assume that the baseline is perpendicular to the optical axes. The co-ordinate of a point $(x,y,z)^T$ in the environment can be measured relative to an origin midway between the lens centres. If the image co-ordinates in the left and right images is (x'_l, y'_l), and (x'_r, y'_r), respectively,

then
$$\frac{x'_l}{f} = \frac{x + \frac{b}{z}}{2} \qquad (17.1)$$

and
$$\frac{x'_r}{f} = \frac{x - \frac{b}{z}}{2} \qquad (17.2)$$

while
$$\frac{y'_l}{f} = \frac{y'_r}{f} = \frac{y}{2} \qquad (17.3)$$

Where f is the distance from the lens centre to the image plane in both cameras. These three equations can be solved for the three unknowns x, y, z. First there is:

$$\frac{x'_l - x'_r}{f} = \frac{b}{z} \qquad (17.4)$$

The difference in image co-ordinates, $x'_l - x'_r$, is called the disparity. Solving the above equations the 3D co-ordinates of a point can be given by:

$$x = b \frac{(x'_l + x'_r)/2}{x'_l - x'_r} \qquad (17.5)$$

$$y = b \frac{(y'_l + y'_r)/2}{x'_l - x'_r} \qquad (17.6)$$

$$z = b \frac{f}{x'_l - x'_r} \qquad (17.7)$$

Using Equation 17.5~Equation 17.7 the 3D co-ordinate of a point $(x, y, z)^T$ can be obtained from two cameras.

The triangulation method has the advantage of not needing special cameras and has a high accuracy. It can be employed for object recognition, positioning and movement guidance. The main disadvantages are that it needs a large memory space and the processing speed is slow as two image frames are required to be stored, and time-consuming algorithms used. A further difficulty in using the method is in finding the corresponding points in the two different images. A frequently used approach for this is to select a point within a small region in one of the images and then attempt to find the best matching region in another image by correlation or other image matching techniques. This technique is called image registration or match. If any mismatching happens in the matching process, all the subsequent results will be incorrect.

A typical example of such a system using triangulation method is 4DI Intelligent Automation System developed by [Wolfson and Gordon, 1997], (see Fig. 17.4). The 4DI is a 3D machine vision system using two or three area cameras and combines a laser projector as structured lighting. Imaging operates in three steps: image acquisition, pre-processing, and correlation/triangulation. A visible diode laser beam is diffracted through a grating, which generates a multi-stripe pattern of 100 parallel lines.

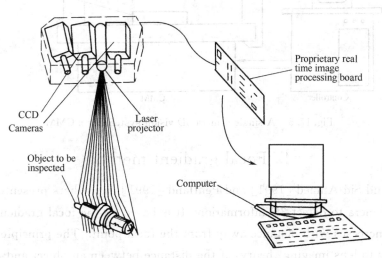

Fig. 17.4 A typical 3D vision system

The reflection of the laser lines on the object is captured by three high-resolution (764× 494 pixel) CCD cameras. The cameras are pixel-synchronized to eliminate ambiguity and decrease image processing times through a proprietary high speed image processing board. This board processes all images in parallel, converting the gray scale image information to sub-pixel stripe position information. The captured images are pre-processed and stored on the image processing board. By the end of a frame cycle, the image has been pre-processed and data relative to the algorithm is stored on the image processing board. The data is then transferred to a PC memory to be processed by the 3D algorithm. The overall computer processing time can range from a few hundred milliseconds to a couple of seconds depending on the details of the application and host computer.

Cho et al. [1995] developed a single camera 3D vision system for workpiece recognition and measuring path planning on a CMM (Fig. 17.5). As shown in Fig. 17.5, a vision camera is mounted on the ram of the CMM. Two images, which are needed for the 3D shape construction by the triangle method, are taken at two positions by moving the ram along the x direction while the z and y coordinates of the camera remain unchanged. Since the CMM is a very accurate machine the calibration of the binocular stereo can be solved by using the position measuring system of the CMM. The advantage of the arrangement is that the distance between the two cameras can be easily changed to obtain more desirable results.

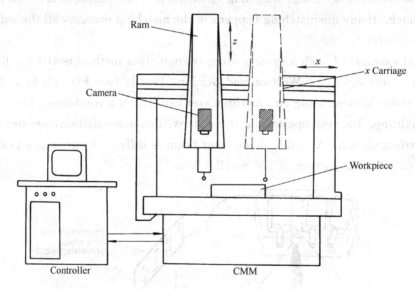

Fig. 17.5 A single camera 3D vision system for a CMM

4. Focal gradient method

Cardillo and Sid-Ahmed [1991] and Pentland [1991] and others presented another way of using one camera to detect 3D information. It is based on the focal gradient, or the error in focus that increases with distance away from the focal point. The principle is as follows.

According to lens imaging theory, if the distance between an object and a lens is l (see Fig. 17.6), the object's image will located at L and the height is H. If l changes, the image height and location will change to H' and $L + \Delta L$ respectively. Since the image plane is fixed, the image is still projected on the same image plane located at L. The result is that the image becomes blurred. Fig. 17.7 shows this situation. In (a) the objects distance $l = 400$mm and the image plane is adjusted at the correct position. Due to that adjustment, the edge of the 9 white dots are sharp and clear. In (b) the $l = 700$mm and the image is blurred. The depth information can be obtained by measuring the amount of blurriness.

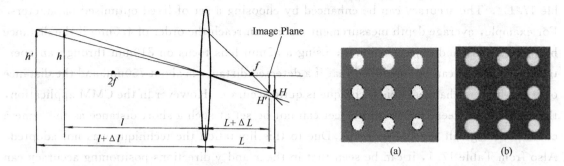

Fig. 17.6 Lens imaging geometry   Fig. 17.7 Lens imaging geometry

Pentland [1991] demonstrated the feasibility of measuring focus blur and applied it to recover relative depth maps. He presented two methods for measuring blur; the first was based on the assumption of sharp scene edges, the second requires a comparison of two or more images taken through different apertures. A more general "depth-from-focusing" method was proposed by [Subbarao, 1944]. He describes a technique for measuring blur similar to Pentland's with the exception that up to three camera parameters may be varied simultaneously. This induces larger measurable changes in the observed image and hence, is more robust.

Absolute positions would be required if this technique were applied in the manufacturing or robotics environment. Cardillo and Sid-Ahmed [1991] presented a calibration scheme that made possible the sensing of absolute 3D positions. An application example is presented in Fig. 17.8. The calibration presented by Cardillo enables the recovery of the absolute 3D position coordinates from image coordinates and measured focus blur.

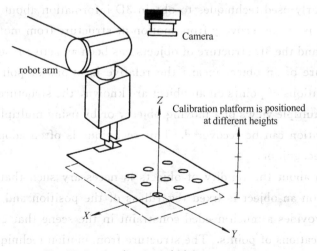

Fig. 17.8 Application of blurriness measure

The advantages of this technique are that it utilises simple hardware and algorithms. Due to the simple algorithm the response speed should be fast with no large memory space requirement. The main disadvantage is that its accuracy for depth information is influenced by the background and an object's surface reflection properties. According to Cardillo and

Sid-Ahmed [1991], the accuracy for different objects and backgrounds are different (see Table 17.1). The accuracy can be enhanced by choosing a set of fixed optimised parameters. For example, average depth measurement errors can reach the order of 4.5mm if the distance between camera and object=750mm; using a 55mm lens focus on 810mm through an aperture of $f/2.8$. It can be concluded that if a detected distance is about 750mm and the distance only has limited changes, this technique is quite accurate. However in the CMM application, the distance between camera and object can not be set at such a short distance as the camera could not image all the CMM frame. Due to this limitation the technique was not adopted. Also from Table 17.1, it can be seen that in the x and y directions positioning accuracy can be high, especially for the situation of white dots on black background. The accuracy could satisfy the requirement for the CMM vision system workpiece position determination. It gives two pointers to help the CMM application: (1) white objects on black background can enhance position determination accuracy and (2) the position determination accuracy of a vision system is capable of reaching 3~4mm in x and y directions.

Table 17.1 Maximum errors for single image system using the focus blurriness technique

Units: mm	White dots on black background			Drilled holes in gray platform		
Distance	x-error	y-error	z-error	x-error	y-error	z-error
400	0.61	0.47	15.35	2.91	4.55	23.43
750	0.33	0.90	13.19	2.91	3.16	22.27
700	0.4	1.45	9.61	3.27	3.13	44.20

5. Shape from Motion

Another popularly used techniques to obtain 3D information about the structure of objects by one camera is shape recovery from motion or structure from motion. Recovery of 3D motion parameters and the 3D structure of objects has been an active research area in machine vision. The structure of an object means the relative locations of points on the object. If some important locations of points on an object are known, the structure of the object can be known. By using multiple views of a moving object, or by using multiple locations of a camera, the 3D information can be recovered. This technique is often adopted by VRS for the purpose of object recognition.

An assumption about the rigidity of objects is necessary such that the geometric relations of the points on an object is fixed regardless of the position and inclination changes. This assumption provides a much-needed constraint in the scene that can be used to determine the relative locations of points. The structure from motion techniques states that given three distinct orthographic projections of four non-coplanar points in a rigid configuration, the structure and motion compatible with the three views are uniquely determined up to a reflection about the image plane. The structure-from-motion theorem provides a precise statement about constraints and possible solutions. By changing the constraints on the types of objects and types of projections, and by using different mathematical approaches, image plane information about objects can be converted to scene information.

Many different approaches have been proposed to solve this under-constrained problem. Weng and Huang [1991] carried out pioneering research in recovering motion characteristics of objects under various conditions. Tan et al. [1993] presented a simple and efficient method to recover vehicle's 3D structure on roads by using a ground plane constraint. This was based on the important fact about traffic scenes that under normal conditions, vehicles are constrained to be in contact with the ground surface which is, at least locally, approximately flat - this was called the ground-plane constraint (GPC). The GPC constraint reduce the degree of freedom of a rigid object from 6 (x,y,z, and α,β,θ) to 3 (x,y,θ). Because of the GPC the height of any point on a vehicle moving on ground plane remains constant. Under this assumption an algorithm was developed by Tan et al. [1993] to solve the depth information. Fig. 17.9 shows an image sequence and a set of points matched in three frames.

Fig. 17.9 An image sequence and a set of points matched in three frames

Although it is theoretically possible to estimate the motion parameters, practical considerations complicate the implementation of the method. It is difficult to use this technique to recognise objects in real times due to the time consuming algorithm. Currently it is mainly used with video tape recording analysis off-line.

Words and Expressions

1. potential　[pə'tenʃ(ə)l]　n. 潜能，电压
2. workpiece　['wə:kpi:s]　n. 工件
3. literature　['litərətʃə(r);(US)'litrətʃuər]　n. 著作，文献
4. Moiré fringe　莫尔条纹
5. contour　['kɔntvə'(r)]　n. 轮廓，等高线
6. vector　['vektə]　n. 向量
7. abnormality　[,æbnɔ:'mæləti]　n. 变态，畸形，异常性
8. ambient　['æmbiənt]　adj. 周围的；　n. 周围环境
9. propeller　[prə'pelə(r)]　n. 螺旋推进器
10. orientation　[,ɔ:riə'teiʃ(ə)n]　n. 方向，定位
11. extrapolate　[ik'stræpəleit]　v. 推断，外推
12. superimpose　['su:pərim'pəuz, 'sju:-]　v. 添加，双重
13. focal　['fəuk(ə)l]　adj. 焦点的，有焦点的，在焦点上的
14. gradient　['greidiənt]　adj. 倾斜的；　n. 梯度，倾斜度，坡度
15. perpendicular　[,pə:pən'dikjulə(r)]　adj. 垂直的，正交的；　n. 垂线

16. disparity [di'spæriti] n. （职位、数量、质量等）不一致，不同，不等
17. registration [redʒi'streiʃ(ə)n] n. 注册，报到，登记
18. subsequent ['sʌbsikwənt] adj. 后来的，并发的
19. diode ['daiəud] n. 二极管
20. diffract [di'frækt] n. 衍射
21. grating ['greitiŋ] n. 门窗的栅栏，[物理] 光栅，摩擦，摩擦声； adj. 刺耳的
22. ambiguity [ˌæmbi'gju:iti] n. 含糊，不明确
23. pixel-synchronized 像素同步
24. calibration [ˌkæli'breiʃən] n. 标度，刻度，校准
25. binocular [bi'nɔkjulə(r)] adj. 用两眼的，给两眼用的；双目并用的
26. stereo [steriəu, 'stiər] adj. 立体的，立体感觉的
27. project ['prɔdʒekt] n. 计划，方案，事业，企业，工程； v. 设计，发射（导弹等），凸出
28. optimize ['ɔptimaiz] vt. 使最优化
29. blur [blə:(r)] v. 使模糊
30. aperture ['æpətjuə(r)] n. （照相机，望远镜等的）光圈，孔径
31. rigidity [ri'dʒidəti] n. 硬度，刚性
32. orthographic [ˌɔ:θəu'græfik] adj. 正交的
33. compatible [kəm'pætib(ə)l] adj. 谐调的，一致的，兼容的
34. constraint [kən'streint] n. 约束
35. uniquely [ju'ni:kli] adv. 独特的，唯一的
36. approximately [əprɔksi'mətli] adv. 近似地，大约
37. non-coplanar 不共面的

Notes

① CMM: Coordinate Measuring Machine 坐标测量机

Exercises

1. Fill in the spaces in your own words according to content of the text.

   (1) Machine vision systems may be divided into three categories according to their functions, ①_____ (VRS), ②_____ (VIS), and ③_____ (VGS).

   (2) VIS is commonly used in _____ for _____, deviations from specifications, or _____. Such systems have an emphasis on checking _____ and shape of objects.

   (3) For a 1D or 2D problem, usually a _____ vision system will be employed, otherwise _____ should be considered. Since the research presents a 3D problem both for the probe and workpiece the literature survey concentrated on stereo vision systems.

   (4) The triangulation method has the advantage of _____ and _____. It can be employed for _____, _____ and _____.

(5) There are four popular working principles for 3D machine vision systems: _____; _____; shape from motion and _____. The triangulation method uses _____ cameras, others employ a single camera.

(6) The triangulation method imitates a human visual system. The (x, y) information can be obtained directly from _____ in any one of the cameras. The position information in the z direction is extracted from _____.

2. Put the following words and phrases in English:

机器视觉系统   视觉识别系统   视觉检查系统   视觉引导系统
三角测量法   光轴   聚焦法   透镜成像理论
参考光栅   物体表面反射特性

Reading Material 17

Theoretical Basis of Image Processing

This text provides an overview of image processing methods and procedures. An evaluation of the approaches has been conducted to identify the main advantages and problems in their adaptation to the CMM vision system application.

1. Image processing procedures

Image processing is the software part of a vision system. Its purpose can be described as the process of extracting, characterizing and interpreting information from images of the 3D world. Gonzalez and Woods, [1993] and Horn, [1993] introduced 6 steps to achieve this purpose. They were: ①sampling; ②preprocessing; ③segmentation; ④description; ⑤recognition; ⑥interpretation. Their relationship is shown in Fig. 17.10.

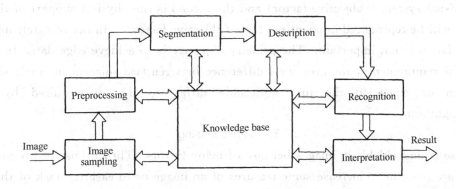

Fig. 17.10 Conventional image processing steps

2. Sampling and Quantification

The function of sampling is to yield visual information. A black-and-white image can be represented by a function $x(u,v)$. Where u and v are two independent space variables. The value of the function $x(u,v)$, at a given point, corresponds to the image brightness at that point. Color images are represented by three functions of this type, one for each primary colour. The brightness $x(u,v)$ is a continuous function of the space variables u and v. Furthermore, although its dynamic range, i. e. the range of permissible values of $x(u,v)$ is finite, it can take any value from an infinite set within this range. To be processed by a computer or a digital processing system, this function needs to be sampled and quantized.

In the spatial domain, Δu, Δv denote the minimum sampled area. For example if a camera has a resolution of (640 pixel wide×440 pixel high) and the scanned 2D area is a rectangle of (1000mm wide×740mm high), the minimum sampled unit is (1000/640)×(740/440)= 1.56×2.04 (mm/pixel).

Another important parameter in sampling is brightness. Brightness is a binary function of light intensity and spectrum. It will influence image quality directly. If the selected camera is sensitive for some light spectrums and has a light source which has a special light spectrum different from day light, the problem of light disturbance can be greatly reduced.

Quantification completes the digitization of the brightness function $x(u,v)$. Usually sampling should be followed by the quantification of samples. The principle of quantification is to divide the brightness dynamic range into a finite number or intervals and to assign the same value at every brightness value within a given interval. The problem is to find the number of intervals and the variation of their width as a function of the brightness.

In areas of an image where the brightness varies very little from one pixel to the next, the quantification will create a constant level. Between two such areas, there will be a sudden jump from one level to another, whereas the original brightness has a continuous variation. These jumps create general falsehoods which do not correspond to any real object. They are known as quantization errors. Quantification errors are mainly depended on the type of A/D converters.

There are two important factors which intervene in the quantification: the first is the human visual system (subjective factor) and the second is the physical support of the image where it will be reproduced in quantized form (objective factor). In the research application the first factor is not important. The primary objective is to achieve edge data. In order to satisfy the requirements, the grey level difference between two adjacent intervals should be less than or equal to the just noticeable difference that is required by correct edge recognition.

3. Preprocessing

Noise is unavoidable in images because of many factors. The purpose of pre-processing is to reduce noise or to increase some features of an image or to ease the task of the subsequent processing by correcting the imperfections of the imaging data. Image smoothing can reduce high frequency noise in image data. Two conventional methods of image smoothing are neighborhood averaging and median filtering. As described in the following paragraphs, neighborhood averaging results in a good smoothing performance while median filtering has a better edge preserving ability.

Neighborhood averaging: It is a straightforward spatial domain technique. Given an image $f(x,y)$, the procedure is to generate a smoothed image $g(x,y)$ whose intensity at every point (x,y) is obtained by averaging the intensity values of the pixel of $f(x,y)$ contained in a predefined neighborhood of (x,y). The smoothed image is given by:

$$g(x,y) = \frac{1}{P} \sum_{(n,m) \in S} f(n,m)$$

Where S is the set of coordinates of points in the neighborhood of $f(x,y)$, including (x,y) itself. P is the total number of points in the neighborhood.

Median filtering. One of the principal difficulties of neighborhood averaging is that it blurs edges and other sharp details. This blurring can be reduced by the use of median filters, in which the intensity of each pixel is replaced by the median of the intensities in a predefined neighborhood of the pixel, instead of by the average.

Neighborhood averaging and median filtering are low pass filtering techniques. They can reduce the influence of high frequency but filtering an image is time consuming. For example, for a picture with 748 pixel×574 pixels and using 3×3 neighborhood averaging method. There are $(748-2) \times (574-2) \times 4 = 3,395,392$ times additions and 424,424 times divisions in the process. The process was found to take 4.112 seconds on a 486/66MHz computer using C language.

Edge detection Edges contain information for further computer analysis, since they are the place where surface orientation of an object changes discontinuously, where one object occludes another, or where a shadow exists. Edge detection is thus an important technique in machine vision. A great deal of literature has been devoted to the edge detection problem, producing numerous algorithms.

4. Interpretation

The function of interpretation is to assign meanings and relationships to recognized objects. The recognized objects do not mean that a vision system has known what the objects are. Because a set of boundary chains codes are the representations of some objects' boundaries. Only after interpretation can it be known what they are. For example after interpretation, the position of the CMM's probe measuring head maybe at (x,y,z) and the included angle between one edge of the workpiece and axis x maybe θ_1.

Interpretation is one of the most active research topics in machine vision and, at the same time, it is in its infancy [Horn, 1993]. There are a number of factors, which make this type of processing difficult, including: occluding bodies, viewing geometry and variations in illumination. For example, to deal with a multiplicity of objects in a 3D scope occlusion will be a difficult problem. Take Fig. 17.11 as an example. A human observer would have little difficulty in

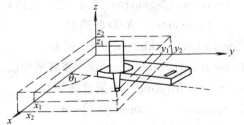

Fig. 17.11 A project of CMM probe image

determining the presence of the workpiece behind the probe. For machine vision, however, interpretation of this scene is a totally different story even if the system is able to perform a perfect segmentation, description and recognition from the image data, the workpiece would still appear as two separate objects in the frame. A circle on the top plane of the workpiece appears as a half circle. Furthermore the exact position of the measuring head is another problem if only one camera is used. It may be at (x_1, y_1, z_1) or at (x_2, y_2, z_2).

5. Knowledge bases

Traditional image processing was presented as 6 steps, each step can have an interaction with a knowledge base. It may say that even the simplest machine vision tasks cannot be solved without the help or support of prior knowledge. This is because the image processing procedure, like the human brain image recognition process, is an analysis and match procedure which compares a visual object with the knowledge stored in memory. A knowledge base is defined as an expert system that contains facts and rules needed to solve problems. For some problems in machine vision the knowledge may be as simple as several parameters which can be coded in a program module. For complicated problems it may be a huge module which is much larger than the main program, for example, an interrelated list of all major possible defects in a materials inspection problem or an image database containing high resolution satellite images of a region in connection with a change detection application. The knowledge base itself can also be quite complex with many layers, types, and structures. Carefully analyses and arranging a suitable knowledge base is a way to enhance a vision system's performance.

Selected from "A single camera vision system for coordinate measuring machines, PhD Thesis, by J. Liao, University of Derby, UK, 1999".

Words and Expressions

1. intervene [intəˈviːn] vi. 干涉，干预，插入，介入，（指时间）介于其间
2. intensity [inˈtensiti] n. 强烈，剧烈，强度；亮度
3. edge detection 边缘识别
4. segmentation [segmenˈteiʃən] n. 分割
5. quantification [ˈkwɔtifikeiʃən] n. 量化
6. spatial [ˈspeiʃ(ə)l] adj. 空间的
7. spectrum [ˈspektrəm] n. 光，光谱，频谱
8. A/D converter A/D 转换器
9. occlusion [əˈkluːʒen] n. 闭塞
10. neighborhood averaging 邻域平均法
11. median filtering 中值过滤法
12. operators [ˈɔpəreitə(r)] n. 算子
13. cross differences 交叉差分
14. region growing 区域增长法

Unit 18　Virtual Reality Applications

> During reading the text, try to answer the following questions:
> 1. What is the VR?
> 2. What is the advantage of the VR?
> 3. Which fields are the VR applied in? Give some examples.
> 4. When have the VR been applied in the engineering?
> 5. Why the full potential of VR cannot be enjoyed today?
> 6. Are there any examples of the application of the VR in the engineering? If there are, please introduce some of them.
> 7. What's the change in the car industry?
> 8. Why VR is perceived as a complementary technology?
> 9. How long was an aero engine designed and measured in the traditional way?
> 10. Why does the aero engine design need the VR?

1. Introduction

The term "virtual reality" (VR) essentially denotes the creation of realistic looking world scenarios by the use of computer graphics simulation techniques which in turn can be connected to Computer Aided Design (CAD) data banks. A distinctive feature of VR products is that the synthetic world scenarios are not static but dynamic: the user can interact with them in various ways in real time.

It has been said that VR is a technology looking for an application. Who ever coined this phrase might have been justified at the time, but today it is no longer true. VR is not so much a technology, but more a mode of computer interaction—and as computers are now firmly integrated into every facet of modern society, VR is here to stay and will become a natural feature of computer systems.

It is very easy to go overboard with ambitious predictions as to how VR systems will be used, but this would serve no real purpose. What is useful is to examine practical applications that are being explored today, and stand a reasonable chance of success.

Virtual environments (VE) have played a significant role in flight training over the past two decades, and they will continue to do so in the future. Their use has demonstrated that they possess distinct advantages over physical scale model, and there is no way that the flight simulation industry could ever return to model making. Models still play an important role in various industries such as architecture, aero engine design, aircraft design, medicine and car design. Although it is hard to imagine that these industries will abandon all forms of physical models in the future, there are obvious reasons why virtual models should be used for visualizations, simulations and assessing new servicing and manufacturing strategies.

Once a virtual object exists, it can be subjected to many forms of manipulative procedures. For example: it can be decorated with colour and texture; illuminated with different lighting configurations; and dimensions can be adjusted to satisfy optimum layouts. The user can explore the environment to obtain an insight into how it would look if it existed. The ramifications of this approach to design create endless possibilities for stage designers, lighting design, animators and car designers. Introduce a fully jointed virtual human figure such as Jack, and the environment can be evaluated for a wide range of ergonomic condition.

A VE can be subjected to Finite Element Analysis (FEA) techniques to identify areas of stress. It can be subjected to Computational Fluid Dynamics (CFD) techniques to discover air or fluid flow around the object, and surface temperature profiles. The VE can even be subjected to other mathematical procedures that can be used to predict its behavior under different physical conditions. All of these techniques are familiar operations in the world of computer graphics, and they are rapidly becoming part of the world of VR where parameters can be adjusted in real time and the user is part of the environment.

Not all applications demand that the user be immersed within a VE. Total immersion will have invaluable benefits in some areas, partial immersion in others, and desktop systems will serve another community. Obviously it would be "exciting" to stand next to a virtual human mannequin as it attempted to reach inside an aero engine to access an oil filter casing, but if immersion does not provide any advantages over a non-immersive system, then there is no need to use it.

2. Engineering and Industrial Concept Design

The virtual domain is not new to the engineering community; for two decades they have successfully applied CAD and CAM techniques to design and manufacturing processes. Preparing 2D schematics of wiring diagrams, floor layouts, designs for PCBs and ASICs are everyday activities in engineering industries. Similarly, 3D CAD systems have been used to design everything from a shoe to an oil rig.

The computer has now become the most powerful design tool ever created. This is not just because of its speed or its ability to display images—it is because of the computer's flexibility to change its role. It can be used to process text and organize documents; but the same machine can be used to develop line drawings, and even construct 3D objects. Geometric information from these objects can be used to control lathes and milling machines, and, with the process of stereo—lithography, create a real physical representation.

For these systems, the virtual domain has been nothing more than a framework for storing descriptions of 2D and 3D entities, and the workstation screen has just been a convenient projection space to view them. VR provides anther role for the computer, whereby the virtual domain becomes 3D spaces that can be explored by the user. Descriptions of engineering components that have been viewed as animated objects. VR has opened a door to a virtual engineering space where objects can be manufactured, inspected, assembled, tested and subjected to all sorts of simulations.

The full potential of VR cannot be enjoyed today as hardware and software tools are still under developing their own systems.

Telecoms engineering

BNR Europe manufactures and supplies telecommunication equipment and services. In the past, planning the installation of a new system has been carried out using a CAD system to design the new products, then building physical models and placing all the equipment into the available space. Using a desktop VR system, they are able to visualize the allotted room and all the equipment, and then make decisions about possible layouts, cable runs and maintenance access.

Industrial concept design

In terms of choice, the car industry has moved from one extreme to another. Henry Ford's secret was mass production of one model type, with one colour. Today's car industry pride itself on its ability to give customers exactly what they want, even to the choice of seat covering, alloy wheels and type of CD player!

To provide this level of flexibility requires complex systems support, and manufacturing a continuous range of car body shapes requires a constant evaluation of concept designs. Fortunately, computers are part of both activities, which is why VR is perceived as a complementary technology.

All sorts of techniques are used to visualize concept designs, from artists impressions and scale models, to life-size working replicas. VR provides another approach, and although it still requires some form of modelling, it does remove the need for any physical representation.

Researchers at the Computer Aided Industrial & Information Design Center at Coventry University are working in collaboration with Division Ltd on an immersive VR system for use in industrial concept design and evaluation. This collaborative project will investigate how designers can interact with virtual concept cars, and how such designs can be evaluated for functional correctness, ease of assembly and even maintainability. In the later stages of the project, the research team expect to use VR to check assembly and fit of their designs in moving or articulated components such as doors. It will also be possible to determine if a mechanic can actually reach certain components. It is hoped that the cost saving VR will bring over conventional mock-up development will allow earlier trials to be performed, increasing design quality and efficiency.

3. Simulator

System Concept

A traditional flight simulator is built using a replica of the cockpit of the aircraft being simulated. Building a replica cockpit is expensive, as a different replica cockpit is needed for every type of aircraft to be simulated, and it is difficult to keep up with changes made to the real aircraft. Conceptually, it would be better to have a virtual cockpit in which the elements of the cockpit are determined entirely by software. Then the expense of the constructing physical replicas could be saved, one simulator can be used for many different types of aircraft, and after the simulators are in service the simulator could be quickly updated to reflect modification of real aircraft.

For a virtual cockpit, the appearance of the cockpit can be represented by computer generated imagery on a head-mounted display (HMD) worn by the user. The fidelity of this approach is limited by the resolution of the HMD and by the realism of the computer generated imagery for display. HMD technology and generated imagery technology are such that the best currently available technology is probably barely acceptable for the application, and even then at relatively high cost. However, current trends toward low cost and improved performance should close the performance gap considerably within a few years' time.

In addition to a visual simulation, a virtual cockpit also needs a simulation of the force and tactile sensations of touching the controls. The controls include primary controls and the instrument panel controls. The primary controls are the joystick and rudder pedals or their equivalents for steering the aircraft. The instrument panel controls include switches, knobs, push buttons, and keypads. Replica controls could be provided to be used with the simulated imagery, but doing so would not meet the objective of having a simulator that is reconfigurable in software [Fig. 18.1].

Fig. 18.1 Concept of positioning instrument controls to be touched in a virtual cockpit

For the prototype virtual cockpit discussed here, replicas would be used for primary controls, but a software reconfigurable approach was adopted for instrument panel controls. Because the simulator user is wearing a head mounted display, and because the user touched only one instrument control at a time, it suffice to present to the user only the single control being touched. This is accomplished by using a collection of a dozen different types of physical replicas of controls, and putting the correct type to correct place to be touched whenever the user actuates a control.

To select the correct type of the control and put it into place, the user's hand and actuated. A user may believe that different toggle switches are being flipped at different places on the instrument panel, but in fact the same toggle switch is being touched in all the different positions. A mechanism must be provided to put the switch in the correct "up" or "down" position while the switch is moved to a new position. Similarly, the rotary controls must be brought into correspondence with the way each control appears in the imagery.

For the concept to be practical, the few replica controls must be moved rapidly to stay ahead of the user's hand motions. The requirements were quantified by analyzing cockpit videotapes taken in flight and also videotapes taken in a lab setup. In the lab, a number of non-pilot subjects were videotaped as they actuated switches and knobs in a prescribed sequence.

Timing requirements were determined by stepping through the videotapes frame-by-frame and recording the times required to reach the controls. The derived requirements were that the controls must be repositioned with an acceleration of up to four g's and a speed of about three meters per second. Maximum acceleration and deceleration are required when closely-spaced controls are actuated in sequence.

System configuration

The system is designed with three major subsystems, one each for robotics, tracking, and visual simulation [Fig. 18.2]. Each subsystem is controlled by its own computer, with communication links transferring data among the three control computers.

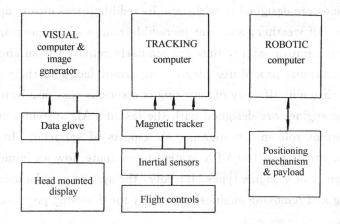

Fig. 18.2 Three major subsystems are used

The tracking subsystem is built around a personal computer running the QNX real time operating system. The tracking computer interfaces with the hardware that measures the position and orientation of the user's head and hands and runs software that filters and extrapolates the tracking data. It determines which switch the user is about to actuate and sends commands to the robotics subsystem to move the selected switch into place. It keeps track of the orientations to which the knobs and toggle switches are moved. It also interfaces to the flight control joystick and throttle and computes the position of the simulated aircraft. The tracking computer sends the positions and orientations of the head and hand, and of the switches, to the visual simulation subsystem, which in turn generates imagery for viewing.

The robotics subsystem includes a VME-rack with a control processor and interfaces, servo power supplies and amplifiers, and power distribution circuitry. The VME-based control processor receives high level commands from the tracking computer over a 56 Kb serial interface. The commands form the tracking computer instruct the robotics subsystem to move each of the servo-driven positioning mechanisms to prescribed locations. The robotics control processor carries out the commands by generating voltage controls for each of the servo-motors. The motors are equipped with digital shaft encoders and each motor channel is run closed-loop with an updated rate of approximately 100Hz. Each channel is tuned for the inertia and spring constants associated with the channels' hardware.

The visual subsystem is built around a Silicon Graphics Onyx computer having a Reality

Engine2 image generator. The visual computer receives data from the tracking subsystem over a dedicated Ethernet link having less than one millisecond latency. The visual computer has a database of polygons modeling the cockpit interior, the user's hand, and terrain outside the simulated aircraft. It assembles the scene from the polygon models, putting each model in its correct relative position. A dataglove worn by the user provides the positions of the fingers directly to the visual computer.

4. Aero engine design

An aero engine involves years of design, and its operational lifetime is often measured in decades. The engines are designed to withstand incredible forces during operation, and must function in all types of weather, and over incredible ranges of temperature and atmospheric conditions. In the pursuit of safety, they are regularly removed from aircraft, serviced and replaced. Such operational procedures play an important factor in their purchase, and any reputation arising through difficulty of servicing is a serious cost disadvantage.

Although aero engines are designed with the lasted CAD systems, full size prototypes still play an important role in investigating all aspects of servicing. In 1994, McDonnell Douglas acquired a Pro Vision 100 VPX system to evaluate how an immersive environment could aid the design of new engine types. Initially, the system is to be used to explore procedures for installing and removing engines, especially for detecting potential interference with other components.

Removing an engine from an aircraft is a complex process, nevertheless, it can be simulated in a virtual environment. An engineer in the VE opens the engine door bay, positions a trailer under the engine bay, and jacks the trailer securing the engine to its housing. The engine is connected to the trailer, then lowered and removed for service. Installation is a similar process performed in reverse. When removed, the virtual engine can be used to evaluate the case with which certain components can be accessed and removed. Collision detection is a powerful technique for discovering whether specific tools can access certain engine parts, and discovering whether components can be easily removed.

The tangible benefits of introducing a VR system are fewer mock-ups and prototypes, earlier design testing and reduced costs.

Rolls-Royce: aero engine maintenance

Rolls-Royce uses Computer Vision's CADDS4X system to design products such as their Trent aero engine. They also rely upon physical mock-ups to assess maintenance issues, before commencing the engine's manufacture. Although these physical mock-ups do not function, their construction must be sound and accurate, which makes them very expensive to build. In 1992, Rolls-Royce approached ARRL (Advanced Robotics Research Laboratory, Salford, UK) now renamed InSys, Ltd, to see whether VR technology could remove the need to construct replicas of their engines.

The first stage in the feasibility study involved an investigation of the portability of the CADDS4X files of the Trent 800 civil engine onto ARRL's VR platform-Division's Super Vision system. This was a non-trivial exercise. Owing in part to the solid modeling nature of CADDS4X. However, by using the CADDS4X stereo-lithography processing option, the first port of the Trent engine casing and lower bifurcation pipe assembly was achieved in the form of simple flat-shaded groups of polygons. Recent work has identified a more efficient and robust CADDS data conversion path, which is being refined at the time of writing.

A series of polygon optimization programs were written to improve the "fly-through" speed of the virtual models. Additional routines were then written to colour-code individual pipe routes selectively, and to segment pipes into groups of objects, thereby allowing detail switching and their removal and manipulation by engineers.

The feasibility study culminated in a successful demonstration of the VR system, and the work continues.

Selected from "1063-6390/97 1997 IEEEE by Roy Latham, 1997".

Words and Expressions

1. distinctive [diˈstiŋktiv]   adj. 与众不同的，有特色的
2. coin [kɔin]   vt. 造新词
3. scenario [siˈnɑːriəv]   n. 想象的场景，游戏的关
4. facet [ˈfæsit]   n. 事物的不同的面，（宝石等的）刻面
5. synthetic [sinˈθetik]   adj. 合成的，综合的
6. demonstrate [demənstreit]   vt. 演示，示例，论证
7. ramification [ræmifiˈkeiʃ(ə)n]   n. 分支，分叉，衍生物，支流
8. visualization [ˌvizjuəlaiˈzeiʃən]   n. 可视化
9. manipulative [məˈnipjulətiv]   adj. 操纵的，控制的
10. ergonomic [əːgənɒmik]   adj. 人类环境改造学的
11. simulator [ˈsimjuleitə(r)]   n. 模拟器，仿真器
12. replica [ˈreplikə]   n. 复制品
13. inertia [iˈnəːʃjə]   n. 惯性；惯量；惰性
14. cockpit [ˈkɔkpit]   n. 驾驶员座舱，战场
15. knob [nɔb]   n. 旋钮，球形捏手
16. fidelity [fiˈdeliti；(US)faiˈdeləti]   n. 保真度，重现精度
17. tactile [ˈtæktail]   adj. 触觉的
18. rudder [ˈrʌdə(r)]   n. 舵，方向舵
19. quivalent [iˈkwivələnt]   n. 等价物，相等物
20. keypad [ˈkiːpæd]   n. 键区
21. oilrig [ɔilrig]   n. 开采石油设备
22. tackle [ˈtæk(ə)l]   vt. 应付（难事等），处理，解决
23. schematics [skiˈmætik]   n. 图表
24. allotted   n. 分配，充当，依靠
25. perceive [pəˈsiːv]   vt. 察觉；   v. 感知，感到，认识到

26. complementary [ˌkɔmpləˈmentəri] adj. 补充的，补足的
27. articulate [ɑːˈtikjuleit] vt. 接合
28. incredible [inˈkredib(ə)l] adj. 难以置信的
29. Rolls-Royce [ˈrəulzˈrɔis] n. 劳斯莱斯（著名的航空发动机生产公司，同时生产顶级汽车）
30. mock-up [ˈmɔkʌp] n. 实验或教学用的实物大模型，伪装工事
31. assess [əˈses] vt. 估定，评定
32. maintenance [əˈmeintinəns] n. 维护，保持
33. commence [kəˈmens] v. 开始，着手
34. sound [saund] adj. 健全的，可靠的，合理的，健康的
35. feasibility [ˌfiːzəˈbiləti] n. 可行性，可能性
36. investigation [inˌvestiˈgeiʃ(ə)n] n. 调查，研究
37. portability [ˌpɔːtəˈbiləti, ˌpəu-] n. 可移植性
38. stereo-lithography 立体印刷术
39. robust [rəuˈbʌst] adj. 鲁棒性，强健的
40. fly-through 浏览
41. bifurcation [ˌbaifəˈkeiʃən] n. 分叉，分歧
42. tangible [ˈtændʒib(ə)l] adj. 切实的
43. polygon [ˈpɔligɔn] n. 多边形
44. collision detection 冲突检测，碰撞检测
45. shaft [ʃɑːft] n. 轴，杆状物
46. servo [ˈsəːvəu] n. 伺服，伺服系统
47. throttle [ˈθrɔt(ə)l] v. 扼杀
48. encoder [enˈkəudə(r)] n. 译码器，编码器
49. latency [ˈleitənsi] n. 反应时间，滞后时间
50. terrain [teˈrein] n. 地形
51. extrapolate [eksˈtræpəleit] v. 传送，推断，外推
52. toggle [ˈtɔg(ə)l] n. 触发器，切换
53. actuate [ˈæktjueit] vt. 开动，促使

Exercise

1. Fill in the spaces in your own words according to content of the text.
   ① The term "virtual reality" (VR) essentially denotes the creation of realistic looking world scenarios by the _____ which in turn can be connected to Computer Aided Design (CAD) data banks. A distinctive feature of VR products is that the synthetic world scenarios are not _____ but _____: the user can interact with them _____.
   ② Once a virtual object exists, it can be subjected to _____. For example: it can be decorated with _____ and _____; illuminated with different lighting configurations; and dimensions can be adjusted to _____.

③ The computer has now become the most powerful design tool ever created. This is not just because of its _____ to display images——it is because of the computer's flexibility to _____.

④ VR provides anther role for the computer, whereby the virtual domain becomes 3D spaces that can be _____. Descriptions of engineering components that have been viewed as _____. VR has opened a door to a virtual engineering space where objects can be _____, _____, _____, to all sorts of simulations.

⑤ An engineer in the VE opens _____, positions _____ under the engine bay, and jacks the trailer _____ to its housing.

⑥ The tangible benefits of introducing a VR system are _____ and _____, _____ and _____.

⑦ A series of _____ were written to improve the "fly-through" speed of the virtual models. Additional routines were then written to colour code individual pipe routes selectively, and to segment pipes into groups of objects, thereby allowing _____ and _____ by engineers.

2. Put the following words and phrases in English:
计算机辅助设计   印刷板电路插座   特定用途集成电路   工业概念设计
虚拟现实   优化设计   有限元分析   计算流体动力学

Reading Material 18

Human Factors Modeling

JACK

The human figure has always posed a tantalizing problem area for computer animation. It is very difficult to model, and to endow it with true-to-life animated behavior is a daunting task. Although the animation community set themselves these problems as interesting challenges in the 1980s, the research is now finding another application in human factors modeling. The challenge today is to develop interactive environments where a fully jointed human figure can be used to evaluate virtual 3D worlds. Jack is probably the most well-known system available today, and was developed by the center for Computer Graphics Research, at the University of Pennsylvania.

PHYSICAL ATTRIBUTES

Jack is a virtual 3D human model incorporating 68 joints—16 of which are in one hand. The torso is segmented and constrained to move within the limits associated with real humans. Joints can be positioned by translations and rotations within predefine constraints, and limb segments possess attributes such as center of mass and moment of inertia. With these qualities, the model can be subjected to dynamic is simulations to reveal its behavior under changes in velocity. Apart from these powerful dynamic features, Jack's anthropometry can be based upon a particular individual or male or female percentiles. An internal database of human characteristics was derived from the General Forces Data ANSUR-88, compiled from 10000 people.

INVERSE KINEMATICS

Jack is animated using inverse kinematics and possesses various motor reflexes such as grabbling, reaching while retaining balance, direction stepping and reorienting behaviors. Thus if instructed to lean forward to grasp an object, it will automatically attempt to retain its balance by adjusting its center of gravity.

When grabbing an object, collision detection is used to ensure that Jack's hand does not penetrate the object being grasped. When its hands are attached to a steering wheel, for example, and the wheel is turned, the entire body will adjust to accommodate the wheel's new orientation.

ERGONOMICS

When Jack is placed inside a virtual environment, it is possible to explore human factors such as reach space, field of view, joint torque load and collision. Thus it can quickly be established whether it can reach controls and see specific parts of moving machinery. It is also possible to discover if the body is placed under any painful strain. This is possible as realistic loadings are known for the joints and limbs, and during any virtual exercise these forces and torques can be monitored for potential overload conditions.

COLLISION AVOIDANCE

Collision avoidance is a property where Jack automatically moves to avoid being hit by a moving object. For instance, if a ball is thrown at the head, Jack will automatically take avoiding action. Furthermore, Jack can be set walking within an environment and instructed to avoid obstacles such as walls or furniture. It can even be endowed with "virtual sight" that enables it to search out an object hidden away behind a wall. This is implemented by "force fields". The hidden object emits an attractive field, while objects emit a repulsing field.

We can imagine many scenarios where Jack could be used to evaluate the suitability of an interior for future use, or the practicality of servicing a complex mechanical structure. Environments that come to mind include the design of cockpits, cars, kitchens, aero engines, ships, spacecraft and military vehicles. In fact, anywhere ergonomic issues are important.

Jack has recently been evaluated as a virtual soldier for training military personnel in various combat duties. When projected onto large video screens, Jack is animated in real time to mimic behavior patterns associated with weapon handling. Real soldiers can then train with Jack to develop appropriate combat skills.

Perhaps it will not be long before we have a virtual assistant to help us undertake a whole range of virtual experiments. Why, for example, should it not be possible to assemble a structure with the aid of someone like Jack? We could even instruct a team of Jacks to collectively solve a problem for us!

Whatever the future holds, virtual humans will play an important role in VR applications, and today we are only at the beginning of a very exciting era of computer simulation.

VIRTUAL SENSORS

Virtual sensors are a software abstraction that provide a simple and consistent programming paradigm for representing and using position and orientation information. They serve as a device independent repository for position and orientation information. From the application programmer's perspective, virtual sensors hide all the issues associated with controlling and monitoring hardware devices. The programmer neither knows nor cares which device generates the information that effects a particular object. From the device programmer's perspective, virtual sensors hide the application program's structures and associations. The device programmer needs only to update one virtual sensor when its associated detector generates a new value. The device programmer does not care that virtual sensor effects multiple objects within the virtual environment.

Virtual sensors decouple the generation of information from its use. This allows us to replace one input device by another input device or even by software that acts like an input device. The decoupling of generation from use also enables concurrency. The code that generates a virtual sensor's data can run concurrently with the code that uses that information.

Virtual sensors act like active values. Device handlers update virtual sensors as soon as they receive new position and orientation information from their devices. Rendering, collision detection, and other application software can perform their computation using a moving object's most recent position and orientation because they have local access to the object's current position and orientation and its associated virtual sensor's position and orientation.

Others have constructed rationalizations of input devices. There are toolkits and commercial VR systems that provide support for plug replaceable input devices. There are software systems that provide control over virtual objects that move. Virtual sensors provide more than a method for replacing devices in a transparent fashion or moving objects in the virtual environment. They provide a coherent methodology for handling any sort of virtual object that moves, whether that object is directly attached to input device or to software that animates its motion. Some definition

In this paper, we use the term *pose* to refer to a six degree-of-freedom position and orientation with respect to some fixed coordinate system. We also distinguish between the terms detector and tracker on the one hand and virtual sensor or sensor on the other.

The terms *tracking device*, *tracker*, and *detector* always refer to physical objects. A tracking device or tracker refers to the hardware box that provides the controlling computer with the pose information for each of its detectors. Detectors, in turn, are associated with each moveable, real-word object whose position and orientation effects the virtual environment. Detectors can wok in a fixed coordinate system associated with the tracker or in one associated with tracked object's initial pose. During a measurement cycle, the tracking device gathers each detector's current pose, packages the poses into a single data record, and transmits the composite record to the computer.

A virtual sensor or sensor is a software abstraction that exists only within the virtual environment. Like detectors, sensors contain pose information and we can associate sensors with objects, but by associating a virtual object with a virtual sensor that object becomes a moveable object. Unlike detectors, a virtual sensor need not have a direct association with a virtual object. Instead, a virtual sensor can serve as a pose repository, an intermediate value, that other sensors can use in computing their poses. In many ways, a sensor acts as the projection of a detector into the virtual world. A virtual sensor in its simplest representation is nothing more than a time-stamped position-orientation matrix——a time-stamped pose. Its pose can come from many sources. The simplest source is a detector. Another view of a sensor is as a projection of a detector onto a virtual sensor. The simplest such projection is the one-to-one mapping of a detector directly onto a sensor.

Selected from "1063-6390/97 1997 IEEEE by Roy Latham, 1997".

Words and Expressions

1. endow [in'dəu] v. 捐赠，赋予
2. tantalizing [tæntəlaiziŋ] adj. 非常着急的
3. daunting [dauntiŋ] adj. 艰巨的，使人畏缩的
4. limb [lim] n. 肢，翼，分支
5. inertia [i'nə:ʃə] n. 惯性，惯量
6. reveal [ri'vi:l] vt. 展现，显示，揭示
7. interactive [intəræktiv] adj. 交互式的
8. torso ['tɔ:səu] n. 未完成的作品（文中指机器人）
9. percentiles 百分位数（值）
10. derive [di'raiv] vi. 起源
11. kinematics [ˌkini'mætiks] n. 运动学
12. anthropometry [ˌænθrə'pɒmitri] n. 人体测量学
13. penetrate ['penitreit] vt. 穿透，渗透
14. mimic ['mimik] adj. 模仿的，假装的
15. torque [tɔ:k] n. 扭矩，转矩
16. repository [ri'pɒzitəri, (US) -tɔ:ri] n. 贮藏室，智囊团，知识库，仓库
17. pose [pəuz] vi. 摆姿势，佯装，矫揉造作
18. paradigm ['pærədaim] n. 范例
19. concurrency [kən'kʌrənsi] n. 并行操作
20. decouple [di:'kʌpl] v. 去耦，分离，减弱
21. rationalization [ˌræʃənəlai'zeiʃən] n. 合理化
22. toolkit n. 工具包
23. time-stamped 时间标记

Unit 19 Bionics Measurement

> Before your reading the text try to answer the following questions:
> 1. What is bionics measurement?
> 2. Why is bionics measurement developped?
> 3. What advant ages does bionics measurement possesses?
> 4. In what cases are bionics measurements usually applied?

In recent years the idea of "learning from nature" is rapidly spreading through a number of scientific communities: computer science (artificial intelligence, artificial evolution, artificial life), engineering (bionics), and robotics (biorobotics). The main goal is to exploit the impressive results achieved by the blind but potent designer "Evolution". Among the most awesome capabilities exhibited by natural systems are the navigational skills of insects. Despite their diminutive brains, many insects accomplish impressive navigation tasks. Desert ants *Cataglyphis*, for example, make foraging excursions that take them up to 200 m away from their nest. On finding a suitable prey, they return home unfailingly and in a straight line (see Fig. 19.1).

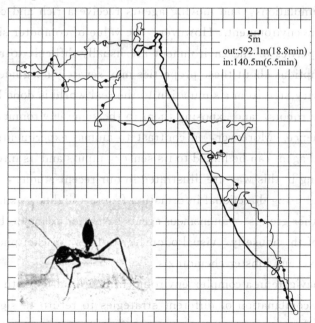

Fig. 19.1 A typical foraging trip of the Saharan ant *Cataglyphis* (inset). Starting at the nest (open circle), the ant searches for food on a random course (thin line) until it finds a prey (position marked with the large filled circle). The food is carried back to the nest on an almost straight course (thick line)

Cataglyphis cannot use pheromones to retrace its trail in order to return back to its nest, since the pheromones evaporate in a few seconds because of the hight ground temperatures. More than two decades of field work have revealed many details about the behavioral repertoire and the underlying mechanisms that *Cataglyphis* employs when homing. The three main strategies used are *path integration*, *visual piloting*, and *systematic search*. Whereas path integration based on compass information gained from the polarization pattern of the sky is the primary navigation strategy of the ants, geocentered information based on landmarks is also used in order to finally pinpoint the nest.

Although there is a large number of behavioral data about the navigation behavior of *Cataglyphis*, and some mechanisms of peripheral signal processing have been unraveled, it is still largely unknown how the navigation system is implemented in the insect's brain. In this paper we use the *autonomous agents* approach to gain additional insights into the navigation behavior of insects. The goal of this approach is to develop an understanding of natural systems by building a robot that mimics some aspects of their sensory and nervous system and their behavior.

This "synthetic" methodology has a number of advantages. Computer simulations of models are a first step of synthetic modeling. While it is often the case that models of biological agents are only described verbally or outlined implicitly, computer simulations require an explicit, algorithmic model, which helps to avoid pitfalls in terms of unwarranted assumptions or glossing over details. Especially the behavior of feedback systems is difficult to predict without simulations, and moving agents receive a rich and complex feedback on their actions from the environment. However, the value of computer simulations is limited by the fact that properties of the environment are usually difficult to reproduce in simulations. Wrong assumptions about these properties may severely misguide the development of models. The necessary step from a simulation to the real world is done by constructing artificial agents (mobile robots) and exposing them to the same environment that also the biological agents experience. Moreover, in contrast to animal experiments, the observed behavior of an artificial agent can be linked to its sensory inputs and its internal state. The advantages of proceeding in this way are illustrated in our recent studies, in which an autonomous agent navigated using directional information from skylight. A similar line of research is also pursued by other groups. Autonomous agents have, for example, been used to study the visuomotor system of the housefly, visual odometry in bees, cricket phonotaxis, six-legged locomotion of insects, and lobster chemotaxis.

The ability to navigate in a complex environment is crucial for both animals and robots. Many animals use a combination of different strategies to return to significant locations in their environment. For example, the desert ant *Cataglyphis* is able to explore its desert habitat for hundreds of meters while foraging and return back to its nest precisely and on a straight line.

The three main strategies that *Cataglyphis* is using to accomplish this task are *path integration*, *visual piloting* and *systematic search*. In this study, we use a synthetic methodology to gain additional insights into the navigation behavior of *Cataglyphis*. Inspired by the insect's navigation system we have developed mechanisms for path integration and visual piloting that were successfully employed on the mobile robot *Sahabot 2*.

On the one hand, the results obtained from these experiments provide support for the underlying biological models. On the other hand, by taking the parsimonious navigation strategies of insects as a guideline, computationally cheap navigation methods for mobile robots are derived from the insights gained in the experiments.

Selected from "D. Lambrinos et al. /Robotics and Autonomous Systems 30 (2000) 39-64" And "Neurobiology Proc. Natl. Acad. Sci. USA Vol. 79, pp. 4451-4455, July 1982".

Words and Expressions

1. artificial [ˌɑːtiˈfiʃəl] adj. 人造的，人工的，假的
2. bionic [baiˈɔnik] adj. 仿生学的，利用仿生学的
3. potent [ˈpəutnt] adj. （药等）效力大的；威力大的
4. awesome [ˈɔːsəm] adj. 令人敬畏的，使人畏惧的，可怕的；棒极了
5. diminutive [diˈminjutiv] adj. 小得出奇的，特小的（指后缀）表示小的
6. excursion [iksˈkəːʃən] n. 远足，短途旅行
7. unfailing [ʌnˈfeiliŋ] adj. 永恒的；无穷的
8. exploit [iksˈplɔit] vt. 开采；开发
9. evolution [ˌiːvəˈluːʃən] n. 演变；进化；发展
10. pheromone [ˈferəmoun] n. 信息素
11. repertoire [ˈrepətwɑː] n. 所有组成部分
12. polarization [ˌpəuləraiˈzeiʃən] n. 极化（作用），两极化
13. unravel [ʌnˈrævəl] vt. 解开；阐明，解决
14. autonomous [ɔːˈtɔnəməs] adj. 自治的
15. natural system 自然系统
16. pitfall [ˈpitfɔːl] n. 陷阱；意想不到的困难；易犯的错误
17. combination [ˌkɔmbiˈneiʃən] n. 结合，组合；联合体，组合物
18. synthetic methodology 合成方法论
19. underlying [ˌʌndəˈlaiiŋ] adj. 根本的，基础的；潜在的
20. biological model 生物模型

Exercises

1. Fill in the blanks in your own words according to the text.

    In recent years the idea of "learning from nature" is rapidly spreading through a number of scientific communities. Among the most awesome (   ) exhibited by (   ) systems are the navigational skills of (   ). Despite their diminutive (   ), many insects accomplish impressive navigation (   ).

    Desert ants Cataglyphis cannot use pheromones to (   ) its trail in (   ) to return back to its (   ), since the pheromones (   ) in a few seconds because of the high ground temperatures. More than two decades of field work have (   ) many details about the behavioral repertoire and the underlying mechanisms that Catalgyphis (   ) when homing. The three main strategies used are path (   ), visual piloting, and (   ).

Although there is a (   ) number of behavioral data about the navigation (   ) of Cataglyphis, and some mechanisms of peripheral signal processing have been unraveled, it is still largely unknown how the navigation system is implemented in the insect's (   ). In this paper we use the autonomous agents (   ) to gain additional insights (   ) the navigation behavior of insects.

The synthetic methodology has a (   ) of advantages. Computer (   ) of models are a first (   ) of synthetic modeling. Moreover, in (   ) to animal experiments, the observed behavior of an artificial agent can be linked (   ) its sensory inputs and its internal state. The advantages of proceeding in this way are illustrated in our recent studies, (   ) which an autonomous agent navigated using directional information from skylight.

2. Put the following into Chinese.

artificial intelligence   navigation task   visual piloting   systematic search
autonomous agent   natural system   computer simulation   algorithmic model
biological model   parsimonious navigation

Reading Material 19

Optical Polarization Based Navigation Technology

MATERIALS AND METHODS

Individually marked bees (*Apis mellifera mellifera*) were trained to an artificial foraging station 400 m away from the hive. Having returned from the foraging station, they performed their waggle dances on a horizontal comb in the center of a translucent Plexiglas hemisphere (Fig. 19.2). This hemisphere depolarized the sky's light completely and thus provided the bees with a homogeneously lit visual surround. Under these conditions the waggle runs were oriented randomly unless the bees were allowed to view at least a single patch of naturally or artificially polarized light through one of the apertures of the hemisphere. When artificial stimuli were used, the light, provided by a xenon arc lamp (400 W), first had to pass through a heat-absorbing filter, a diffuser, a UV filter (UG 11; Schott), and a polarizer (HNP'B; Polaroid) before entering the aperture. The waggle dances were recorded by a video setup and were analyzed later by measuring the directions of the individual waggle runs. To ensure that, while foraging, the bees were exposed to the whole pattern of polarization, all experiments reported here were performed on cloudless days.

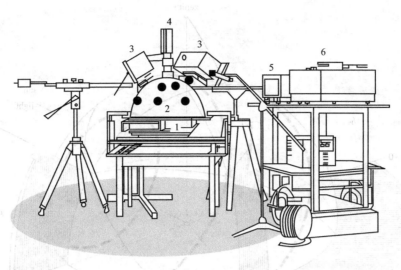

Fig. 19.2 Experimental setup.

1, Horizontally arranged hive containing a single comb. The hive can be moved in the x and y directions. 2, Translucent Plexiglass hemisphere (radius, 33 cm); if the apertures (black dots) are opened, either natural sky light or artificially polarized light can be presented to the bees. 3, Xenon lamps equipped with heat filters, diffusers, spectral filters, and polarizers. 4, TV camera. 5, Monitor. 6, Video recorder.

Now consider the cases shown in Fig. 19.3, Fig. 19.4. This line of maximal polarization positioned 90° off the sun and the antisun forms a prominent line of symmetry of the e-vector pattern.

The situation becomes more complicated when the pattern of sky light is described in terms of the terrestrial system of coordinates, defined by meridians converging toward the zenith (Fig 19.3). Within this system of coordinates a second line of symmetry is defined by the solar and the antisolar meridian. Because, during daytime, the more highly polarized part of the sky is subdivided by the antisolar meridian, its direction can be used as a reference direction ($\phi=0°$) for defining the azimuth direction (ϕ) of any point in the sky presented at a given elevation μ. The directions of polarization (χ) are measured relative to the meridians. The directions of those e-vectors that lie along the line of maximal polarization are indicated by χ_{Pmax}. μ_0 defines the elevation of the sun.

Armed with this knowledge, let us emphasize some important spatial and dynamic characteristics of the e-vector pattern (compare Fig. 19.4). (i) Irrespective of the elevation of the sun, the horizontal e-vectors ($\chi=90°$) are located exclusively along both the solar and the antisolar meridian. (ii) The positions of all other e-vector directions vary as a function of the elevation of the sun. (iii). Within the e-vector distribution realized at a given elevation (χ/ϕ function), any one e-vector direction usually occurs twice. The one that is farther from the sun is more strongly polarized than its counterpart closer to the sun. (iv) At least in the upper region of the sky ($\mu>30°$), the azimuth position of any given e-vector direction lying along the line of maximal polarization (χ_{Pmax}) varies only slightly during the

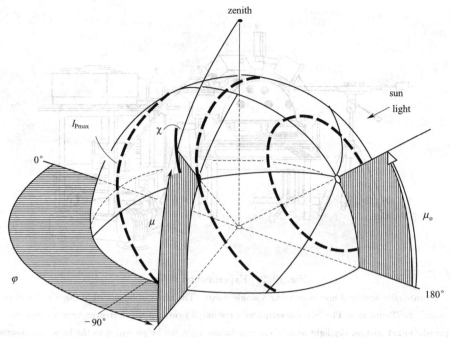

Fig. 19. 3 Pattern of polarized sky light (e-vector pattern) and definitions. The directions of the bars plotted across the celestial sphere denote the e-vector directions; the widths of the bars symbolize the degrees of polarization. Note that the most highly polarized area of the sky occurs at 90° from the sun (I_{Pmax}, line of maximal polarization representing a prominent intrinsic line of symmetry of the e-vector pattern). μ_0, Elevation of the sun. μ, Elevation of a given point in the sky. ϕ, Azimuth position of a given point as measured relative to the antisolar meridian. χ, e-vector direction as measured relative to the meridian. ϕ and χ are positive when counted clockwise and negative when counted anticlockwise.

course of the day. (V) No ambiguities occur within the χ_{Pmax}/ϕ functions. As the only exception to this rule, the vertical e-vectors ($\chi_{Pmax}=0°$) occur twice (opposite to each other and at right angles to the antisolar meridian).

Which of these characteristics of sky-light polarization are known to the bees? The question is answered by displaying to the bee's single patches (diameter, 10°) of polarized UV light. If the bees were informed about the spatial distribution of the e-vectors in the sky, the waggle dances guided by any one e-vector should be oriented correctly—i. e., they should point toward the feeding station. However, such is not the case. Bees exhibit orientation errors that reflect the difference between the actual azimuth position of the given e-vectors in the sky and the corresponding azimuth position assumed by the bees.

Some examples are given for an elevation of $\mu=60°$ and elevations of the sun $60°\geqslant\mu_0\geqslant 30°$. During the course of the experiment, different e-vector directions were displayed, including $\chi=90°$, $+45°$, $-45°$, and $0°$. No orientation errors occurred when horizontal e-vectors ($\chi=90°$) were presented. The bees always interpreted them as lying along the antisolar meridian, as actually is the case in the natural sky. As the sun decreases in elevation from $\mu_0=60°$ to $\mu_0=30°$, the actual azimuth positions of the e-vectors $\chi=+45°$ ($-45°$) as

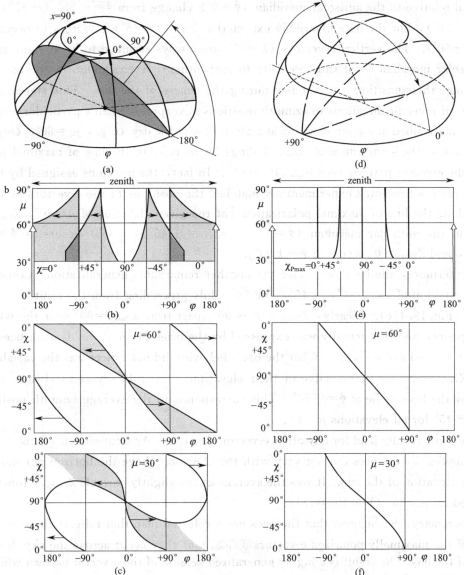

Fig. 19.4 Distribution of e-vector directions in the sky. (a) The e-vector directions are always perpendicular to the plane defined by the direction of the sun and the observed point in the sky. Consequently, with the sole exception of the horizontal e-vectors ($\chi = 90°$) that are positioned along the solar and the antisolar meridian, all e-vectors move toward the climbing sun. In the figure this is demonstrated for a vertical e-vector. The path of the sun is marked by the open arrow. (b) Celestial map (cylindrical equal-spaced projection) showing the azimuth positions of the e-vector directions $\chi = 90°$, $+45°$, $-45°$, and $0°$ (stippled areas) as they vary with the elevation of the sun ($0° \leq \mu_0 \leq 60°$). The solid arrows indicate the direction in which the e-vectors move when the sun moves up (open arrow). $\phi = 0°$ and $\mu = 0°$ mark the antisolar meridian and the horizon, respectively. (c) e-vector distribution for two elevations ($\mu = 60°$ and $\mu = 30°$) and different elevations of the sun ($0° \leq \mu_0 \leq 60°$). The solid arrows indicate the direction in which the e-vectors move when the sun moves up. Note that, at a given elevation, identical e-vector directions may occur twice (the stippled areas mark those e-vectors that are farther from the sun). In the text, these e-vector distributions are referred to as χ/ϕ functions. (d) When the sun moves up (open arrow), the line of maximal polarization tilts down. Thus, during the course of the day, all directions of polarization $0° \leq \chi \leq 90°$ get exposed along the line of maximal polarization. (e) Celestial map (cylindrical equal-spaced projection) showing the azimuth positions of $\chi_{Pmax} = 90°$, $\pm 45°$, and $0°$, as set by the daily movement of the line of maximal polarization. It is important to note that this map does not represent any actual pattern in the sky but comprises the azimuth positions of χ_{Pmax} as they occur during the course of the day (compare d). $\phi = 0°$ and $\mu = 0°$ mark the antisolar meridian and the horizon, respectively. (f) Distribution of the maximally polarized e-vectors for elevations $\mu = 60°$ and $\mu = 30°$ [(χ_{Pmax}/ϕ) functions]. The functions result from the daily movement of the line of maximal polarization.

measured relative to the antisolar meridian ($\phi=0°$) change from $\phi=-85°$ ($+85°$) to $\phi=-55°$ ($+55°$), but the bees invariably expect the $+45°$ ($-45°$) e-vectors to occur at $\phi=-50°$ ($+50°$). The vertical e-vectors ($\chi=0°$) are always assumed to lie at right angles to the antisolar meridian (and thus opposite to each other), even though in the natural sky they change their position continuously during the course of the day. This stereotyped assignment of e-vector directions to azimuth positions also applies when a particular e-vector direction is not realized at a given elevation at a given time of the day (e.g., $\mu_0=60°$, $\chi=0°$).

To assess the significance of these findings let us refer to the line of maximal polarization of the e-vector pattern (see Fig. 19.4(e)). In fact, the positions assigned by the bees to the e-vectors presented experimentally matched the positions of the e-vectors as they occurred along the line of maximal polarization [at the given elevation of $\mu=60°$, $\chi_{Pmax}=90°$ occurs on the antisolar meridian ($\phi=0°$), $\chi_{Pmax}=+45°$ ($-45°$) occurs at $\phi=-48°$ ($+48°$), and $\chi_{Pmax}=0°$ occurs at $\phi=\pm90°$].

Furthermore, the bees performed yet another remarkable generalization. Consider the azimuth position of $\chi_{Pmax}=0°$, $\pm45°$, and $90°$ while proceeding from the zenith toward the horizon (Fig. 19.4(e). Clearly, $\chi_{Pmax}=0°$ is $90°$ apart from $\chi_{Pmax}=90°$ over the whole celestial sphere, and this actually was expressed by the orientation of the dancing bees whenever they viewed a $0°$ e-vector. What the bee's behavior did not reflect was the variable position of $\chi_{Pmax}=\pm45°$. Irrespective of their elevation, the $\pm45°$ e-vectors always were assumed by the bees to lie at $\phi=\mp50°$. This corresponds to the average azimuth positions of $\chi_{Pmax}=\pm45°$ for all elevations $\mu>30°$.

The same results held for any other e-vector direction. As a consequence, the χ/ϕ function as applied by the bees did not vary with the elevation above the horizon nor did it vary with the elevation of the sun. It was the average of the slightly variable χ_{Pmax}/ϕ functions as computed for $\mu>30°$ (Fig. 19.4(f)).

In summary, we suggest that the bees use a celestial map that reflects the mean distribution of the maximally polarized e-vectors (χ_{Pmax}) as they occur across the sky during the course of the day. The result is a highly generalized version of the e-vector pattern which does not vary during the day.

Several additional findings support this hypothesis. First, in assigning e-vector directions to azimuth positions, the bee uses its generalized χ/ϕ function when confronted not only with an artificial e-vector but also with patches of the natural blue sky. Even when it views a rather large part of the sky, subtending a visual angle of $40°$, it makes exactly the mistakes that can be predicted from its χ/ϕ function. Second, the bee's stereotyped χ/ϕ function also applies when, at a particular elevation, a given e-vector direction is realized twice (see Fig. 19.4(c)).

Selected from "Neurobiology *Proc. Natl" Acad. Sci. USA* Vol. 79, pp. 4451-4455, July 1982".

Words and Expressions

1. translucent [trænz'luːsnt] adj. 半透明的

2. depolarize [ˌdiːˈpəuləraiz] vt. 去极化，去偏极，去偏光
3. homogeneous [ˌhɔməˈdʒiːnjəs] adj. 同性质的，同类的
4. azimuth [ˈæziməθ] n. 方位角
5. meridian [məˈridiən] n. 子午圈，子午线
6. irrespective [ˌirisˈpektiv] adj. 不考虑的，不问的，不顾的
7. ambiguity [ˌæmbiˈgjuiti] n. 歧义，模棱两可的意思
8. waggle [ˈwægl] n. 来回摇动；摇摆
9. generalization [ˌdʒenərəlaiˈzeiʃn] n. 概括，归纳；概说
10. celestial [siˈlestjəl] adj. 天体的，天体导航法的
11. hypothesis [haiˈpɔθisis] n. 假说，假设，前提
12. confront [kənˈfrʌnt] vt. 勇敢地面对，正视，遭遇

Unit 20 Embedded System Supporting Control Process

> Before reading the text try to answer the following questions:
> 1. What is embedded system?
> 2. What important constrains of digital controller of embedded system hardware are normally included?
> 3. What application case of embedded system can be seen in industry?
> 4. Of what application characteristic (s) usually is an embedded system?

1. Overview

Embedded systems are usually single function applications. Various functional constraints associated with embedded systems are low cost, single-to-fewer components, low power, provide real-time response and support of hardware-software co-existence. A general methodology used in designing an embedded system is shown in Table 20.1.

The decision on the kind of digital platform to be used takes place during the system architecture phase as each embedded application is linked with its unique operational constraints. Some of the constraints of a digital controller of embedded system hardware include (in no particular order) the following:

- Real-time update rate
- Power
- Cost
- Single chip solution
- Ease of programming
- Portability of code
- Libraries of re-usable code
- Programming tools.

Table 20.1 Embedded system design flow

Design Phase	Design Phase details
Requirements	Functional and non-functional reqirements(size,weight,power consumption and cost)
User specifications	User interface details along with operations needed to satisfy user request
Architecture	Hardware components(processor, perihperals, programmable logic and ASSPs), software components (major programms and their operations)
Component design	Pre-designed components, modified components and new components
System intergration (hardware and software)	Verification scheme to uncover bugs quickly

2. Case Study

For understanding different digital design platforms. this text uses the design of a digital controller for a robot as a case study. The robot is a hypothetical, vertically articulated robot system for an automated assembly line. The process of desigining this controller will help in understanding various digital design concepts. Figure 20. 1. shows the various components of an assembly line robot. Each robot consists of live electric motors that work as actuaters for different joints of the robot. A programming pendant or workstation is used to program the movements of the robot along with a communications network to link this robot to other robots on the assembly line. Various sensors are interfaced to the robot control system.

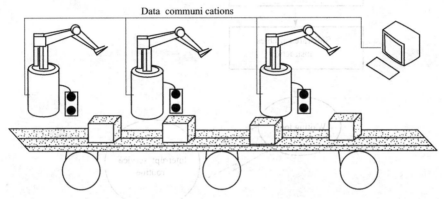

Fig. 20. 1 Verically articulated robot system
used in an assembly line environment

Till the 1970s, electronic system designs were based on discrete analogue components such as transistors, operational amplifiers, resistors, capacitors and inductors. These circuits offered concurrent processing but had problems of parameter drift with temperature and ageing. The coming of TTL-based components laid the foundation of digital design. The Intel 4004 microprocessor became the first digital platform which was configurable using software. Table 20. 2 lists the major contemporary digital designs along with their relative merit.

Table 20. 2 Digital design platforms

Digital design platform	Merit
Microprocessors	Reconfigurable using software. Good for computations
Microcontrollers digital signal controllers	Combination of peripherals and CPU
Application specific standard product(ASSP)	A specialized peripheral with the ability to communicate with a bost processor
Field programmable gate array(FPGA)	Ability to combine the strengths of processor. controller and ASSP

The microprocessor has changed digital design methodology like no other digital component. It started out as a 4^2 bit programmable CPU in 1971 and still continues to be the digital controller of choice across several application areas. The microprocessor brought the concept of instruction set architecture (ISA), assembler and compiler. There are many real-time applications, with fast update rates require programming the microprocessor in its native assembly language. This is usually done when the size of available memory is a constraint. Even though most commercial microprocessors used today cater to data-centric applications, there are microprocessor cores embedded in microcontrollers for real-time control applications.

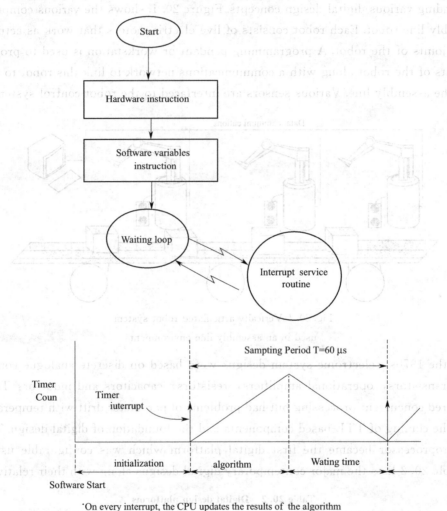

Fig. 20. 2 Interrupt service routine (ISR) based processing scheme of processor-controller control scheme

Digital control systems, like the robot application use a processor by using interrupts for real-time processing. There are interrupts for calculation of robot arm trajectory, encoder and sensor feedback control of motors and networks. Each interrupt will occur based on the update time requirement of the given task. Fig. 20. 2 shows a generic nature of interrupt processing, where an interrupting device seeks CPU attention. A microprocessor-based robot controller carries out the task of arm positioning based on the flowchart shown in Fig. 20. 3.

Because most single core general purpose processors (GPP) are single-threaded (can process one instruction at a time), the processor use can become very high when managing multiple interrupts from different tasks of the robot controller where processor CPU use increases linearly with each motor.

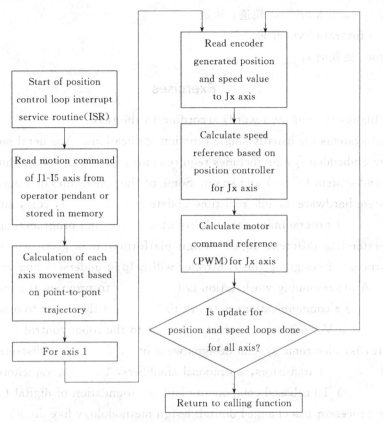

Fig. 20.3 Processor-interrupt-based flowchart needed for computing a control action

Words and Expressions

1. coexistence [ˌkəuigˈzistəns] n. 共存
2. architecture [ˈɑːkitektʃə] n. 构造，结构
3. unique [juːˈniːk] adj. 独一无二的，仅有的，唯一的
4. constraint [kənˈstreint] n. 强制；限制，约束
5. single chip solution 单片解决方案
6. portability of code 代码的可移植性
7. hypothetical [ˌhaipəuˈθetikəl] adj. 假设的，假定的；有待证实的
8. automated assembly line 自动装配线
9. actuator [ˈæktjueitə] n. 执行器，传动装置（机构），拖动装置
10. communication network 通信网络
11. interface [ˈintə(ː)ˌfeis] vi. 连接
12. discrete [disˈkriːt] adj. 分离的，不相关联的
13. operational amplifier 运算放大器
14. concurrent [kənˈkʌrənt] adj. 同时发生的，并存的；合作的
15. configurable [kənˈfigjureit] vt. 使成形，形成

16. contemporary [kən'tempərəri] adj. 当代的，同时代的，同属一个时期的
17. compiler [kəm'pailə] n. 编译程序
18. trajectory ['trædʒiktəri] n. 轨迹；轨道
19. interrupt [ˌintə'rʌpt] vt. 中断
20. update time 更新时间

Exercises

1. Fill in the blanks in your own words according to the text.

Embedded systems are usually single function applications. A general methodology used in designing an embedded system includes requirements, User (   ), architecture, component (   ) and system (   ) and so on. Some of the constraints of a digital controller of embedded system hardware include real-time update rate, (   ), cost, single (   ) solution, ease (   ) programming, portability of (   ) and programming (   ) etc.

For understanding different digital design platforms, it is given a case study as followed. The process of designing this controller will help in understanding various digital design concepts. A programming workstation is (   ) to program the movements of the robot along (   ) a communications network to (   ) this robot to other robots on the assembly (   ). Various sensors are (   ) to the robot control (   ).

Till the 1970s, electronic system designs were based (   ) discrete analogue components such (   ) transistors, operational amplifiers, (   ), capacitors and (   ). The coming (   ) TTL-based components laid the foundation of digital (   ).

The microprocessor has changed digital design methodology like no other digital component. The microprocessor brought the concept (   ) instruction set architecture, assembler and compiler. There are many real-time applications, with fast update rates require programming the microprocessor in its (   ) assembly (   ).

2. Put the following into Chinese.

embedded system   low power   real-time   automated assembly line
be linked with   single chip solution   update rate   portability of code

Reading Material 20

The High-performance Microcontroller of Embedded System—ATmega 8

Overview

The ATmega8 is a low-power CMOS 8-bit microcontroller based on the AVR RISC architecture. By executing powerful instructions in a single clock cycle, the ATmega8 achieves throughputs approaching 1 MIPS per MHz, allowing the system designer to optimize power consumption versus processing speed.

Block Diagram

(See Fig. 20. 4)

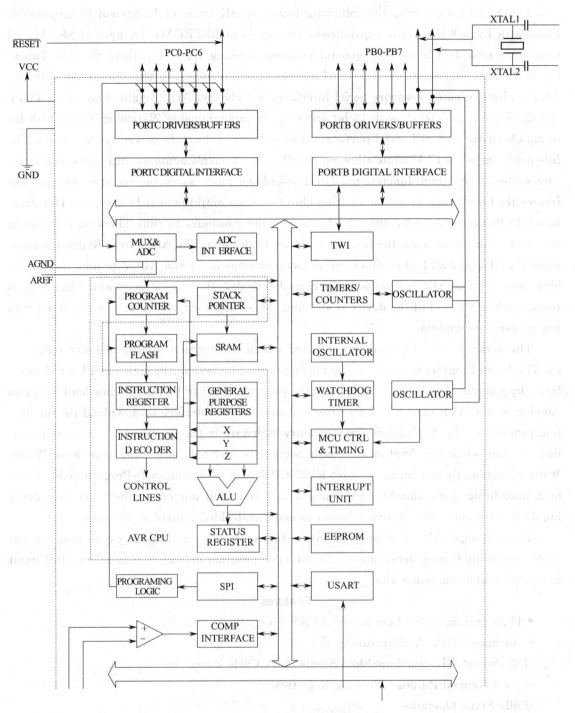

Figure 20.4 Block Diagram

The AVR core combines a rich instruction set with 32 general purpose working registers. All the 32 registers are directly connected to the Arithmetic Logic Unit (ALU), allowing two independent registers to be accessed in one single instruction executed in one clock cycle. The resulting architecture is more code efficient while achieving throughputs up to ten times faster than conventional CISC microcontrollers.

The ATmega8 provides the following features: 8K bytes of In-System Programmable Flash with Read-While-Write capabilities, 512 bytes of EEPROM, 1K byte of SRAM, 23 general purpose I/O lines, 32 general purpose working registers, three flexible Timer/Counters with compare modes, internal and external interrupts, a serial programmable USART, a byte oriented Twowire Serial Interface, a 6-channel ADC (eight channels in TQFP and QFN/MLF packages) with 10-bit accuracy, a programmable Watchdog Timer with Internal Oscillator, an SPI serial port, and five software selectable power saving modes. The Idle mode stops the CPU while allowing the SRAM, Timer/Counters, SPI port, and interrupt system to continue functioning. The Powerdown mode saves the register contents but freezes the Oscillator, disabling all other chip functions until the next Interrupt or Hardware Reset. In Power-save mode, the asynchronous timer continues to run, allowing the user to maintain a timer base while the rest of the device is sleeping. The ADC Noise Reduction mode stops the CPU and all I/O modules except asynchronous timer and ADC, to minimize switching noise during ADC conversions. In Standby mode, the crystal/resonator Oscillator is running while the rest of the device is sleeping. This allows very fast start-up combined with low-power consumption.

The device is manufactured using Atmel's high density non-volatile memory technology. The Flash Program memory can be reprogrammed In-System through an SPI serial interface, by a conventional non-volatile memory programmer, or by an On-chip boot program running on the AVR core. The boot program can use any interface to download the application program in the Application Flash memory. Software in the Boot Flash Section will continue to run while the Application Flash Section is updated, providing true Read-While-Write operation. By combining an 8-bit RISC CPU with In-System Self-Programmable Flash on a monolithic chip, the Atmel ATmega8 is a powerful microcontroller that provides a highly-fiexible and cost-effective solution to many embedded control applications.

The ATmega8 AVR is supported with a full suite of program and system development tools, including C compilers, macro assemblers, program debugger/simulators, In-Circuit Emulators, and evaluation kits.

Features

- High-performance, Low-power AVR® 8-bit Microcontroller
- Advanced RISC Architecture

-130 Powerful Instructions-Most Single-clock Cycle Execution

-32 x 8 General Purpose Working Registers

-Fully Static Operation

-Up to 16 MIPS Throughput at 16 MHz

On-chip 2-cycle Multiplier

- High Endurance Non-volatile Memory segments

-8K Bytes of In-System Self-programmable Flash program memory

-512 Bytes EEPROM

-1K Byte Internal SRAM

-Write/Erase Cycles: 10000 Flash/100000 EEPROM
-Data retention: 20 years at 85℃/100 years at 25℃ [1]
-Optional Boot Code Section with Independent Lock Bits
In-System Programming by On-chip Boot Program
True Read-While-Write Operation
-Programming Lock for Software Security
● Peripheral Features
-Two 8-bit Timer/Counters with Separate Prescaler, one Compare Mode
-One 16-bit Timer/Counter with Separate Prescaler, Compare Mode, and Capture Mode
-Real Time Counter with Separate Oscillator
-Three PWM Channels
-8-channel ADC in TQFP and QFN/MLF package
Eight Channels 10-bit Accuracy
-6-channel ADC in PDIP package
-Six Channels 10-bit Accuracy
-Byte-oriented Two-wire Serial Interface
-Programmable Serial USART
-Master/Slave SPI Serial Interface
-Programmable Watchdog Timer with Seperate On-chip Oscillator
-On-chip Analog Comparator
● Special Microcontroller Features
-Power-on Reset and Programmable Brown-out Detection
-Internal Calibrated RC Oscillator
-External and Internal Interrupt Sources
-Five Sleep Modes: Idle, ADC Noise Reduction, Power-save, Power-down, and Standby
● I/O and Packages
-23 Programmable I/O Lines
-28-lead PDIP, 32-lead TQFP, and 32-pad QFN/MLF
● Operating Voltages
-2.7~5.5V (ATmega8L)
-4.5~5.5V (ATmega8)
● Speed Grades
-0~8 MHz (ATmega8L)
-0~16 MHz (ATmega8)
● Power Consumption at 4 Mhz, 3V, 25℃
-Active: 3.6mA
-Idle Mode: 1.0mA
-Power-down Mode: 0.5μA

Pin Configuration Figures

See Fig. 20.5

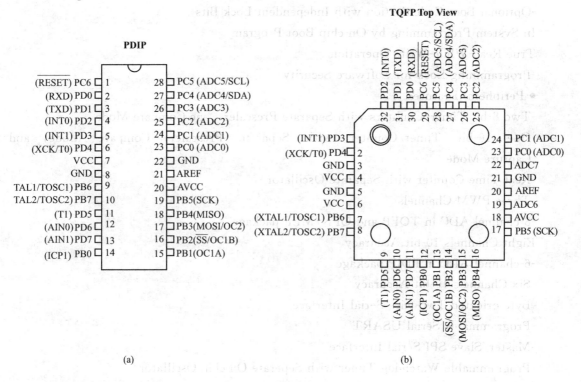

(a)

(b)

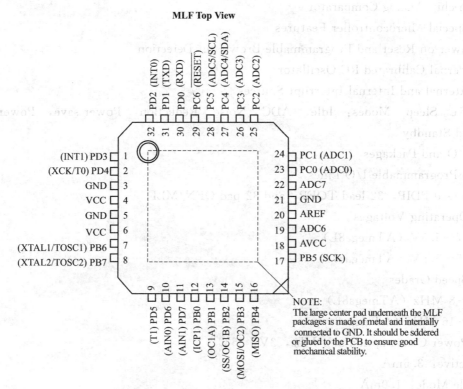

(c)

Fig. 20.5 Pin Configuration

Pin Descriptions

VCC	Digital supply voltage.
GND	Ground.
Port B (PB7 PB0) XTAL1/XTAL2/ TOSC1/TOSC2	Port B is an 8-bit bi-directional I/O port with internal pull-up resistors (selected for each bit). The Port B output buffers have symmetrical drive characteristics with both high sink and source capability. As inputs, Port B pins that are externally pulled low will source current if the pull-up resistors are activated. The Port B pins are tri-stated when a reset condition becomes active, even if the clock is not running.

Depending on the clock selection fuse settings, PB6 can be used as input to the inverting Oscillator amplifier and input to the internal clock operating circuit.

Depending on the clock selection fuse settings, PB7 can be used as output from the inverting Oscillator amplifier.

If the Internal Calibrated RC Oscillator is used as chip clock source, PB7.6 is used as TOSC2.1 input for the Asynchronous Timer/Counter2 if the AS2 bit in ASSR is set.

The various special features of Port B are elaborated in "Alternate Functions of Port B" on page 58 and "System Clock and Clock Options" on page 25. |
| Port C (PC5~PC0) | Port C is an 7-bit bi-directional I/O port with internal pull-up resistors (selected for each bit). The Port C output buffers have symmetrical drive characteristics with both high sink and source capability. As inputs, Port C pins that are externally pulled low will source current if the pull-up resistors are activated. The Port C pins are tri-stated when a reset condition becomes active, even if the clock is not running. |
| PC6/$\overline{\text{RESET}}$ | If the RSTDISBL Fuse is programmed, PC6 is used as an I/O pin. Note that the electrical characteristics of PC6 differ from those of the other pins of Port C.

If the RSTDISBL Fuse is unprogrammed, PC6 is used as a Reset input. A low level on this pin for longer than the minimum pulse length will generate a Reset, even if the clock is not running. The minimum pulse length is given in Table 15 on page 38. Shorter pulses are not guaranteed to generate a Reset.

The various special features of Port C are elaborated on page 61. |
| Port D (PD7~PD0) | Port D is an 8-bit bi-directional I/O port with internal pull-up resistors (selected for each bit). The Port D output buffers have symmetrical drive characteristics with both high sink and source capability. As inputs, Port D pins that are externally pulled low will source current if |

the pull-up resistors are activated. The Port D pins are tri-stated when a reset condition becomes active, even if the clock is not running.

Port D also serves the functions of various special features of the ATmega8 as listed on page63.

RESET　　Reset input. A low level on this pin for longer than the minimun pulse length will generate a reset, even if the clock is not running. The minimum pulse length is given in Table 15 on page 38. Shorter pulses are not guaranteed to generate a reset.

Selected from "Product Data Sheet, ATMEL, AEmega8 ATmega8L Summary, 2008".

Words and Expressions

1. microcontroller [ˌmaɪkrəkənˈtrəʊlə] n. 微控制器
2. single clock cycle 单时钟周期
3. consumption [kənˈsʌmpʃən] n. 消费，消耗
4. Arithmetic Logic Unit (ALU) 算术逻辑单元
5. conventional [kənˈvenʃənl] adj. 常规的，通常的，传统的
6. oscillator [ˈɔsɪleɪtə] n. 振荡器
7. asynchronous [eɪˈsɪŋkrənəs] adj. 异步的
8. non-volatile memory 非易失存储器
9. SPI serial interface SPI 串行接口
10. multiplier [ˈmʌltɪplaɪə] n. 乘法器

附　　录

附录一　关于如何撰写英文的学术论文

在国际刊物或国际学术会议上发表专业论文，是向国际学术界阐述专业思想、学术贡献，从而博得同行与关注者的了解、重视与支持的一个重要手段。目前，绝大部分国际权威性刊物和会议论文集以英语作为语言工具。

一篇典型的英文学术论文主要分为十一大部分：标题、作者姓名、作者单位与联系地址、摘要、关键词、引言、主要内容、总结、参考文献清单、图形描述、公式、注释。全文的基本篇幅一般不超过 6 页（一般按 5 号字算），若超过，则需按要求支付一定附加金额。以下针对所附的例子具体介绍。

一、论文标题

论文标题一般采用比正文大一、二号的黑体字，对称地写在文章首行的正中央，不宜过长（一般不超过两行）。除介词、连词外，标题中每个词的词首必须大写，也有些学术会议论文集的论文标题的所有字母都大写。标题内容要求简单明了，道出核心内容及意义。可以采用主、副标题和破折号形式，一般要求将整个标题构成一个名词性词组。如："A Digital Processor of Neural Networks"、"Modeling Petri Nets in Express"等。

二、论文作者姓名

论文作者姓名写在论文标题的正下方中央处。第一作者（担任论文主要工作、起决定作用的作者）的姓名排在最前面。可以在姓名的右上角标上阿拉伯数字序号或标识符，以便下一步相应地标明单位和联系地址；也可以不这样标明，但一般要求在下一行说明谁是第一作者。中国作者的姓可写在名字的前面或后面，视具体要求而定；姓和名的首写字母都要大写；名字中的两个字（如果是双字结构的话）之间可以用破折号隔开，或直接连写，视具体要求而定。各作者的姓名之间空一格，各人的姓与名之间也空一格（见例一、例二、例三）。

三、作者单位与联系地址

先写作者所在单位，后写联系地址，也可二者合一，如例一、例二、例三。不同的单位和地址按行分开，顺序要和作者名称一样。若某个单位是多层次的，则小单位排在大单位之前，例如：

"Department of Measurement/Control Technology and Instrument　Institute of Information Science and technology　Beijing University of Chemical Technology（北京化工大学信息科学与技术学院　测控技术与仪器系）"、"Department of Electronic Science and Technology Beijing University（北京大学　电子科学与技术系）"。

有些刊物要求作者姓名和联系地址（包括单位）分成两部分写，有些刊物则要求每个作者的联系地址紧跟在该作者姓名之后，但按行分开。

例一

Double Description and Separate Identification
of Non-linear Multi-variable Systems
Jianguo Han Xiangyu Wei Yuming Li and Yaanshan Lu
Beijing University of Chemical Technology
Beijing 100029, China

（引自"1996 IEEE International Conference on System, Man and Cybernetics, Volume 3 of 4, 96ch359229"，这篇论文已于 1997 年被 EI[①] 录入）

例二

An LMI approach to the design of a robust observer with application
to a temperature control problem for space vehicle testing
Massimilian Mattei
Departimento di Informatica, Electronica e Trasporti, Università Mediterrania di Regio Calabria
Via Graziella (Feo di Vito), 89100 Regio Calabria, Italy

（引自"Automatica A Journal of IFAC [②] The International Federation of Automatic, Control, Vol. 37, 2001"）

例三

Foundational algorithm and computational codes for the light
beam propagation in high power laser system
Guo Hong (郭弘)[1], Hu Wei (胡巍)[1], Liu Chengyi (刘承宜)[1]
& Deng Ximing (邓锡铭)[2]

1. Laboratory of Light Transmission Optics, South China Normal University, Guangzhou 510631, China
2. National Laboratory on High Power Laser and Physics, Shanghai Institute of Optics and Fine Mechanics, Chinese Academy of Science, Shanghai 201800, China
Correspondence Should be addressed to Guo Hong (Email: hguo@scnu.edu.cn)

（引自"Science in China (Series E)[③], Vol. 44 No. 1, February 2001"），

四、摘要（Abstract）

摘要应以精练的语言简单扼要、重点突出地讲明本文所介绍或阐述的新成果（包括新技术、新理论、新算法、新观点等）的主要内容、意义、创新点、验证情况、应用范围，并融合地点明本文所要介绍的主要内容。使得读者或审稿人能够很快一目了然，予以足够重视。摘要的篇幅不宜过长，一般不超过 200 个单词。

在层次较高的刊物中，一般要求摘要里使用第三人称（多用被动语态），而不使用第一、第二人称。例如：对于"此项算法，已经过计算机仿真验证。"这句话，用英文写成"This algorithm is tested by using computational simulation."是正确的，而写成"We have tested this algorithm by using computational simulation."就不符合许多刊物的要求。

例四

Abstract

In this paper, a new control scheme for high temperature trajectory following problems is presented. The problem of reproducing on proper test articles the thermal stress conditions occurring on parts of space vehicles during ter entry into atmosphere is considered. The model of the thermal process, in the lumped parameter domain, is described by a quasi-linear system depending on a number of parameters that are uncertain and varying with the operating conditions. An ad hoc trajectory following control system is proposed together with a robust performance analysis which makes use of the concept of quadratic stability with a H_x norm bound. The analysis technique allows to evaluate the stability of the close loop system in the presence of time varying parameters and uncertainties, and the rejection of disturbances acting at the system input. An LMI based observer synthesis procedure is proposed to increase the closed loop system performance.
(引自"Automatica", Vol. 37, 2001, P1979~1987.)

五、关键词（Key words）

紧随摘要之后，专立一段写本文所涉及的关键词。关键词就是最能够集中反映本文的理论、技术特点的关键性技术单词或词组。单词（或词组）总个数一般不超过 5 个。

例五

Key words: Temperature control; Quadratic stability; H_x control; Robust control; Convex optimization

（资料来源同上。）

六、引言（Introduction）

引言应以明快的语言从背景、发展、需求等情况入手，阐明本文核心问题提出的缘由，从而引入到正面的阐述，使读者对本文的宗旨、核心理论、核心技术和目标能较快地有所了解。从而为深入阅读、理解本文主要内容作好思想准备。在必要时还可重点地介绍本文所介绍的成果与历史上已有的相关成果相比自身有何特色或者新的贡献等。

例六

Introduction

For remote sensing spacecraft (SCs) there is the need to orient the line-of-sight to a predetermined part of the Earth's surface (to scan in designated direction, when charge-coupled devices are used) and to compensate the image motion (velocity stabilization) at the onboard optical telescope's focal plane, moreover, for low-orbital SCs these requirements are expressed by rapid angular variable vector of angular rate. The increased requirements to SCs' attitude control systems (ACSs) efficiency, reliability as well as to reasonable mass, size and energy characteristics have motivated intensive development of ACSs with executive devices in the form of moment gyrocomplex (MGC) on the basis of excessive number of single gimbal control moment gyroscopes (CMGs) -gyrodines (GDs). We classify these ACSs of remote sensing rodines in according with the structure exceptions and select them in spatial rotation manoeuvres (SRMs) for which nonlinear problem of synthesis are quite actual.

Mathematical aspect of SC's attitude control under it's SRM were represented in a number of research works, among which monograph J. L. Jinkins and J. D. Turner stands out. This book investigates optimization problems of SRM for SCs controlled by jet engines and reaction wheels. However the method of elimination reaction wheels' angular momentums as state space coordinates owing to the available integral of the system's angular momentum (AM) can not be applied for SRM optimization of a SC with MGC on the basis of GDs. The recent results of B. R. Hoelsscer and S. R. Vadali on the optimal open-loop and the feedback control that spacecraft's gyromoment ACSs are based on methods of the numerical optimization and the Lyaapunove functions, whereas the exact feedback linearization (EFL) technique was applied to the problem of SC's using CMG. In this paper, our new results on optimization and the nonlinear dynamic synthesis of such ACSs are discussed.

（引自 "1996 IEEE International Conference on System, Man and Cybernetics[④], Volume 3 of 4, 96ch359229"，这篇论文已于1997年被EI录入）

文中的第一段简单介绍了本文所讨论技术的实际意义和发展背景，也就是问题的提出。第二段简单介绍了业已问世的有关成果，并在此基础上阐明了本文所介绍的新成果所处的水平。

七、正　文

正文的宗旨一般是要阐明作者所要推出的成果的基本内容、理论依据、正确性、实现方法、仿真的和/或实验的验证方法及其结果分析。要求推理论证严密、论述简明准确、分析与介绍条理清晰而重点突出，全文层次清楚、结构严谨、逻辑关系完整而封闭。

为突出重点，一般不要叙述研究、试验过程和具体情节（除非与说明当前结论密切相关）。

为加强效果，可适当采用层次合理的多维复合句型，如：

"According to the fundamental algorithm the corresponding codes are worked out and some simulation results are derived for the light beam propagation through the spatial filter with the different pinhole".

（引自 "Automatica A Journal of IFAC The International Federation of Automatic, Control, Vol. 37, 2001"）

此句可译成"根据这一基本算法，相应的代码已经编制出来，并且还推演出一些有关光束在带有各种微孔的空间滤波器中传播的仿真结果。"

作者在此句中同时点明了两项新贡献—— "corresponding codes"（相应的编码）和 "simulation results"（仿真结果），并交代了新成果的产生依据 "the fundamental algorithm"（基本算法），以及后一成果的具体内容。

有些刊物在 Abstract 之后的部分往往允许适当地使用第一人称，如："We classify these ACSs of remote sensing rodines in according with the structure exceptions and select them in spatial rotation manoeuvres (SRMs) for which nonlinear problem of synthesis are quite actual."

（引自 "1996 IEEE International Conference on System, Man and Cybernetics, Volume 3 of 4, 96ch359229"，这篇论文已于1997年被EI录入）

正文可按内容和目的划分为若干部分，用粗体字小标题组开头。如例七。

例七

"1. Introduction

　　…　…　…

2. Neural Network Model Based on Hierarchical Structure

　　…　…　…

3. Fast Learning Algorithm Based Hierarchical Multiobjective Optimization

　　…　…　…

4. Experiments and Discussion

　　…　…　…

5. Conclusion

　　…　…　…"

（引自 International Conference on Neural Information Processing（ICONIP'95），Volume 1 of 2，China，Beijing，Oct. 30～Nov. 3，1995）

八、结论或总结（Conclusion 或 Summary）

结论或总结的宗旨一般是让读者对本文所介绍成果的精髓、意义、成功之处及验证结果有一个全貌的了解。常常还要简单介绍该成果可以被推广到的重要领域，并可点出值得进一步探讨和解决的问题。

由于这种介绍是在读者已完成对全文了解的基础上进行的，因此，它比前面的摘要和引言要更高一层、更深一层，可以采用在正文中建立起来的专业性较强的术语。

例八

Conclusion

To meet the demand of real-time signal processing in practice, the globally exponential stability for a class of CNN is defined in this paper. The conditions for the network without [network 1] and with [network 2] synapse delay to have a unique equilibrium are derived, then the criteria for the equilibrium to be globally exponential stable are given. The conditions and criteria do not require the feedback matrix to be symmetric and are quite easy to verify.

For network (1) having a unique globally exponential equilibrium, a formula for estimating its exponential convergence speed is also derived, thus making it possible to define a time constant for the network, which may serve as a measure to check whether the network meets the demand of real-time applications.

（引自 "Automatica A Journal of IFAC The International Federation of Automatic, Control，Vol. 37，2001"）

此段引文中的第一段总结了本文作者的新贡献：the globally exponential stability for a class of CNN is defined；The conditions for the network without [network 1] and with [network 2] synapse delay are derived；the criteria for the equilibrium are given. 第二段重点指出了一个最新的贡献［"For network (1)，…a formula for estimating its exponential convergence speed is also derived"］、它的意义（"…thus making it possible to define a time constant for the network"）和应用价值（"…which may serve as a measure to check whether the network meets the demand of real-time applications. ")。

九、参考文献

在论文的最后部分应以清单形式列出论文所涉及的参考文献。一般以粗体字"References"开头，然后依次列出各篇参考文献的索引条，列出的顺序一般需与其在本论文中被提及的顺序一致。每个索引条的内容和顺序一般为：①用阿拉伯数字表示的索引条序号（有或无，以及序号是否用中括号括起来，要视具体要求而定）；②作者姓名（格式同上）；③论文标题（加引号或不加，视具体要求而定）；④论文所在刊物或书籍名称，卷数；⑤论文所属国际会议名称；⑥出版社名称；⑦出版时间；⑧页数。

所引用和列出的参考文献要力求精简、准确，重点突出，不要使用过多篇幅（参看例九、例十）。

例九

References

Ambrosino. G., Celentano. G., & Mattei. M. (2001). Modelling and control of a plasma wind tunnel. Mathematical and Computer Modelling of Systems. 7 (1), 109~207.

Anderson. J. D. (1989). Hypersonic and high temperature gas dynamics. New York: McGraw Hill.

Barmish. B. R. (1983). Stabilization of uncertain systems via linear control. *IEEE Transaction on Automatic Control*. 28. 848~850.

Becker. G., & Packard, A. (1994). Robust performance of linear parametrically varying systems. System & Control Letters. 23, 205~215.

Boyd. S., El Ghaoui. L., Feron. E., & Balakrishnan. V. (1993). Linear matrix inequalities in system and control theory. Philadelphia: SIAM Press.

Colaneir. P., Geromel. J. C., & Locatelli. A. (1997). Control theory and design. An $RH_2 - RH_r$ viewpoint. London: Academic Press.

（摘自"Automatica"，2001）

例十

References

1. Sacks, R. A., The PROP 92 Fourier Beam Propagation Code, UCRL-LR-105821-96-4.
2. Williams, W. H., Modeling of Self-Focusing Experiments by Beam Propagation Codes, UCRL-LR-105821-96-1.
3. User guide for FRESNEL software.
4. Hunt, J. H., Renard, P. A., Simmons, W. W., Improved performance of fusion lasers using the imaging properties of multiple spatial filters, Appl. Opt., 1977, 16: 779.
5. Deng Ximing, Guo Hong, Cao Qing, Invariant integral and statistical equations for the paraxial beam propagation in free space, Science in China (in Chinese) Ser. A, 1997, 27 (1): 64.
6. Goodman, J. W., Introduction to Fourier Optics, New York: McGraw-Hill, 1968.
7. Born, M., Wolf E., Principles of Optics, New York: Pergamon Press, 1975.
8. Siegman, A. E., Lasers, New York: Mill Valley CA, 1986.

9. Fan Dianyuan, Fresnel number of complex system, Optica Sinica (in Chinese), 1983, 3 (4): 319.
10. Lü Baida, Laser Optics (in Chinese), Chengdu: Sichuan University Press, 1992.
 (摘自 "Sience in China", 2001)

Words and Expressions

1. remote sensing　远距离检测
2. control scheme　控制方案
3. quasi-linear system　准线性系统
4. ad hoc trajectory　['æd'hok'trædʒiktəri]　特定轨道
5. time varying parameters　时变参数
6. uncertainties　不确定性
7. rejection　[re'dʒekʃən]　n. 拒绝
8. remote sensing　远距离检测
9. designate　['dezigneit]　vt. 指定
10. executive devices　执行装置
11. gyromoment　['dʒaiərou'moumənt]　n. 旋转矩
12. linearization　[ˌliniərai'zeiʃən]　n. 线性化
13. gyrodine　['dʒaiəroudain]　n. 装有螺旋桨的直升机
14. globally　['gloubəli]　a. 地球的
15. equilibrium　[i:kwi'lipriəm]　n. 平衡,保持平衡的能力
16. synapse delay　神经连接滞后

Notes

① EI: "The Engineering Index Monthly" ("工程索引月刊"),是 IEEE 主办的一个大型国际性刊物。由美国 "Engineering Information Inc., lCastle Point Terrace" 出版。IEEE 是指 "国际电子、电气工程师协会"。

② Automatica: 是 "Intenational Federation of Automation Control" ("国际自动控制学会",缩写为 IFAC) 主办的一个专门刊登该学会隔年一度的学术会议重要论文的期刊。

③ Science in China (Series E): "中国科学期刊",是中国的一个最高层次的科技刊物之一,由中国科学院主办。该期刊一共分为 5 个系列。系列 A (月刊):数学、物理、天文;系列 B (双月刊):化学;系列 C (双月刊):生命科学;系列 D (双月刊):地球科学;系列 E (双月刊):技术科学。

④ IEEE International Conference on System, Man and Cybernetics: "IEEE 系统、人与控制国际学会" 是 IEEE 主办的一年一度的国际学术会议之一。

附录二 关于如何参加一次国际 IEEE 学术会议

在国际上，大约每隔一年或者两年都会召开由国际 IEEE 组织主办、某个下属机构或有影响的单位或个人经办的涉及几乎各个现代学科领域的专业性国际学术会议。这些会议一般

图 1 ICNC'08 国际会议网页首页

都是依次在相关国家召开。要投稿并参加这样的会议，需要经过查询、写稿（并做相应的构思和实验）、投稿、改进并标准格式化（若经评审后被录取）后再次上传、注册缴费、办理签证（若会议是在国外召开）、购机票和预订宾馆客房、前去报到并入住旅馆、倾听主会场重要报告、出席分会/宣读论文/解答问题、倾听其他发言等一系列活动过程，并且在会议期间还可以利用机会进行会下交往从而结识许多国内外科技专业界朋友。下面以 2007 年的一位专业人员查询、投稿并出席 2008 年的 ICNC 国际会议的具体事宜及过程为例简述如下。

一、会议信息查询

若要寻找次年将要召开的相关专业的国际会议信息，可以查看权威性刊物上的征稿通知或在百度、雅虎、搜狐、大图书馆的信息栏上输入关键词。例如，在百度首页搜寻栏上输入"Conference on Natural Computation 2008"，便可获得 4rd International Conference on Natural Computation（ICNC'08）的信息和会议网页首页如图 1 所示。

在首页上，可以看到会议召开的时间、地点、主要内容、论文摘要或初稿上传的截止时间、录取通知颁发时间、终稿上传截止时间以及会议的水平和所属层面；是否、或者在什么样的条件下能够被国际权威性文献索引机构 EI、ISTP 或 SCI 收录等。

二、初稿构成与投递

1. 选题并成稿

点击开启"Topics"栏，可查阅到此次会议所包括的各个子专题及其基本要求（当然，一些

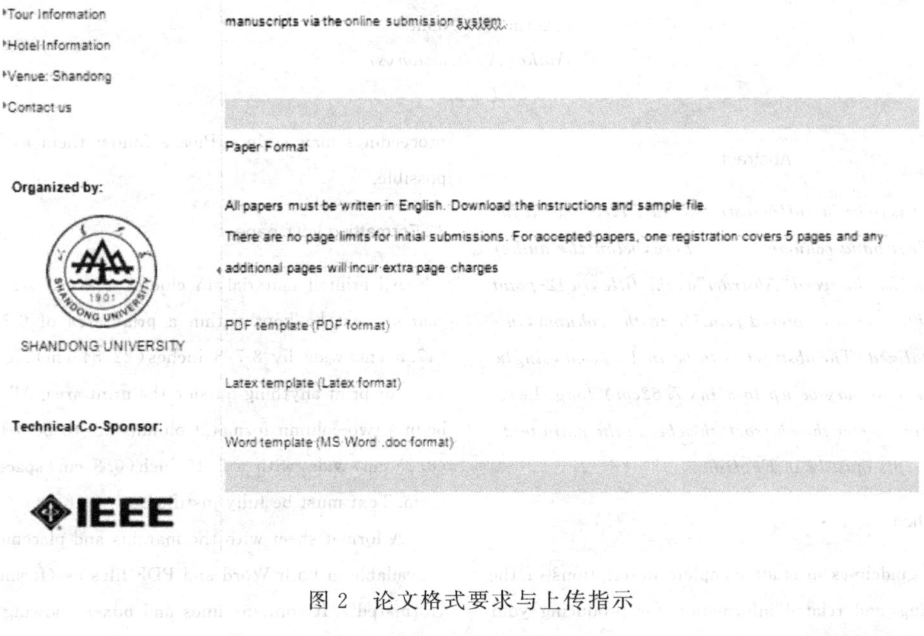

图 2　论文格式要求与上传指示

超出已有专题范围但十分优秀的论文也会被录用),投稿者可以按照所列范围选定自己已获初步成果的课题或论文雏形进行构思、提升,构成符合要求的论文初稿并在原理、推导、过程、实验、结果交代与分析和基本英语语法、常用术语、习惯用语和语言的流畅性上严格把关。

2. 初稿上传

点击"Submission"栏,按指示下载论文格式模板,初步按照模板完成初稿或论文综述(Abstract),并按照指示进入投稿栏、上传初稿或综述(参看图2~4)。

上传成功后,将会在自己给会议所提供的电子邮箱上收到自己所投稿件的标题、全部作者的有关信息和会议秘书处给这篇论文初稿所标定的 ID 号和密码。

A Novel Non-Invasive Medical Measurement
Based on Parallel Neural Computation Supported by the Grid

姓名1	姓名2	姓名3
单位名称1	单位名称2	单位名称3
电子邮箱1	电子邮箱2	电子邮箱3

Abstract

The Grid serving optimized by newly developed workflow engine and in computer embedded parallel-operating intelligent-base based on FPGA, helps the medics and patients in benefiting from the on-line diagnosis medical measure method, so that they can determine the personal illness/health situation convenienthy, quickly, resource sharing, non-invasively, on-line, and remotely. These contributions to domains of computing science, information technique and bio-medicine are developed and combined into a so called CAD Grid (China-Austria Data Grid) on-line diagnosis medical measure system (CAD-ODMM) by the research group of the project called China-Austria On-line Diagnosis Medical Measure Grid, and suggested in this paper. The CAD-ODMM frame poses the advantages, such as intelligent resource sharing, completely parallel processing, non-invasive-, on-line-, and remote-medical measuring, with the help of soft-sensing with neural computing, based on classical Chinese human-meridian theory, Grid computing technology, micro-electronic technology on FPGA, and computer PCI buss structure, thus, facing a considerable application future refers to the domains such as multivariable-, non-linear-, on-line-, real-time-, and remote-control and soft sensing.

图3 论文综述

Author Guidelines for 8.5x11-inch Proceedings Manuscripts
Author(s) Name(s)
Author Affiliation(s)
E-mail

Abstract

The abstract is to be in fully-justified italicized text at the top of the left-hand cohumn as it is here, below the author information Use the word "Abstract" as the title, in 12-point Times, boldface type, centered relative to the cohumn, initially capitalized. The abstract is to be in 10-point, single-spaced type, and may be up to 3 in (7.62cm) long. Leave two blank lines after the abstract, then begin the main text. All manuscripts must be in English.

1. Introduction

These guidelines in clude complete descriptions of the fonts, spacing, and related information for producing your proceedings manuscripts. Please follow them as closely as possible.

2. Formatting your paper

All printed material, in cluding text, illustrations, and charts, must be kept within a print area of 6-7/8 inches (17.5 cm) wide by 8-7/8 inches (22.54 cm) high. Do not write or print anything outside the print area. All *text* must be in a two-column format. Columns are to be 3-1/4 inches (8.25 cm) wide, with a 5/16 inch (0.8 cm) space between them. Text must be fully justified.

A format sheet with the margins and placement guides is available in both Word and PDF files as ⟨formatdoc⟩ and ⟨formatpdf⟩. It contains lines and boxes showing the margins and print areas. If you hold it and your printed page up to the light, you can easily check your margins to see if your print area fits within the space allowed.

3. Main title

The main title(on the first page) should begin 1-3/8 inches(3.49 cm) from the top edge of the page, centered, and in Times 14-point, boldface type. Capitalize the first letter of nouns, pronouns, verbs, adjectives, and adverbs, do not capitalize articles, coordinate conjunctions, or prepositions (unless the title begins with such a word). Leave two blank lines after the title.

4. Author names(s) and affiliation(s)

Author names and affiliations are to be centered beneath the title and printed in Times 12-point, non-boldface type. Multiple authos may be shown in a two or three-column form at, with their affiliations below their respective names. Affiliations are centered below each author name, italicized not bold. In clude e-mail addresses if possible. Follow the author information by two blank lines before main text.

5. Second and following pages

The second and following pages should begin 1.0 inch (2.54 cm) from the top edge. On all pages, the bottom margin should be 1-1/8 inches(2.86 cm) from the bottom edge of the page for 8.5 x 11-inch paper, for A4 paper, approximately 1-5/8 inches(4.13 cm) from the bottom edge of the page.

6. Type-style and fonts

Wherever Times is specified, Times Roman, or New Times Roman may be used. If neither is available on your word processor, please use the font closest in appearance to Times that you have access to. Please avoid using bitmapped fonts if possible. True-Type 1 fonts are preferred.

7. Main text

Type your main text in 10-point Times, single-spaced. Do not use double-spacing. All paragraphs should be indented 1 pica (approximately 1/6-or 0.17-inch or 0.422 cm). Be sure your text is fully justified—that is, flush left and flush right. Please do not place any additional blank lines between paragraphs.

Figure and table captions should be 10-point Helvetica (or a similar sans-serif font), boldface. Callouts should be 9-point Helvetica, non-boldface. Initially capitalize only the first word of each figure caption and table title. Figures and tables must be numbered separately. For example. "Figure 1. Database contexts"。 "Table 1." Input data. Figure cap-

tions are to be *below* the figures. Table titles are to be centered *above* the tables.

8. First-order headings

For example "1。Introduction", should be Times 12-point boldface, mitially capitalized, flush left, with one blank line before, and one blank line after. Use a period(". ") after the heading number, not a colon.

8.1. Second-order headings

As in this heading, they should be Times 11-point boldface, initially capitalized, flush left, with one blank line before, and one after.

8.1.1. Third-order headings. Third-order headings, as in this paragraph, are discouraged. However, if you must use them, use 10-point Times, boldface, initially capitalized, flush left, preceded by one blank line, followed by a period and your text on the same line.

9. Footnotes

Use footnotes sparingly(or not at all!) and place them at the bottom of the column on the page on which they are referenced. Use Times 8-point type, single-spaced. To help your readers, avoid using footnotes altogether and include necessary peripheral observations in the text(within parentheses, if you prefer, as in this sentence).

10. References

List and number all bibliographical references in 9-point Times, single-spaced, at the end of your paper. When referenced in the text, enclose the citation number in square brackets, for example [1]. Where appropriate, include the name(s) of editors of referenced books.

[1]A. B. Smith, C. D. Jones, and E. F. Roberts, "Article Title", *Journal*, Publisher, Location, Date, pp. 1-10.

[2]Jones, C. D. , A. B. Smith, and E. F. Roberts, *Book Title*, Publisher, Location, Date.

11. Copyright forms and reprint orders

You must include your fully-completed, signed IEEE copyright release form when you submit your paper. We must have this form before your paper can be published in the proceedings. The copyright form is available either as a Word file, ⟨copyrightdoc⟩, or as a PDF version, ⟨copyrightpdf⟩. You can also use the form sent with your author kit.

Reprints may be ordered using the form provided as⟨reprintdoc⟩or⟨reprintpdf⟩.

图 4 论文模板

三、论文的修改

如果一篇论文的初稿或综述符合会议的专题范围和水准,特别是具有在国际上有影响的创新性,就会被会议录用。这样,投稿人便会在会议首页所标定的时间收到录用通知书电子邮件。在此邮件上,将展示一篇评审人对论文的评价和修改要求。修改要求一般包括:图形和公式不清楚之处、某些具体的技术或原理的细节有不够令人理解或信服之处,要求加以修正、补充、进一步的描述或提高性的阐述(参看图5、图6)。

ID:P1344

Password:45508208

http://www.icnc-fskd2008.sdu.edu.cn

The 4th International Conference on Natural Computation and the 5th International Conference on Fuzzy Systems and Knowledge Discovery

OpenConf Conference Management System
OpenConf Home
Email Chair

Paper Submission

Thank you for your submission. Your paper number is P1344 Please write this number down and include it in any communications with the conference committee.

Below is the information submitted. We have also emailed a copy to the contact author. If you notice any problems or do not receive the email within 24 hours, please contact the General Chair.

Paper ID:P1344

Title:A Novel Non-Invasive Medical Measurement Based on Parallel Neural Computation Supported by the Grid.

Author 1
·· Name:姓名1
·· Position/Degree:Professor
·· Org:单位名称1
·· Country:China
·· Email:邮箱1

Author 2
·· Name:姓名2
·· Position/Degree:Lecturer
·· Org:单位名称2
·· Country:China
·· Email:邮箱2
   ··············

图5 录用通知书

Some points to note when you format your paper.

1. Do not capitalize all letters in your paper title. Capitalize only the first letter of each word.

2. In each author name, put the surname (family name) last and put given name first. Do not capitalize all letters of the surname (family name). Capitalize only the first letter.

3. For color figures, please make sure that the figures are legible when they are printed in black and white (printed proceedings will be in black and white).

4. In your reference list, do not add things like [J] and [C].

5. Avoid using undefined acronyms, i.e., if you wish to use an acronym, you must first define it in your paper, e.g.,

fuzzy neural network (FNN).
6. Please also do a thorough spelling check.

Comments from Reviewer 1.

This is an inter esting paper which give us a novol method. However, the manuscript should be checked against formal technical criteria (structure of submission, adherence to the Guide for Authors and English language usage), Please also make sure that every aspect of the manuscript is in accordance with the Guide for Authors which is always available on the ICNC08-FSKD08 Website.

Comments from Reviewer 2.

mnovation of the paper is not enough.
very poorly written.

Comments from Reviewer 3.

suggestions to author(s): (1) The paper gives an an application example of processing 300 simulated blood glucose values with developed system. It will be appreciated, if a practical human measurement is provided in the paper. But I don't think this affect the publication. (2) Please check the word "functuin" and "circeuite" which is suspected to be mistyped in Writing Process of 3-3.

图 6　评审人意见和修改要求

四、终稿形成与注册缴费

　　如果论文初稿经改进提高后符合会议要求,将会收到会议秘书处对终稿的修改要求通知。

　　此时,投稿者必须按照通知要求和模板对初稿进行"Camera ready"即符合对稿件进行激光扫描、编入会议论文集过程所要求的格式形成工作,并按通知要求进入终稿上传路径,将终稿上传。

　　与此同时或此后,还会收到注册缴费手续通知(参看图 7)。投稿人可按通知的指示汇款并将表填好、连同汇款证明复印件一起发还会议秘书处。

Registration Form

We would greatly appreciate it if you could complete this form and send it to nc2008@sdu.edu.cn, together with your payment confirmation, i. e., scanned copy of bank transfer or credit card payment confirmation.

Author Name		Nationality	
Organization			
Phone			
E-mail(as used to submit your paper)		Paper ID(s)	
Paper Title(s)			
Registration Fee			
Extra Page Fee			
Total Fee Paid(as Shown on the Payment Confirmation Attached)			
Any Remarks			

图 7　注册表

五、论文录用条件

一篇科技论文若要获得会议录用,至少应具备如下条件。
① 有扎实的科研成果作为基础。
② 有国际上尚未出现的如下创新中的一条:新发现、新理念、新观点、新原理、新方法、新技术或者有影响的新实验结果。
③ 语法、术语、习惯用语、科技描述基本正确。
④ 基本内容阐述、论述、介绍清晰。
⑤ 有真实的如下验证之一:实验验证、推理验证、数学验证或计算机仿真验证。
⑥ 没有一稿多投或抄袭他人成果之嫌。

六、应邀审稿

一些比较成熟的或有影响的专家、教授、学者投稿人往往在投稿之后收到会议秘书处发来的邀请投稿通知书和一批待审稿件,这时,投稿人应尽可能做出符合要求的评审以协助会议成功召开。评审工作内容包括:对论文的现实意义、学术价值、论文水平等方面做出评价并在表格上给出评审等级分数以及提出需要改进的地方(包括内容和格式)。

附录三　关于"工程索引"EI

EI 全称"The Engineering Index Monthly",译为"工程索引月刊"。这是由美国工程信息公司（Engineering Information Inc.）于 1884 年创办的一个国际权威性刊物（月刊）。它对全世界各科技领域的技术性论文进行跟踪搜寻,并进行选择、组织和编辑。覆盖范围包括所有正式出版的学报、期刊、技术报告、会议记录、会议论文集以及其他技术资料。描述方式包括索引和摘要两个方面。另外,它还有一个年刊 PIE,即"Publications in Engineering",专门刊载 EI 在一年中所涉及的所有材料的清单。与 EI 对应,还有一个 EI 的 PC 可读版（machine readable version）,名为"EI Compendex",即 COMPuterized Engineering InDEX。它可通过若干种网上方式、CD-ROM 和磁盘来阅读。可直接通过"Internet"网从 EI Compendex Web 那里读到。相应的软盘文件 Machine-readable file 可向 EI 的销售部"EI ales Department"租用或获得特许使用。

EI 的具体内容主要分为两部分：索引和摘要,具体通过文摘索引、作者索引和标题索引三个栏目来完成。

在内容部分第一页的标题行"THE ENGINEERING INDEX MONTHLY"（其下紧随的一行写着月份和年）下面,开始按主题词首字母的英文字母顺序列出本刊该月份所索引的论文、资料的索引条。从这些索引条中可看到被索引资料的主题、序号、主要内容、作者姓名、资料来源。每条以较大号的大写形式简略写出主题开始,紧接着从下面一行开始以略小一号的标准字体列出索引条件的内容：①索引序号（按本月排序）；②内容摘要（基本上与论文本身的摘要"Abstract"相同）；③作者全称（第一作者后面括号内简略地写着他（她）的地址或单位）；④资料来源（刊物名称、卷数、出版社、出版地、出版时间、页数）。本栏参看"THE ENGINEERING INDEX MONTHLY January 2000"

THE ENGINEERING INDEX MONTHLY January 2000

A

ABS RESINS

000001 Numerical simulation of acrylonitrile-butadiene-styene material's vacuum forming process. In this paper a vacuum forming simulation together with the experimental results is presented. In order to establish a material model which could describe the polymers deformation behavior precisely, the authors conducted uniaxial tensile tests using the newest type of Meissner rheometer with an acrylonitrile-butadiene-styrene (ABS) material. The tests were conducted for constant strain-rates varying from 0.01 to 1 ($1s^{-1}$), at temperatures ranging from 150 to 200℃. A new material model, based on the test data was proposed, in which the combined effects of strain-hardening, strain-rate sensitivity, and temperature variation can be taken into account. Excellent agreement with uniaxial tensile test data was obtained. The vacuum forming processes of a square cup, under different initial temperatures, were simulated employing the proposed material model and the results compared with those of experiment, the simulated final thickness distribution showing a good correspondence to the measured thickness values. (Author abstract) 11 Refs.

Wang, S. (Inst of Physical and Chemical Research, Tokyo, Jpn); Makinouchi, A.; Tosa, T.; Kidokoro, K.; Okamoto, M.; Kotaka, T.; Nakagawa, T. J Mater Process Technol v

91 n 1 1999 Elsevier Science S. A., Lausanne, Switzerland, p 219～225.

AIR POLLUTION CONTROL

000100 Climate policy with multiple sources and sinks of greenhouse gases. This paper studies how inclusion of many sources, sinks and reservoirs-a comprehensive approach-affects climate policy, compared with a control merely of CO_2. Two questions of particular importance arise in such an analysis. One is how to aggregate the emissions of different climate gases, and the other is how to include all relevant measures in the analysis. To aggregate gases properly, an intertemporal analysis should be carried out. To assure that all relevant measures are included, we suggest that certain measures to reduce emissions of greenhouse gases are specified explicitly and evaluated together with indirect measures, such as carbon charges. A numerical analysis based on an optimal control model indicates that direct measures may play an important role in the design of climate policy, especially for the control of the emissions of greenhouse gases other than CO_2. Similar to other studies of the timepath for abatement efforts, the bulk of abatement should be taken by the end of the planning period. This result is significantly strengthened if gases with short lifetimes in the atmosphere, such as methane, are subject to control. (Author abstract) 25 Refs.

Aaheim, H. Asbjorn (Univ of Oslo, Oslo, Norway). Environ Res Econ v 14 n 3 1999 Kluwer Academic Publishers, Dordrecht, Netherlands, p 413～429.

在摘要索引栏内容结束后，紧跟着的内容是作者索引。这一部分的内容在"AUTHOR INDEX"标题之下，按第一作者的姓的首字母的英文字母排列顺序列出。每个索引条先列出每一作者的姓，然后是名，最后是索引序号。根据这个序号，可以查到与之对应的内容摘要索引条。本栏参看 AUTHOR INDEX。

AUTHOR INDEX

Each author name appearing in this list is followed by Ei Abstract Number (s) which appear in sequential order in the body of the book. Guide numbers are provided at the top of the page to aid in the location of desired abstracts. The guide number at the top of the left hand page refers to the first abstract on that page; the guide number at the top of the right hand page refers to its last abstract.

A

Aaheim, H. Asbjorn, 000100
Aaron, J. J., 001510
Aaron, Kim M., 003975
Aarsvold, J. N., 001440
Aarts, Jan, 000812
Aase, Sven Ole, 007579
Aasmundtveit, K., 001596
Aasmundtveit, K. E., 001612, 007250
Abacherli, V., 008392
Abad, Carlos, 002745
Abad, M. j., 002802, 006232
Abam, T. K. S., 008730
Abare, A. C., 007142
Abbar, B., 007057
Abbas, E., 002415
Abbate, E., 003625
Abbon, P., 006692
Abbott, B., 004753
Abbott, Michael B., 001179
Abboud, Nicolas, 003210
Abd-El-Galil, Mohamed E., 002235
Abd El-Hameed, Hamdy, 004954

在紧跟着作者索引栏目之后，在"SUBJECT INDEX"标题下，用大写字母按文章标题首字母的英文字母顺序列出了被索引的论文、资料的标题。每个标题后面紧跟着索引号。本栏参看 SUBJECT INDEX。

SUBJECT INDEX

Headings from Ei controlled vocabulary appear in boldface. Headings which are free language terms and phrases appear in lightface. Each entry in the Subject Index is followed by the appropriate Ei Abstract Number (s) which appear in sequential order in the body of the book. Guide numbers are provided at the top of each page to aid in the location of desired abstracts. The guide number at the top of the left hand page refers to the first abstract on that page; the guide number at the top of the right hand page refers to its last abstract.

2D STRING	002030

A

A POSTERIORI ERROR ESTIMATE	002824
A PRIORI INFORMATION	006324
A TIME OVER THRESHOLD MACHINE	004753
AB INITIO BASIS	007414
AB INITIO PLANE WAVE PSEUDOPOTENTIAL METHOD	007266
AB INITIO QUANTUM CHEMICAL METHODS	005519
ABAQUS ELASTICITY FORMULATION	002716
ABDOMEN	001449 008566
ABE-LAN NETWORK	002679
ABEL TRANSFORMS	002471
ABERRANT OBSERVATIONS	005991
ABERRATIONS	005622 005659

下面举一个从作者姓名开始查询的例子。

假设某人姓名是 Aheim H. Asbjorn，另一位关心他的研究动向的人想查询他某年某月是否有新的论文被 EI 索引。

首先，可翻到 AUTHOR INDEX 栏目，在"A"为标题的姓名清单中找到了这个姓名（第 723 页，左上角）。在姓名后面紧跟着查到索引号是 000100。说明他的论文已被索引。下一步是查询被索引的论文的标题和主要产品内容。于是翻到 THE ENGINEERING INDEX MONTHLY 栏目，按顺序找到了序号 000100。在此序号的后面可以看到"Climate cpolicy with…are subject to control"，这就是论文的主要内容。就在这一索引条的后半段，可以看到第一作者的单位、联系地址、文章来源。

附录四 总词汇表

abnormality   n. 变态，畸形，异常性
abstract image   抽象的映像
abstract range space   抽象域空间
abstract symbol   抽象符号
accelerometer   n. 加速度计
accommodate   vt. 供应，供给，使适应
accommodation   n.（眼睛等的）适应性调节
accounting charge   结算费用
acquisition of information   信息采集
acronym   n. 只取首字母的缩写词
actual empirical quantity   实际经验的数量
actual measurement signal   实际测量信号
actual output   实际输出
actuator   n. 执行器，传动装置（机构），拖动装置
actuate   vt. 开动，促使
actuator   n. 执行器，激励
adaptive gain   适应性增益
A/D converter   A/D 转换器
additional letter   附加字母
adequate   adj. 适当的，足够的
adipic acid   n. 己二酸
adjust   vt. 调整，调节，调理
adjustable quantity   可调量
afterthought   n. 事后产生的想法
air to close   气关
air to open   气开
alarm function   提示功能，警告功能
algorithm   n.［数］运算法则，算法
allotted   n. 分配，充当，依靠
allowable bandwidth   允许的带宽
alloy   合金；贱金属；成色
alphanumeric   adj. 文字数字的，包括文字与数字的
alter   vt. 改变
alternative   n. 二中择一，可供选择的办法，事物   adj. 选择性的，二中择一的
altimetry   n. 测高学，高度测量法（以海平面为基准）
ambient   adj. 周围的   n. 周围环境
ambiguity   n. 含糊，不明确
ambitious   adj. 有雄心的，野心勃勃的

amount of drift   漂移量
amount of overrange   超出范围的数量
amplifier   n. 放大器
amplitude   n. 广阔，丰富，振幅，物理学名词
amplitude distribution function   振幅分布函数
analog   adj. 模拟的
analogy   n. 类推，类比，类推法
a necessary and not a sufficient aspect   一个必要而非充分的条件
annotation   n. 注释，注解
annunciate   vt. 告示，通知
anthropometry   n. 人体测量学
anticipation   n. 预期，预料
aperture   n.（照相机，望远镜等的）光圈，孔径
approach   n. 接［逼］近；近似法［值］；途径，方法
approximately   adv. 近似地，大约
arbitrary   adj. 专横的，专断的，反复无常的
arbitrary moment   任意时刻
arbitrate   v. 做出公断
arc   n. 弧，弓形，拱；弧光；adj. 逆三角作用的
architecture   n. 构造，结构
area controller   装置控制器
area level   装置级
arithmetic unit   算术单元
artefact   n. 人工品
articulate   vt. 接合
artificial   adj. 人造的，人工的，假的
artificial neural nets（ANN）   人工神经网络
ASCII   美国信息交换标准码
a specified set of condition   一系列的特定条件
assemble product   装配产品
assess   vt. 估定，评定
assignment algorithm   分配算法
assimilate   vt. & vi. 吸收，消化
asymmetry   n. 不对称，不均匀
asyachronous   adj. 异步的
automated assembly line   自动装配线
automatic control system   自动控制系统
automatic transmission   自动驾驶
autonomous   adj. 自治的

auxiliary   adj. 辅助的，补助的
auesome   adj. 令人敬畏的，使人畏惧的，可怕的；棒极了
azimuth   n. 方位角
balanced condition   平衡条件
bandwidth   n. 带宽
barometric   adj. 大气压力
batch control   批量控制
be based on   基于
be cognizant of   认识到
bell-shaped   钟形的
bias   n. 偏差，偏见，偏爱
bifurcation   n. 分叉，分歧
bimetauic   adj. 双金属的；复本位制的
binary   adj. 二进位的，二元的
binocular   adj. 用两眼的，给两眼用的；双目并用的
biological model   生物模型
bionic   adj. 仿生学的，利用仿生学的
biosensor   n. 生物传感器
blend   vt. 混合；n. 调和，合而为一；混杂
block diagram   方框图
blur   v. 使模糊
boldface   n. [印刷]黑体字，粗体铅字
Boolean programming method   布尔编程方法
branchline   n. 分支
breakdown   n. 故障，损坏
bulb   n. 鳞茎，球形物
bullet hole   子弹孔
bumpless transfer   无扰动切换
bus protocol   总线协议
calibrate   vt. 校准
calibrated point   校正点
calibration   n. 标度，刻度，校准
calibration curve   标定曲线
calibration deviation   校验误差
calibration facility   校准装置
calibration history   校验记录
calibration procedure   标定过程，检验方法
calipers   n. pl. 弯脚器，测径器
camcorder   n. 可携式摄像机
candela   n. 烛光； adj. 小雪茄烟的
canonical   adj. 规范的
cardinal measurement   最重要的测量
carrier   n. 载波，载流子
cartridge   盒式磁盘[带]（机）；夹头；（粉）盒
cascade control   串级控制

catatonic state   紧张性精神病的状态
categorize   vt. 分类
category   n. 种类，别，[逻] 范畴
cathode   n. 阴极
cathode ray tubes (CRTs)   n. 阴极射线管
celestial   adj. 天体的，天体导航法的
cell level   单元级
celsius   adj. 摄氏的
central control room   中央控制室
central microprocessor   中心元处理器
certification   n. 证明
change in the load   负载变化
channel   n. 通道，信道；频道
characterize   vt. 描绘……的特性
chemical property   化学性质
chloride   n. [化学] 氯化物；漂白粉
chore   n. 家务杂事
chronic schizophremia   adj. 慢性的精神分裂症
circuitry   n. 电路，线路
circumflex   n. 昂低音符，长音符；音调符号；声调符号
cite   vt. 引用
class   vt. 分类
client-server model   客户端服务器模型
clockwise   adj. 顺时针方向的；adv. 顺时针方向地
closed-loop   闭环
closeness   n. 接近，近似
coaxial   adj. [数] 同轴的；[电] 同轴电缆的
cockpit   n. 驾驶员座舱，战场
coding   n. 编码
coefficient   n. [数] 系数
coercivity   n. [电] 矫顽（磁）力，矫顽（磁）性
coexistence   n. 共存
coherent sampling   相干采样
coil   n. 线圈，螺旋；vt. 盘绕
coin   vt. 造新词
collaborative   adj. 合作的，协作的，协力完成的
collapsed   n. 崩溃，破裂；压缩；[微软] 折叠
collision   n. 碰撞，冲突
collision detection   冲突检测，碰撞检测
combination   n. 结合，合并
commence   v. 开始，着手
communicating equipment   通信设备
communication network architecture   通信网络层
communication sophistication   通信混合系统
communication standard   通信标准

compatibility n. 兼容性
compatible adj. 谐调的，一致的，兼容的
compensate vt. 补偿
compiler n. 编译程序
complementary adj. 补充的，补足的
complex number 虚数
component n. 成分，组成
composition n. 成分
comprehensible a. 可理解的
computer analysis 计算机分析
computer database 计算机数据库
computer-assisted simulation 计算机辅助仿真
computer-integrated manufacturing（CIM） 计算机集成制造
conclusion n. 结论
concurrency n. 并行操作
concurrent adj. 同时发生的，并存的；合作的
condense v. 精简
conduct v. 引导，传导
conductivity n. 传导性，传导率
cone n. ［数、物］锥形物，圆锥体，（松树的）球果 vt. 使成锥形
configurable vt. 使成形，形成
configuration register 配置寄存器
confirmation n. 证实，确认
conformance testing 相似测试，一致性测试
confront vt. 勇敢地面对，正视，遭遇
congruent representation 适合的表述法
consecutive a. 连续不断的
consistently ad. 一贯地，固守地
constrain vt. 约束，强制，局促
constraint n. 约束
construction drawing 结构图
consultant n. 顾问
consumer goods 消费商品
consumption n. 消费，消耗
contemplate v. 凝视，沉思，预期，企图
contemporary adj. 当代的，同时代的，同属一个时期的
continuous adj. 连续的
continuous manner 连续方式
contour n. 轮廓，等高线
control action 控制动作
control strategy 控制策略
controlled variable 被控量
controller n. 控制器

controller output 控制器输出
control mode 控制模型
control system 控制系统
control valve 控制阀
controversy n. 论争，辩论，论战
conventional adj. 常规的，通常的，传统的
cornea n. ［医］角膜
correction n. 改正，修正
corrective action 正确行为
corrective effect 纠正作用
correlation n. 相互关系，相关（性）
corrosion n. 侵蚀，腐蚀状态
corrupt vt. 使恶化
cost-effective 节省成本的
crank n. 曲柄
credit n. 信任，信用，声望，荣誉，［财务］贷方，银行存款 vt. 相信，信任，把……归给
criterion n. 标准，准则，规律
cross differences 交叉差分
crossover point 交叉点
cruising vi. 巡游，巡航；n. 巡游，巡航
crustiness n. 外壳，硬壳，面包皮；vt. 盖以硬皮 vi. 结硬皮
crystal adj. 结晶状的；n. 水晶，水晶饰品，结晶，晶体
cumbersome adj. 讨厌的，麻烦的，笨重的
customizing computer 用户化计算机
cutter n. 刀具；切割机；快艇
cylinder n. 圆柱体；汽缸；圆柱形的容器
daisy chain n. 雏菊花环，〈美〉链，环
damper n. 阻尼闸
data processing 数据处理
data reduction 数据简化
data routing 数据路由
daunting adj. 艰巨的，使人畏缩的
dead band 死区
decimal adj. 十进位的；小数的
decoding n. 解码器
decouple v. 去耦，分离，减弱
de facto adj. ［拉］事实上的，实际的
degradation v. 鉴别
degree of conformity 一致程度，相似度
demanding adj. 过分要求的，苛求的
demodulation n. 解调
demonstrate vt. 演示，示例，论证
denote vt. 指示，标志

dependency n. 从属，从属物
deploy v. 展开，配置
depolarize vt. 去极化，去偏极，去偏光
derate vt. 减免
derivative mode 微分模型
derive vt. 得自；vi. 起源
description n. 描述
descriptive adj. 描述的，叙述的
descriptive statistics 描述性统计
designation n. 指示，指定，选派，名称
designation system 指定的系统
desired value 期望值
destination n. 目的地，［计］目的文件，目的单元格
detectable adj. 可发觉的，可看穿的
deterioration n. 退化，变坏
deviation 背离
diagnosis n. 调查；诊断
dial n. 刻度盘，钟面，转盘，（自动电话）拨号盘 v. 拨
dial-pulse 脉冲拨号
dial-tone 音频拨号
diaphragm n. 振动膜
diffract n. 衍射
digital adj. 数字的
dimension n. 尺寸，尺度，维（数），度（数），元；尺寸，量纲，维面积
diminutive adj. 小得出奇的，特小的，（指后缀）表示小的
diode n. 二极管
direct current 直流
direct input 直接输入
direct machine control 直接机器控制
disastrous adj. 灾难性的，造成灾害的
discernible adj. 可看出的，可辨别的
discrepancy n. 差异不一致，不符，差异
discrete adj. 离散的
discrete step 分离的步骤
disparity n. （职位、数量、质量等）不一致，不同，不等
dispersion n. 分散
dissipation n. 消散，分散，挥霍，浪费
distinctive adj. 与众不同的，有特色的
distribute vt. 分发，分布
distributed real-time system 分布式实时系统
distribution of value 数据分布
disturbance n. 骚动，打扰，干扰
documentation n. 文件
drive vt. 驱动
drive controller 驱动控制器
due date 期限，到期日
duplex ［计］路由器（读取每一个数据包中的地址然后决定如何传送的专用，智能性的网络设备）
dynamic adj. 动力的，动力学的，动态的
edge detection 边缘识别
elaborate control system 精细控制系统
elapse n. 过去，消逝
electrical domain 电气域
electrical potential difference 电势差
embed vt. 使插入，使嵌入，深留，嵌入
empirical data 经验数据
empirical domain space 经验域空间
empirical world 经验的世界
employed measurement system 被使用的测量系统
enable vt. 使……有能力
encoder n. 译码器，编码器
endow v. 捐赠，赋予
enormous adj. 巨大的，极大的，庞大的
enthusiasm n. 狂热，热心，积极性
entity n. 实体
enumeration n. 计数，列举，细目
envelope n. 包络线
environmental control 环境控制
enzyme n. ［生化］酶
equidistant adj. 等距离的；同比例的
equip vt. 装备
erase vt. 抹去，擦掉，消磁，〈俚〉杀死
ergonomic adj. 人类环境改造学的
error detector 误差检测器
established standard 现有标准
establish equality 建立等式
etch v. 蚀刻
ethical adj. 与伦理有关，民族的，民族特有的
event-sequenced control 事件顺序控制
euolution n. 演变，进化，发展
evolve vt. （使）发展，（使）进展，（使）进化
exaggeration n. 夸张，夸大之词
exclusive adj. 专用的，独家的，高级的，奢华的
excursion n. 远足，短途旅行
execute vt. 执行，实行，完成，处死，制成，［律］经签名盖章等手续使（证书）生效

experienced operator　有经验的操作者
experimental precision　精确实验
expertise　n. 专家的意见,专门技术
exploit　vt. 开采,开发
extent　n. 范围,程度
external power supply　外部电源供应,外部供电
external signal　外部信号
extract　vt. 吸取,摘取
extrapolate　v. 传送,推断,外推
fabricate　vt. 制作,构成,捏造
facet　n. 事物的不同的面,(宝石等的)刻面
factory floor　厂地
fatigue　n. 疲乏,疲劳
feasibility　n. 可行性,可能性
feasible　a. 可行的
feature　n. 面貌的一部分(眼、口、鼻等)特征,容貌,特色,特写　vt. 是……的特色,特写,放映　vi. 起重要作用
feedback　反馈
ferric　adj. 铁的;含铁的
fertilizer plant　化肥厂
fidelity　n. 保真度,重现精度
fieldbus　现场总线
file record　文件记录
final control element　最终控制单元
finalize　v. 把……最后定下来
flexibility　n. 适应性,机动性
flexible　adj. 柔性的
flow　n. 流量
flow rate　流通率
flow transmitter　流量变送器
fluctuate　vi. 波动
flux　n. 磁通,(电、磁、光)通量;焊剂;流动
fly-through　浏览
focal　adj. 焦点的,有焦点的,在焦点上的
follow-up system　随动系统
food-processing plant　食品加工厂
foreseeable　adj. 可预知的,能预测的,能看透的
formal　adj. 外形的,正式的,合礼仪的,形式的,整齐匀称的　n. 正式的社交活动
formalism　n. 拘泥形式,(艺术或宗教上的)形式主义,虚礼
format　n. 开本,版式,形式,格式;vt. 安排……的格局(或规格),[计] 格式化(磁盘)
forward path　前向路径
fovea　n. 凹,小凹(尤指视网膜的中央凹)

fragile　adj. 易碎的,脆的
frame　vt. 构成,设计;　n. 帧,画面,框架
frequency　n. 频率,周率,发生次数
frequency band　频率段
frequency response　频率响应
frequency spectrum　频谱
front panel　前面板
fuel flow　燃料流量
full-scale　adj. 与原物大小一样的,全面的,未经删节的;n. 全尺寸,满标度
function　n. 功能,作用
functionality　n. 功能性,泛函性
fuzzy　adj. 失真的,模糊的
fuzzy logic　模糊逻辑
gage　n. (= gauge)标准度量,计量器　vt. (= gauge)精确计量,估计
gain　n. 增益
galaxy　n. 星系,银河,一群显赫的人,一系列光彩夺目的东西
gateway　n. 门,通路,网关
gathered information　收集到的信息
general instrument symbol　通用仪器符号
general level　通用层
generalization　n. 概括,归纳;概说
geometric　adj. 几何的,几何学的
geometry　n. 几何,几何学;几何图形,几何结构
gradient　adj. 倾斜的;　n. 梯度,倾斜度,坡度
graphical form　图解形式
grating　n. 门窗的栅栏,[物理]光栅,摩擦,摩擦声;　adj. 刺耳的
gravitational　adj. 重力的
grid　n. 格子,栅格
gyro　陀螺仪,回转仪
handicapped　adj. 残疾的
hardness　n. 硬,硬度
harsh environment　恶劣的环境
heating system　加热系统
heuristic　adj. 启发式的
heuristics　n. [计] 试探法
hierarchical structure　递阶结构,层次结构
highly subjective　高度主观的
histogram　n. 直方图,柱状图,矩形图
homogeneous　adj. 同性质的,同类的
horizontal traffic　水平通信
household　adj. 普通的,平常的,家庭的
hover　v. 盘旋

hub　n. 网络集线器，网络中心
hue　n. 色调，样子，颜色，色彩
human control　人工控制
human dialogue　人对话，交互
humidity　n. 湿气；潮湿；湿度
hybrid　n. 混合物；adj. 混合的，杂种的
hydraulic line　水力线
hype　n. 皮下注射，欺骗，骗局
hypothalamus　n. 丘脑下部
hypothesis　n. 假说，假设，学说；pl. hypotheses
hypothetical　adj. 假设的，假定的；有待证实的
hysteresis　n. 滞后作用，[物]磁滞现象
ideal value　理想值
identical　a. 同一的，相似的
identification code　识别码
identifier　n. 标识符；标识号
illuminance　n. (=illumination) 照明[度]，启发
image set　映像集
immunity　n. 免疫力
impart　vt. 给予（尤指抽象事物），传授，告知，透露
impedance　n. [电]阻抗，全电阻，[物]阻抗
implementation　n. 执行
impractical　adj. 不切实际的
inaccurate calibration　不准确的刻度
inanimate　adj. 死气沉沉的，没生命的，单调的
in contrast　比较
incorporate　vt. 合并，包含
incredible　adj. 难以置信的
increment of measurement　测量值增量
indication deflection　指示偏差
individual　n. 个人，个体；adj. 个别的，单独的，个人的
individual model　单独的模型
inductive　adj. 诱导的，感应的
industrial computer　工业计算机
industrial distributed system　工业分布式系统
industrial operation　工业操作
industrial relay　工业继电器
inertia　n. 惯性，惯量
inertial navigation　惯性导航
information　n. 信息
infrastructure　n. 基础构造
inherently　adv. 天性地，固有地
initiate　vt. 开始，发动，传授；v. 开始，发起

input signal　输入信号
installation　n. 安装
instructor　n. 指导
instrumentation　n. 仪器使用
instrument identification　设备鉴定
integral mode　积分模型
integrated　adj. 综合的，完整的
intelligent sensors　智能传感器
intensity　n. 强烈，剧烈，强度；亮度
interact　vi. 互相作用，互相影响
interaction　n. 交互作用，交感
interactive　adj. 交互式的
interchange method　交换法
interconnection　n. 互相联络
interface　n. [地质]分界面，接触面；[物、化]界面，接口
intermediate　n. 媒介；vt. 起中介作用
in terms of　就……而论，在……方面
internal register　内部寄存器
international standards organization (ISO)　国际标准化组织
interoperability　n. 互用性，协同工作的能力
interpolation　n. 篡改，添写，插补
interpret　vt. 解释，翻译
interpretation　n. 解释，阐明，口译，通译
interrogation　n. 审问，问号；询问
interrupt　vt. 中断
intervene　vi. 干涉，干预，插入，介入，（指时间）介于其间
intuitive understanding　直觉理解
invariant　adj. 无变化的，不变的；n. [数]不变式，不变量
inventory　n. 详细目录，存货，财产清册，总量
inversely　adj. 倒转的，反转的；n. 反面；v. 倒转
invert　vt. 转换
investigation　n. 调查，研究
invoked　v. 调用
involve　vt. 包括，笼罩，潜心于，使陷于
iris　n. [解]虹膜
irrespective　adj. 不考虑的，不问的，不顾的
irreversible process　不可改变的进程
isobaric　adj. 表示等压的，同重元素的
isolated measurement　隔离测量，独立测量
isolated value　分离量
isomorphic　adj. 同形的，[数]同构的
iterative　adj. 重复的，反复的，[数]迭代的；n.

反复体
jolt　v. 重击，摇撼
keep track of　跟踪，记录
kerr rotation　克尔旋度，克尔旋转
key factor　关键因素
keypad　n. 键区
kinematics　n. 运动学
knob　n. 旋钮，球形捏手
known accuracy　已知精确度
Laplace transform　拉普拉斯变换
largest step　最大的刻度
latency　n. 反应时间，滞后时间
lathe　n. 车床
layer structure　层次结构
legal transformation　合法转换
legibility　n. 易读性，易辨认，易理解
lens　n. 透镜，镜头
level　n. 液位，水平，水平面
level transmitter　液位变送器
limb　n. 肢，翼，分支
linguistic　adj. 语言上的，语言学上的
link layer　［计］链路层
liquid crystal (LCD)　液晶
literature　n. 著作，文献
local/remote setting　本地/远程设置
location　位置，特定区域
logic unit　逻辑单元
lower range limit　范围下限
lubricating oil　润滑油
luminous flux　n. ［物］光通量（其单位为流明 lumen）
machine control system　机器控制系统
machine level　机器层
machinery　n. 机器
magnetic　adj. 磁的，有磁性的，有吸引力的
magnetic fields　磁场
magneto optic　adj. ［物］磁光的，磁场对光线的影响的
magnetoresistive　a. ［物］磁滞电阻的
magnetostrictive　adj. 磁力控制的，磁致伸缩的
magnitude　n. 大小，数量，巨大，广大，量级
mainframe computer　大型计算机
maintenance　n. 维护，保持
maintenance tracking　跟踪维护
malfunction　n. 障碍；故障；　vi. 发生故障
manipulated variable　操作量

manipulative　adj. 操纵的，控制的
manual control　手动控制
manufacturing process　制造过程
mapping of elements　元素的映射
mapping　n. 映射，绘制……之地图，计划
martian　n. 火星人；adj. 火星的
master control　主控制
material handling　原料处理
mathematical computations　数学计算
matrix　n. 矩阵
meaningful manner　有意义的方式
measurable　a. 可测量的
measurand　n. 被测物理量［性质，状态］，被测对象
measured value　被测量
measured variable　被测变量
measurement constitute　测量组成
measurement instrument　测量工具
measurement instrument's output　测量装置的输出
measurement process　测量过程
measurement result　测量结果
measurement strategy　测量策略
measuring mean　测量值
measuring point　测量点
mechanical linkage　机械连接体
median filtering　中值过滤法
membrane　n. 膜，隔膜
memory　n. 内存，存储器
mental disorder　精神错乱
meridian　n. 子午圈，子午线
methodology　n. 方法学
metric information　公制信息
microcontroller　n. 微控制器
microelectronics　n. 微电子学
microfossils　n. 微体化石，微化石
midband amplitude　频带中心振幅
millivolt　n. 毫伏
mimic　adj. 模仿的，假装的
miniature　n. 缩小的模型，缩图，缩影；adj. 微型的，缩小的
minimal effort　最小的努力
misinterpret　vt. 曲解
misinterpretation　n. 误译，曲解
mismatched impedance　不匹配的阻抗
mock-up　n. 实验或教学用的实物大模型，伪装工事

moderate adj. 中等的,适度的,适中的 v. 缓和
modify vt. 更改 修改
modify variable 修改变量
modulation n. 调制
Moiré fringe 莫尔条纹
moisture n. 潮湿,湿气
monitor n. 监听器,监视器,监控器; vt. 监控 v. 监控
monotonic adj. 单调的;没有变化的
monotonic function 单调函数
motor n. 发动机,电动机
multiple adj. 多样的,多重的 n. 倍数,若干 v. 成倍增加
multiple data path 多路数据路径
multiple standard 多重标准
multiplex v. 多路操作
multiplexing n. 多路技术
multiplier n. 乘法器
mutual induction 互感
myriad clone 大量复制
nanometer n. 纳米 (10^{-9} m)
narrow-band 窄波段
natural system 自然系统
nature n. 本性,本质
needle n. 针
neighborhood averaging 邻域平均法
network layer 网络层
neural adj. 神经的,神经系统的
nonlinearity n. 非线性,非直线性
nonuniform adj. 不一致的,不均匀的
nonvolatile adj. (尤指物质)非挥发性的,不挥发的,非易失的
non-volatile memory 非易失存储器
nonzero adj. 非零的
non-coplanar 不共面的
notify vt. 通报
numerical control 数值控制
Nyquist theorem 奈奎斯特定律
objective adj. 客观的
objectivity n. 客观性
object of measurement 测量目标
obscure vt. 使暗,使不明显
observational data 观测数据
observer n. 观察者;观察器
occlusion n. 闭塞
off-line adj. 不连接到线上的,脱机的,离线的

oil refinery 炼油厂
oilrig n. 开采石油设备
onboard adj. 随车携带的
on line 在线
on-off control 开关控制
open systems interconnection (OSI) 开放式系统互连
open-loop 开环
operating environment 操作环境
operating system 操作系统
operating temperature 操作温度,工作温度
operational amplifier 运算放大器
operational architecture 操作体系结构
operational description 操作描述
operation manual 操作指南
operators n. 算子
optimization n. 最佳化,最优化
optimize vt. 使最优化
optoelectronil adj. 光电子的
orientation n. 方向,定位
orthographic adj. 正交的
oscillator n. 振动器,振动子,振荡器
oscilloscope n. 示波器,示波管 (OSP)
outperform vt. 做得比……好,胜过
output signal 输出信号
output span 输出范围
overlap v. (与……) 交迭
overload vt. 过载
packet switching 分包交换
pancake n. 薄烤饼
paradigm n. 范例
parameter n. 参数,参量 [口] 起限定作用的因素
parametric adj. [数][物][晶]参(变)数的,参(变)量的
parasitic quantity 寄生量,附加量
parity n. 奇偶
passive device 被动装置
pattern recognition 模式识别
peak n. 最高值,峰值
penetrate vt. 穿透,渗透
perceive vt. 察觉; v. 感知,感到,认识到
percentiles 百分位数(值)
performance n. 履行,执行,成绩,性能,表演,演奏
performance check 性能检查
performance limitation 性能限制因素,性能极限
periodic adj. 周期的,定期的

permanent change 永恒的变化
perpendicular adj. 垂直的，正交的； n. 垂线
perspective n. 远景，前途，观点，看法，观察
pervasive adj. 普遍深入的，渗透的
phase n. 阶段，状态，相，相位 v. 定相
phase angle 相位角
phase difference 相位差
pheromone n. 信息素
phosphor n. 磷，启明星
photopic n. 光适应，眼对光调节
physical activity 身体的运动
physical construction 物理建筑
physical property 物理性质
physical quantity 物理量
physical-link 物理连接
pickoff n. 以牵制球使出局
piezoresistive adj. 压阻现象的，压阻的
pitfall n. 陷阱；意想不到的困难；易犯的错误
pixel n. （显示器或电视机图像的）像素
pixel-synchronized 像素同步
plant floor 装置层
plant level 厂级
plausible adj. 似是而非的
pneumatic adj. 风力的，汽力的； n. 气胎
pneumatic control valve 气动控制阀
pneumatic tube 大气管道
polarize v. （使）偏振，（使）极化，（使）两极分化
polarization n. 极化作用，两极化
polygon n. 多边形
portability n. 可移植性
portability of code 代码的可移植性
pose vi. 摆姿势，佯装，矫揉造作
potent adj. （药量）效力大的；威力大的
potential n. 潜能，电压
potentiometric n. 电位计，分压计；adj 电势测定的
power assist 辅助动力
practicable adj. 能实行的，行得通的，可以实行的
preserve vt. 保护，保存
pressure drop 压降
pressure transmitter 压力变送器
prime n. 最初，青春，精华；adj. 主要的，最初的，有青春活力的，最好的，第一流的，根本的，[数]素数的；v. 预先准备好
problem location 问题所在

process control 过程控制
process control system 过程控制系统
processed data 已处理过的数据
process output variable 过程输出变量
process progress 进程
programmable controller 可编程控制器
progressive drift 逐渐的漂移
project n. 计划，方案，事业，企业，工程； v. 设计，发射（导弹等），凸出
propeller n. 螺旋推进器
proportional adj. 比例的，成比例的，相称的，均衡的
proportional mode 比例模型
protocol n. 草案，协议
psychological experiment 心理试验
pupil n. 瞳孔
purchasing decision 采购决策
pyramid n. 金字塔
pyramidal model 金字塔模型
QoS=quality of service 服务质量
qualitative measurement 质量测量
quanta n. pl. 量子（quantum 的复数）
quantification n. 量化
quantitative data 定量数据
quantitative measurement 数量测量
quivalent n. 等价物，相等物
quotient n. [数]商数
ramification n. 分支，分叉，衍生物，支流
random errors 随机误差
randomly adv. 随便地，未加计划地
random sampling 随机采样
range n. 范围
rationalization n. 合理化
raw n. 生的，未加工的
raw or unprocessed data 原始或未处理数据
real-time control 实时控制
reciprocal adj. 互惠的；n. 倒数
reconstructed signal 重建的信号
recovery time 回复时间
rectilinear n. 直线
redundancy n. 冗余
reference n. 参考
refract vt. 使折射，测定……的折射度
region growing 区域增长法
registration n. 注册，报到，登记
regular system 调节系统

regulator system 调节器系统
relational system 相关系统
relay n. 继电器
reliability n. 可靠度
reliability condition 可靠条件
repeatable a. 可重复的
repertoire n. 所有组成部分
repetition n. 重复，循环
replica n. 复制品
repository n. 贮藏室，智囊团，知识库，仓库
reproducible adj. 能繁殖的，可再生的，可复写的
resolution n. 分辨率
respective characteristic 各自的特性
respond to 响应，作出反应
response n. 回答，响应，反应
response-time error 反应时间误差
restrict vt. 限制 约束
retina n. ［解］视网膜
retrieval n. 取回，恢复，修补，重获，挽救，拯救 检索，查找
reveal vt. 展现，显示，揭示
revolution per minute 每分转数
ribbon n. 带状电缆，扁平柔性电缆；（打印机的）色带；［微软］带状条；格式栏
rifle n. 来复枪
rigidity n. 硬度，刚性
rms abbr. root-mean-square 均方根
robotic n. 机器人
robotics n. 机器人技术
robust adj. 鲁棒性，强健的
robustness n. 鲁棒性
rod n. 杆，棒
Rolls-Royce n. 劳斯莱斯（著名的航空发动机生产公司，同时生产顶级汽车）
room condition 室内条件
rough handling 粗处理
rounding number 四舍五入数
round-even 约偶，舍偶
rudder n. 舵，方向舵
rudimentary adj. 根本的，未发展的，基本的
rule n. 规则
sacrifice n. 牺牲，献身；v. 牺牲，献出，供奉
sake n. 为了……之好处，出于对……的兴趣，缘故，理由
sample n. 采样值
sample mean 样本均值

sampling oscilloscope 采样示波器
saturation n. 饱和（状态），浸润，浸透 饱和度
saturation effect 饱和效应
saturn n. 土星
scan time 扫描时间
scarcity n. 缺乏，不足
scatter vt. 使分散，驱散，散布，挥霍； vi. 消散，溃散
scenario n. 想象的场景，游戏的关
schematically 概要地
schematics n. 图表
scientific way 科学方法
scotopic adj. ［医］暗适应的，暗视的
scratchpad memory ［计］暂时存储器
segmentation n. 分割
selectivity n. 选择性
self-diagnosis 自诊断
self-tuning 自调谐［校正］
sense vt. 检测，感知
sensing element 检测元件
sensitivity n. 敏感，灵敏（度），灵敏性
sensitivity drift 敏感性漂移
sensor n. 传感器
sensor networks 传感器网络
sequential control 连续控制
sequentially adv. 顺序地
serial adj. 连续的
serial number 序列号
service vt. 保养，维修
servo n. 伺服，伺服系统
servomechanism n. 伺服机构（系统）
servo system 伺服系统
setpoint n. 给定值
setpoint value 设定值
set theory 集合论
shaft n. 轴，杆状物
share n. 共享，参与； vt. 分享，共有
sigmoidal n. S形曲线，S形的，反曲的
signal line 信号线
signal transducer 信号变送器
significant digits 有效数字
simplicity n. 简单地
simplistic adj. 过分单纯化的
simulator n. 模拟器，仿真器
simultaneously adv. 同时地
single clock cycle 单时钟周期

single control system 单回路控制系统
single chip solution 单片解决方案
single step 单步
single-value 单值
sinusoidal signal 正弦信号
size relationship 量值关系
skipped period 跳跃区间
sodium n. 钠
software n. 软件
sophisticated adj. 久经世故的；高度发展的；富有经验的
sophistication n. 混合
sound adj. 健全的，可靠的，合理的，健康的
source set 源集
span n. 跨度，跨距，范围 v. 横越
spatial adj. 空间的
spatially adv. 空间地，存在于空间地
specific application 特殊应用
specified limit 指定的限度
specified period 特定时期
spectrum n. 光，光谱，型谱，频谱
spherical adj. 球的，球形的
spinal column 脊柱
SPI serial interface SPI 串行接口
stack n. 堆，一堆，堆栈 v. 堆叠
standardization n. 标准化
static characteristics 静态特征
static value 静态值
statistical inference 统计性推论
statistical parameter 统计学参数
statistical processing 统计处理
statistics n. 统计学
stereo adj. 立体的，立体感觉的
stereo-lithography 立体印刷术
stimulate vt. 激励，鼓励
storage n. 存储器，内存，存放处；[动] 存储
strain n. 过度的疲劳，紧张，张力，应变
stroboscopic adj. 频闪观测仪的
structural information 结构信息
styli （留声机上的）唱针，日晷指针
sublevel n. 子层，子级，次层，次能级
subsequent adj. 后来的，并发的
substantial adj. 坚固的，实质的，真实的，充实的
substantial agreement 实质上的一致
substitution method 代入法
subtend vt. 对着，对向

superimpose v. 添加，双重
surveillance n. 监视，监督
swap v. 交换
switch n. 开关，转换； vt. 转换，转变
symbol n. 符号，记号，象征
synthetic adj. 合成的，综合的
synthetic methodology 合成方法论
syrup n. 糖浆，果汁
systematic adj 系统的；规划的；有计划的
systematic errors 系统误差
systematics n. 分类学，分类法；系统学
system design 系统设计
system expansion 系统扩展
system integrator 系统集成器
tabular form 表格形式
tabulate vt. 把……制成表格；列表，制表
tackle vt. 应付（难事等），处理，解决
tactile adj. 触觉的
tagging of instrument 仪器标志
tailor vt. 剪裁，缝制（衣服）～，适应，适合
tally n. 标签，记数器，记数； vt. 计算，记录，加标签；vi. 符合，记分
tangible adj. 切实的
tantalizing adj. 非常着急的
technical paper 资料
telemetry n. 遥感勘测，自动测量记录传导
temper v. （冶金）回火，锻炼，调和，调节
temperature transmitter 温度变送器
temporal adj. 暂时的（现世的） n. 暂存的
temporarily store 临时存储
terminology n. 术语学，专门名词
terrain n. 地形
theorem n. 定理；法则
theoretical calculations 理论计算
theoretical model 理论模型
thermal equilibrium 热平衡
thermometer n. 温度计，体温计
thermosensitive adj. [化] 热敏的
thermostat n. 自动调温器
threshold n. 阈，阈值，门限，门槛
throttle v. 扼杀
tight pattern 紧凑的方式
time delay 时延
timeliness n. 合时，时
time multiplexing 时间多重操作
time-sequential control 时间顺序控制

time-stamped 时间标记
timing relationship 时间关系
toggle n. 触发器,切换
token n. 表示,象征,记号,代币; adj. 象征的,表意的
tolerance limit 公差极限
toolkit n. 工具包
tool management 工具管理
topography n. 地形,地势,地形学
topology n. 拓扑,布局 拓扑学
torque n. 扭矩,转矩
torso n. 未完成的作品(文中指机器人)
touch-tone 音频按键
traceable adj. 可追踪的,起源于
trajectory n. 轨迹,轨道
transaction n. 办理,处理,会报,学报,交易,事务,处理事务
transducer n. 传感器,变频器,变换器
transfer function 传输函数
transformation function 转换功能
translucent adj. 半透明的
transmission n. 播送,发射,传动,传送,传输,转播
transmit vt. 传输,转送,传达,传导,发射,遗传,传播; vi. 发射信号,发报
transmitting measurement signal 测量信号发送
transponder n. [无]异频雷达收发机
trigger registers 触发寄存器
troposphere n. [气]对流层
troubleshoot v. 排除故障
troubleshooting n. 发现并修理故障
truckline n. 主干
tweak vt. 扭,捏,拧
ultrasonic adj. 超音速的,超声的; n. 超声波
unambiguous adj. 不含糊的,清楚的,明确的
underlying adj. 根本的,基础的,潜在的
undesirable change 不期望的变化
unidimensional adj. 单向的,单向性的
unfailing adj. 永恒的,无穷的
uniform means 统一方法
unimaginable adj. 想不到的,不可思议的

unigue adj. 独一无二的,仅有的,唯一的
uniquely adv. 独特的,唯一的
unravel vt. 解开,阐明,解决
upgrade vt. 升级
upper cutoff frequency 频段上截
upper range limit 范围上限
update time 更新时间
user manual 用户手册
uset-programmable 用户可编程的
user protocol 用户协议
utilization n. 利用
utilize vt. 利用
validation n. 确认
valid representation 有确凿根据的陈述
valuable a. 有用的,有价值的
valve n. 阀
vapor n. 水汽,水蒸气,无实质之物
variable n. [数]变数,可变物,变量 adj. 可变的,不定的,易变的; [数]变量的
VDT=Video Display Terminals 视频显示终端
vector n. 向量
veiling n. 罩以面纱,面纱,面纱布料,帐幔
velocity n. 速度,速率,迅速,周转率
versatile adj. 可使直立的,通用的,万能的,多才多艺的,多面手的
versatility n. 多功能性
vertical adj. 垂直的,直立的,顶点的,[解]头顶的; n. 垂直线,垂直面,竖向
vertically adv. 垂直地
vestigial adj. 发育不全的,退化器官的
vibration n. 振动,颤动,摇动,摆动
video tape 录像磁带
visualization n. 可视化
wafer n. [无]晶片,圆片,薄饼,干胶片
waggle n. 来回摇动,摇摆
wireless communications system 无线通信系统
withstand vt. 抵挡,经受住
workpiece n. 工件
yield v. 出产,生长,生产 vi. (~to)屈服,屈从 n. 产量,收益
zero drift 零点漂移